Community Media

Critical Media Studies
Institutions, Politics, and Culture

Series Editor
Andrew Calabrese, University of Colorado

Advisory Board

Recent Titles in the Series

Community Media

A Global Introduction

Ellie Rennie

ROWMAN & LITTLEFIELD PUBLISHERS, INC.
Lanham • Boulder • New York • Toronto • Oxford

ROWMAN & LITTLEFIELD PUBLISHERS, INC.

Published in the United States of America
by Rowman & Littlefield Publishers, Inc.
A wholly owned subsidiary of The Rowman & Littlefield Publishing Group, Inc.
4501 Forbes Boulevard, Suite 200, Lanham, Maryland 20706
www.rowmanlittlefield.com

P.O. Box 317, Oxford OX2 9RU, UK

British Library Cataloguing in Publication Information Available

Library of Congress Cataloging-in-Publication Data

Rennie, Ellie.
  Community media : a global introduction / Ellie Rennie.
    p. cm. — (Critical media studies)
  Includes bibliographical references and index.
  ISBN-13: 978-0-7425-3924-2 (cloth : alk. paper)
  ISBN-10: 0-7425-3924-5 (cloth : alk. paper)
  ISBN-13: 978-0-7425-3925-9 (pbk. : alk. paper)
  ISBN-10: 0-7425-3925-3 (pbk. : alk. paper)
    1. Local mass media—Social aspects. 2. Communication—Social aspects. 3.
  Community life. 4. Social participation. I. Title. II. Series.

  HM1206.R46 2006
  307—dc22

                                                                2005036287

Printed in the United States of America

∞™ The paper used in this publication meets the minimum requirements of
American National Standard for Information Sciences—Permanence of Paper for
Printed Library Materials, ANSI/NISO Z39.48-1992.

Contents

Acknowledgments

The Creative Industries Research and Applications Centre at Queensland University of Technology provided me with the time and resources to write this book. Christina Spurgeon, in particular, gets my wholehearted thanks. Her generosity, pragmatism, and enthusiasm made it an achievable and enjoyable task. Above all, she helped me to see that community media is a fascinating object of study.

Stuart Cunningham taught me to run with the difficult ideas rather than run away from them. For that I am eternally grateful. The Community Broadcasting Association of Australia provided valuable training in communications policy. Thanks to Barry Melville for his immensely useful comments and guidance (which even navigated me through the corridors of Parliament House). Thanks also to Andrew Brine, David Sice, and Jan McArthur, whose collaboration on policy projects influenced this book without them knowing it. *SKA TV* (Jeff Riley, Cam Manderson, Peter Lane, Rose Field, Ntennis Davi, and everyone else) taught me more about community media than a book ever could. They were my introduction to community media—and now they are the introduction to this book.

Thanks to everyone who agreed to be interviewed or offered their networks internationally, including: Nicky Edmonds, Steve Buckley, Sylvia Harvey, Jeni Vine, John Trevitt, Chris Hewson, Dave Rushton, Hitesh Popat, the *Undercurrents* team, Nick Couldry, Peter Lewis, Margaret Gillan, Sean O'Siochru, Ollie McGlinchey, Nick Jankowski, Martina Huyzenga, Erik van der Schaft, Jürgen Linke, Jonathan Levy, Zane Blaney, Denise Brady, Ron

Cooper, Kari Peterson, Ruben Abrue and others at MNN, DCTV, Tara Mateik and Carlos Pareja at Paper Tiger, Kevin Howley, Curtis Henderson, Isabelle Voyer, André Desrochers, the Federation of Community Television Stations in Quebec, Peter Foster, Paul Baines, Cathy Edwards, Bunnie Riedell, Nantz Rickard, Jim Blackman, Bevin Yeatman, Tracy Naughton, Christina Alvarez, Kath Letch, everyone from OURMedia, the International Association of Media and Communication Rsearch (IAMCR) Community Communication section, Pete triDish, and the World Association of Community Radio Broadcasters (AMARC).

I am grateful to Rowman & Littlefield for taking on this project. Finally, thanks to John Hartley—a brilliant writer and a generous mentor.

Introduction

In 1998, I signed up to volunteer on a community television program called *Access News*, ticking the box that said "no prior experience." Digital technologies were just about to become part of daily life for a great many people, and would result in new levels of media participation. Even to a media novice like me community radio and video groups, which had existed in Australia for decades, seemed a bit old-fashioned. Now I think that they were ahead of their time. This book explains the use, possibilities, and ideals of community media—past and present—across the globe.

It also looks at the notion of *community* and the role it plays in contemporary politics. This is essential to any theorization of community media, and unavoidable for community media practice. I noticed on my very first encounter with *Access News* that there was an overwhelming amount of activity taking place around me. Stories were everywhere. We filmed a massive structure of entangled metal that blocked a Melbourne wharf. It was built by members of the Maritime Union of Australia and they called it "public art," intended to "cheer the place up."[1] The steel wall of railway lines welded together wasn't just there for aesthetic reasons—it conveniently prevented trucks from entering the terminal during the longshoremen's long protest against the company's (and government's) attempt to curtail workers' rights. In another instance, a superhero known by the name of Starpower, who was known to enjoy the odd rave, was arrested for carrying a toy gun. A seemingly spontaneous dance party formed on the court steps during Starpower's trial in a show of solidarity for identity rights. On the other side of the city, residents released yellow balloons into the sky in disapproval of their local park being used as a racecourse for the Grand Prix. Onlookers who were unaware of their protest must have thought someone was throwing a large picnic.

The city appeared to be a complex and active place that year, full of people contesting spaces and government "reforms." They used whatever tactics they could come up with to get themselves noticed by the mainstream media, who would intermittently pay attention. But always nearby were small groups with cameras and microphones from Melbourne's community media sector, reporting not just the controversial stuff but the stories, songs, and "artworks." *Access News* would often hold screenings and the people in the communities represented would come along and cheer when they saw themselves on television. We wondered if anyone was at home watching.

Getting the show to air was always hard work. When I arrived, the tapes were kept in someone's living room as the group had been evicted from its office at the back of a local pub. There was one sturdy SVHS camera and an old editing suite that another program, *Challenge*, kindly allowed us to use. The *Challenge* edit suite lived up to its name on many occasions. But the most difficult piece of equipment to make sense of was the old black filing cabinet that everyone seemed to steer well clear of. As the rest of the group worked hard to produce our weekly program (which they managed on an almost weekly basis), I sorted through files trying to make sense of the group's history, finances, and structure. I wanted to figure out whether an easier future was possible. I then discovered other video centers, radio stations, print media, and online forums that were doing similar work and realized that we were, in fact, part of a large network. Eventually I came to suspect that the history of community media held some valuable lessons for media participation in the digital age.

But the future of community media cannot be contemplated without research into the reasons for its existence and how it has been treated thus far. Why has it met with such enormous resistance and/or disinterest from governments the world over? Why is it so poorly resourced, and how has it managed to survive at all? What motivates communities and individuals to produce media? Can it ever have any impact on culture and society at large? In the end I never produced much content for *Access News*. But hopefully this book can explain some of the doubts that plague community media in policy and academic arenas and help sort through the messy filing cabinet of community media history.

Defining Community Media

Community media is local television in Denmark, microradio and public access television in the United States (chapter 2), local newsletters produced by women in Bengal, and the web-based Indymedia that operates in seventy cities around the world (chapter 6). This book discusses all of these examples and more. But what is it that they have in common that defines them all as "community media"? The terms "participation" and "access" apply to most community media endeavors, meaning that nonprofessional media makers are encouraged to become involved (participation), providing individuals and communities with a platform to express their views (access). Community media is often defined by the parameters within which groups have to work, including organizational structure, production techniques, and programming. Here's how the experts describe community radio:

> Community is defined geographically, as well as in terms of interest, language, cultural or ethnic groupings. Many stations will serve multiple overlapping communities, and it is of the essence of this type of radio that each community or interest group participates in station policy, programme, production and operation. This is achieved by a variety of democratic structures that ensure representation in the management body of both listeners and station staff, paid and unpaid. The presence of volunteers is not the result of cost-saving calculations but is an essential means of contact with the community or communities involved, ensuring that they are represented in the day-to-day running of the station. Community stations of this type are non-profit in aim, and generally attempt to diversify their sources of funding in order to avoid dependency on any one source. Public funding, listener subscription and advertisements of a limited kind and quantity constitute a major part of these sources in different countries, although one or other are objected to on ideological or pragmatic grounds in some places.[2]

All of this is pretty much true. Community media is usually run on a not-for-profit basis and provides community members with an opportunity to participate in the production process. However, community stations do vary immensely in their finances, structures, and the audiences for which they are intended. Particular qualities have also been prescribed to community media enterprises in different parts of the world. In Europe, community media is often described as "local media," while in Third World contexts it is often called "participatory media." As discussed throughout this book, community media has a tendency to defy any assumptions we might have of it. Although policy makers have imposed criteria upon community media (in countries where there is community media policy), these boundaries get challenged all the time. I prefer a more general definition of community media. A group within the International Association of Media and Communication Research (IAMCR) came up with the following: Community media "originates, circulates and resonates from the sphere of civil society. . . . This is the field of media communication that exists outside of the state and the market (often non-government and non-profit), yet which may interact with both."[3] This description is broad enough to encompass the many platforms that community media has been distributed across (print, broadcast, cable, and new media) but it is narrow enough to discount community uses of commercial or public media. I will return to definitions and terminology throughout this book as descriptions say much about the expectations we place upon community media, and determine, at least in part, the parameters within which it performs. Community media is distinguished by its aspirations and motivations as much as by its methods and structures. This book attempts to explain these aspirations and where they fit into the intellectual history of media studies.

Radio is the dominant medium for community expression in most parts of the world. Its content is relatively easy to produce and radio receivers are still far cheaper than television sets. In places where there are low levels of literacy, radio is used to convey information on health and services. It also plays an important cultural role by promoting local music, stories, and opinions, all of which reinforce community memory and history. Television content is more expensive and complicated to produce, but this is becoming less of an issue as cameras and editing software reach a larger market. In First World countries in particular, the community television campaign has been important as it has challenged the way that cable and broadcast platforms are managed.

Radio and television must exist within regulated media environments—it is where the battles over community access have been fought out. Print media has had its fair share of legal obstacles (and worse under repressive regimes), but in democratic states people are free to publish print media without permission from their government. Although some of the issues in this book will relate to print media, I recommend the work of media studies author Chris Atton for more detailed analysis specific to that form.[4] Community broadcasting requires that spectrum is set aside for community purposes. In doing so, governments must endorse "community" as a sphere of activity outside of the state and economy that requires attention, status, and resources. Through this process, communities are named and validated—named as having a substantial interest, if not a right, to broadcast.

From Broadcast to Digital

The broadcast era began with the large-scale adoption of radio and television, enduring—and flourishing—through the second half of the twentieth century. With limited channels, people across a given nation listen to or watch the same content; it is a form of *mass media*. Analogue broadcasting is also a one-way technology, meaning that it goes from the broadcaster to the receiver/audience. Broadcasting has become highly regulated in most countries for reasons of cultural protection and economic stability. A nation's government controls who is allowed to broadcast and places restrictions on the type of content that is transmitted. Broadcasting is also regulated for technical reasons. When content is transmitted "over-the-air," stations' signals can interfere with one another if they are not allocated a space of their own. Community media appears to have been a marginal priority when the distribution of spectrum across all nations is tallied up.

The new digital media era is different. The Internet has demonstrated that widespread participation in media technologies is both possible and desirable. People still consume media content, but they can also distribute it on the Internet without having to gain permission. Although broadcasting is still regulated, digital broadcasting technologies mean that, at least in principle, many more broadcast channels are possible. Information transmitted digitally over-the-air can be compressed, thereby making room for more information in the same space. Community media has, in the past, been excluded or marginalized on the grounds of "spectrum scarcity"—meaning that it would be a waste of a channel that could potentially be used for commercial or government use. With more channels available, this argument is less convincing. Community media may therefore be better accommodated in the new media environment.

Revisiting the struggle for citizen-led media that occurred during the analogue broadcast era can help to understand the theoretical and policy challenges of participatory new media. It also offers some valuable insights into why the mass media functioned the way it did and why that model endures. The hopes and contradictions of community media—the most neglected aspect of media history—can help us to understand the media at large.

Throughout the broadcast era, community radio and television have existed in direct tension with dominant cultural policy objectives. In Europe, community media offered an alternative definition of the public interest and sought the breakdown of public service broadcasting monopoly structures. In North America, the legalistic execution (in both senses) of free speech by commercial players has hindered the efforts of civil society groups to establish community access policies. Australian cultural policy has organized and sanctioned multiculturalism, yet relegated the unpredictable community broadcasting sector to the fringes of culture. In organizations such as the World Association of Community Radio Broadcasters (AMARC) community broadcasting has been promoted as a means to Third World development. The following chapters are an attempt to understand what community media of the broadcast era meant—not only for those involved in its production, but for administrators and the public(s) it claimed to represent.

This is essentially a theoretical task. Community media is a surprisingly underrepresented area within media studies. Public service and commercial broadcasting have both been studied as a part of the public sphere, as the promotion and enactment of citizenship and in relation to the laws and policies of government. This is not the case with community media; its vision has not been clearly articulated or its contradictions exposed. Media studies research has devoted many pages to the role that the media plays in promoting, maintaining, or restricting democratic processes. *Democracy*—meaning to rule in the interests of the people—is also a central concept in community media studies as access and participation have been pursued out of a belief that people have a right to directly represent themselves within the media. This has an impact upon how power—symbolic and political—is circulated.

To get closer to a theorization of community media, this book also makes reference to some long-standing debates around *communitarianism* and *liberalism*. These theories articulate the contentious place of community-directed laws and structures. Liberalism came out of the Enlightenment, an intellectual period that spanned the seventeenth and eighteenth centuries in France, England, Scotland, and America. It is a philosophy based on individual reason that is concerned with the role of the sovereign state and the limits that should be placed upon it in order to maintain individual freedom. It holds that a secure social environment, maintained by the state, allows individuals to pursue their own interests without infringing upon the rights of others. The free market is considered one of the mechanisms through which liberty is pursued. Communitarianism is a revision of liberalism. It maintains that community must be factored into the way social and political institutions are built as individuals do not live in isolation; it is a *social* conception of freedom. Nationality, languages, group ties, interests, identity, and family have an impact upon the way we live. Communitarians argue that if this is not taken into account, inequality may result. Liberalism, on the other hand, generally considers community to be a derivative of liberty and equality. These concepts have been exposed and challenged at the day-to-day level through community media. Is the community sphere an essential component of democratic societies? If so, should we be supporting community communication? Or are the commercial and government media more effective and efficient uses of media resources?

At the core of the book is the notion of civil society and its revival. *Civil society* is sometimes referred to as the "third sector." It is the sphere of formal and informal networks and groups, such as associations, clubs, and cultural allegiances, and the social bonds that tie communities together. It is considered to be a necessary part—if not a product—of modern liberal democracies. The practical and ideological obstacles that community broadcasting has had to deal with are a reflection of the status and treatment of civil society. Over the past decade, civil society has become a prominent concept in political thought. New political approaches are emerging that seek to utilize the community sphere as a means to subtle and context-sensitive political change. They have been expressed through some diverse global trends, including recent participatory communications approaches to Third World development, third way politics (discussed in chapter 1), and the innovation commons in new media theory (discussed in chapter 6). As a result, community media's demands for access and community empowerment—as well as the alternative models of action and organization that it offers—have taken on new significance. A whole new set of questions for community media arises: Can community media be seen as part of a wider political and social ambition? Do these approaches offer new ways of conceptualizing and constructing community media? How is community broadcasting inhibited by outdated ideologies? What does it mean to implement communications policies that involve the unknowable and "messy" domain of community?

When community media entered policy and academic debates in the 1970s there was some hope that it could disrupt the rise of transnational media conglomerates and provide an alternative to the mainstream media. Three decades on, community media is far from a united force and it feels misdirected to even expect that it could be. At the same time, activist networks and social movements have demonstrated that communities can make a difference and community-based media has been a part of that. Community media's role now needs to be rethought.

Community Media Policy

A great deal of cultural studies work has concentrated on the intersection of culture and government, including a prolific published debate over the worth of such analyses (known in Australia as the "policy moment" of the 1990s).[5] It was argued that policy studies allowed for an engagement with the national and cultural infrastructure that could not be reached by focusing only on grand theories. For Stuart Cunningham, linking cultural studies to policy was a means to expand the field "but with methods far more modest and specific than those to which we are accustomed," making it "sensitive to what is possible as much as to what is ideal."[6] He argued that not only could an emphasis on policy create more socially relevant studies, but that theory itself could benefit from an understanding of the processes, ideas, and structures created through the technologies of government. This approach incorporated the notion of *governance*. At its most general, this means "any strategy, tactic, process, procedure or programme for controlling, regulating, shaping, mastering or exercising authority over others in a nation, organization or locality."[7] It is an enabling category, rather than one of policy/government standing over and against the individual and civil society. Its application is broad, referring also to mechanisms such as the ethical competence of the individual as well as interactions and interdependencies of various actors—public, private, and voluntary.[8]

Those opposing the turn towards policy study pointed out that such analysis risks becoming the "handmaiden of practice," of selling-out to a particular trend.[9] It was further argued that the social utility of policy analysis could not be proven over the broader influences of critical theory and inquiry. Although there is always this danger, policy analysis is very much needed in community media studies as it gets away from notions of community media as something resistant to government and the economy.[10] Community broadcasting is dependent upon and intersects with both, as any investigation into governments' various attempts to accommodate the sector within broadcasting policy clearly shows. To ignore these dynamics risks denying important aspects of an already neglected area of the media.

In researching this book, I used policy documents as "road maps" to determine the guidelines, resources, and restrictions that have shaped the radio and television stations discussed. Where possible, I met with policy makers to hear their insights and reflections on the community broadcasting sector, as well as their personal difficulties in attempting to deal with a sector that is not easily defined or managed. Material collected from industry associations has been another primary source of policy information. I also gathered stories from practitioners in various countries. Community media is, after all, about the stories we tell.

The term "public philosophy" describes the wider context that I am interested in—not the theoretical, authored philosophies that are learned and debated amongst scholars, but the related philosophies upon which institutional design, values, and the beliefs and biases of society are based.[11] The term "corporate liberalism," used intermittently throughout this book, is one such public philosophy (see chapter 2). The term is useful "to emphasize the ways in which the institution is the product of social and political choices, not of accident or impersonal economic or technological forces alone."[12] This restores agency and intentionality to the way in which broadcasting is constructed, reminding the reader that different choices and models are possible. The commitment to freedom of speech within the notion of community access is another such public philosophy—a derivative of notions of liberty that guides and informs the way in which broadcasting is managed. Philosophy, political science, and cultural studies theory are all used within this book as a means to discuss the "public philosophies" that inform community media.

Themes and Chapters

This book is structured thematically, with each area of inquiry focusing upon a different geographical region (or regions). The first chapter reviews and synthesizes a number of existing theoretical approaches to community media. Community media theory emerged out of advocacy efforts to democratize the media. These early discourses depicted community media as oppositional and kept community media out of touch with developments in media studies at large.[13] A number of theorists working within alternative media are now acknowledging the inadequacies of this tradition, and are producing definitions of alternative media based on empowerment and citizenship.[14] These works are discussed in chapter 1, although I also try to steer away from alternative media theory. Community media is not always intended to be an alternative to the mainstream or alternative in its values. Theories of community media need to encompass its conservative, ordinary, and mundane elements and not just that which is radical or alternative. The second part of the chapter introduces some key political theories that help us understand the intellectual traditions that community media theory sits within. Liberalism and communitarianism are most usefully seen as providing a dialogue that allows us to dispute and to engage with the institutional realization of both individual rights and the social whole. These concepts are important in understanding the way in which community media is constructed and managed and why different approaches have emerged.

Chapter 2 looks at the principle of "access" and the obstacles it has encountered in the United States. In its most extreme form, community access means allowing anyone to broadcast whatever they want. This policy can result in programming that very few will be tempted to watch or listen to. In recent years, public, educational, and government (PEG) access cable television stations have been attempting to move beyond straightforward free speech conceptions of community broadcasting and cablecasting (the minimalist, individual rights-based model) towards new notions of access based upon a more complex idea of empowerment. Stations see their role as doing more than simply opening the door in the morning; they actively encourage communities to step forward and express their concerns, and structure their volunteer programs to involve those most in need of training. In chapter 2, both the on-the-ground station management policies and the legal contracts and licenses that permit access are explored, demonstrating the ways in which civil society is being helped or hindered through the access model. At the regulatory level, the dominant paradigm of broadcasting and cablecasting in the United States has presented significant obstacles for the development of community media. Access television has sought federally mandated laws for community media but has managed to survive mainly through support from municipal governments. Community radio, on the other hand, has had to operate illegally in many instances due to inadequate nationwide regulations for community media.

European community media demonstrates a different set of problems. Although models of community media within Europe vary greatly, international developments since the emergence of community broadcasting have left stations throughout the region facing a common set of issues. The literature on the early community radio and television trials yields two recurring themes: The first is concerned with community media's role in decentralization—in particular whether it played a part in the breakdown of monopoly public broadcasting systems and led the way for the influx of commercial broadcasting. The second is that community broadcasting was seen to promote amateurism; it was a threat to the high standards that public service broadcasting promoted. These two themes are explored in chapter 3 via the history of pirate radio in Europe, the community cable television trials, and recent local television efforts. Community media offers an alternative idea of the public interest and this sets it apart from public service broadcasting.

Some of the strongest policy approaches to community media have been based upon notions of cultural diversity, in particular, multiculturalism. Are these approaches capable of encompassing the myriad of identities, groups, and issues arising out of globalization and new technologies? Chapter 4 addresses this question via community media policy in Australia. Australia has a long tradition of community media, which it considers the "third tier" of broadcasting. Despite this, community media has been treated as marginal by policy makers, leaving it with an uncertain future in the new digital television environment. Recurring policy dilemmas relating to localism, spectrum allocation, and financial models are now being played out in that context.

Chapter 4 also examines Indigenous broadcasting in Australia. Community media policy has been important for Indigenous Australians, allowing them an autonomous media service that has been much harder to achieve through public service broadcasting and commercial avenues. However, for Indigenous communities this (community) media is mainstream media. This chapter raises the issue of whether a separate Indigenous broadcasting license may be more suitable.

Chapter 5 looks at the deployment of community media as a development strategy in both First and Third World countries. Many community media projects are established on the assumption that they can lead to positive social change. In this rationale, community is seen as a legitimate partner for government and development agencies. However, community media projects may also be judged by criteria that they find they cannot conform to. Much development-based community media is designed to achieve economic or political outcomes, such as overcoming poverty or peace building. Can community media achieve its aims and still comply with government and donor criteria? If community media's achievements work at the local level, can this have an impact upon the forces of globalization? In chapter 5, postdevelopment theory and participatory communications are used to unpack current issues facing community media, including: tensions between localism and the effort to articulate into the knowledge economy via community projects, the problems of attempting to define communities as knowable and measurable entities, and the relationship of these discourses to new social movement theory.

Chapter 6 compares regimes of access in community broadcasting with new media developments. The Internet is said to have produced an *innovation commons* where people can build upon existing technologies without obtaining permission. This has produced a type of media participation that is collaborative and voluntary, and where ownership of ideas is shared. "Access" is conceived of as openness or "intercreativity," rather than as "access to" an otherwise controlled system. The way we think of amateurism and voluntarism are changing as a result. These terms are now being used in discussions of innovation and changing patterns in work and consumption. Chapter 6 discusses how these shifts might contribute to the formation of new policy justifications for community media in the digital broadcasting environment. It offers a conception of community media that is generative rather than oppositional. However, the commons approach also raises new problems. It endorses an unquantifiable approach to social and cultural goods which requires something of a leap of faith from policy makers. Furthermore, notions of participation that reconcile commercial and noncommercial motives may complicate community media goals. Nonetheless, the commons is an important theory that demonstrates how the public interest is changing in the digital environment.

Chapter 7 synthesizes the arguments of previous chapters and offers some further thoughts as to what media democracy in the digital age might look like. Community media has always been about self-expression—and seeing ourselves as part of the society in which we live. Democracy is said to be in a predicament over the perceived distance between the people and the institutions that represent them, which results in political apathy. Can participation in the media help close that distance? E-government models suggest direct input into the policy process by citizens. Is this desirable? Being able to represent oneself in the media paves the way for a more visible, transparent, and responsive model of democracy. Community media may not solve the problems of the mass media, but it does offer some valuable lessons for e-democracy.

The chapter themes are not restricted to the geographical regions I have located them within. They intersect with and influence each other and change over time. The geographical focus is used to highlight the importance of the overriding policy objectives and traditions within which community media must function. To some extent, it also works to show how and why community media debates have acquired different preoccupations in North America, for instance, than they have in the Third World or Europe.

Community media is not an easy object of study. If you have seen or heard much community media content then this will not surprise you—it defies generalization, is unconventional at its best, and ambitious in what it sets out to achieve. But it is also persistent; community media has proven again and again it is here to stay and it demands to be taken seriously.

Notes

1. *Access News*, www.accessnews.skatv.org.au/site/awards/arts/arts.htm (accessed February 1, 2005).

2. Peter M. Lewis and Jerry Booth, *The Invisible Medium: Public, Commercial and Community Radio* (Basingstoke: Macmillan, 1989), 9.

3. IAMCR Community Communication, www.iamcr.net/secannounce/comcom/index (accessed February 1, 2005).

4. Chris Atton, *Alternative Media* (Thousand Oaks: Sage, 2002).

5. Stuart Cunningham and Terry Flew, "Policy," in *Television Studies*, ed. Toby Miller (London: British Film Institute, 2002). See also Tom O'Regan, "Some Reflections on the Policy Moment," *Meanjin* 51, no. 3 (1992).

6. Cunningham cited in O'Regan, "Some Reflections on the Policy Moment," 524. See also Stuart Cunningham, "The Cultural Policy Debate Revisited," *Meanjin* 51, no. 3 (1992).

7. Nikolas Rose, *Powers of Freedom: Reframing Political Thought* (Cambridge: Cambridge University Press, 1999), 15.

8. Cunningham, "The Cultural Policy Debate Revisited."

9. O'Regan, "Some Reflections on the Policy Moment," 526.

10. Gay Hawkins, *From Nimbin to Mardi Gras: Constructing Community Arts* (Sydney: Allen & Unwin, 1993).

11. As used by Michael J. Sandel, *Democracy's Discontent* (Cambridge, Mass.: Harvard University Press, 1996), 3.

12. Thomas Streeter, *Selling the Air: A Critique of the Policy of Commercial Broadcasting in the United States* (Chicago: University of Chicago Press, 1996), 6.

13. Clemencia Rodriguez, *Fissures in the Mediascape* (Cresskill, N.J.: Hampton Press, 2001).

14. Atton, *Alternative Media*; Nick Couldry, *The Place of Media Power: Pilgrims and Witnesses of the Media Age* (London: Routledge, 2000); John Downing, *Radical Media: Rebellious Communication and Social Movements* (Thousand Oaks: Sage, 2001); Rodriguez, *Fissures in the Mediascape*.

CHAPTER ONE

Community

Melbourne's community television station, Channel 31, had a well-known fish tank in its presentation studio. Whenever the station was without a program to broadcast, a staff member would point the camera at the fish tank for a live *Fish TV* broadcast. Televisions across the city were turned into aquariums—fairly murky ones when the station was short of volunteers. One year Channel 31 found itself in a serious financial crisis. To stay on the air they launched a fund-raising campaign and urged programmers to raise money within their local communities. One particularly quiet night, a young volunteer crept into the studio and stuck a handwritten ransom note to the fish tank. It read "pay up or the fish get flushed." The note prompted an influx of calls, many from distressed children and animal welfare groups, but also a few from viewers making donations. The goldfish survived, as did the station, which continues to be one of the most interesting and successful community television stations in the world.

There is nothing better than a crisis to make a community visible. It became apparent during Channel 31's difficult year that as a community station, Channel 31 carried a range of emotive and ideological associations for its viewers. Many who were not even represented by a group or interest at the station still thought it deserved to exist. There was a sincere sentiment from supporters that communities are necessary and worthwhile, even though—as I discovered on many occasions—communities could also be extraordinarily difficult to predict and manage.

Community media holds a promise of a different way of doing things—not just in terms of aesthetic qualities and production practices, but in terms of organization. This chapter is concerned with the question of community and what it represents within today's society. Later chapters examine how community media has fared with the values it espouses: free speech, the public interest, access, and social change. All of these concepts are caught up in a politics of community, one that is deeply rooted in democracy's intellectual traditions. *Community* can be used as a type of governance—an identifiable means to achieve certain political outcomes—and it is at this level that community media attracts the "for" or "against" arguments that have dominated theoretical and policy writing. In other words, community media carries some complex aspirations into political life by nature of its very organization, and these are often at odds with the dominant system. Community organizations challenge us to reassess the way in which liberal democracy itself is managed, in particular the status granted to nongovernment, noncommercial institutions working in the sphere of civil society. The second half of this chapter will explore the meaning of civil society and the role that community media plays within it.

Although our media institutions are structured according to political systems, there is a limit to how much political science literature can teach us about the media. This is partly due to the striking absence of communication and the media from most political science debates—an inexcusable oversight when the media's role in the flow of knowledge (and hence power) is taken into consideration. It is partly the task of this book to bring together these two separate areas of study to see what each may learn from the other, particularly in regards to community media policy. However, there are other aspects of community media that cannot be understood through this political science approach, such as content or text, the individual's engagement, and the motivation behind participation. A small body of work exists that has attempted to define the meaning and use of community media. This is discussed first in order to see where community media studies began and where it is heading.

Community Media Studies

Community media has received surprisingly little scholarly attention, even within the field of media studies itself. If anything, this deficiency reinforces the assumptions of marginality that surround community media. Some scholars have begun to address this shortfall, amongst them John Downing, Clemencia Rodriguez, Chris Atton, Nick Jankowski, Peter Lewis, and Nick

Couldry (all discussed below). Academic work on community media does not always refer to "community media"—"alternative" media, "radical" media, and "citizens' media" are terms more often used. Texts that use these terms generally deal with a specific area within community media rather than the broader public philosophies that this book is concerned with. However, these works do contribute substantially to the project of discovering community media's unique attributes and can assist in uncovering why community media has made it into policy agendas in a particular way. A rethink of community media is certainly needed if the challenges of the digital era are to be understood. The revival of community media studies is still a new project, but one with the promise and potential to yield new policy directions.

Community media studies first emerged out of efforts to "democratize" the media. It was a challenge to the domination of the corporate media and the economic and political media structures that favored some interests over others. In 1976, UNESCO established a commission to examine international communications issues, in particular the inequality of information flows between the First and Third Worlds. The Latin American scholars who dominated the debate argued that underdevelopment of the South (Third World) was partly due to the unequal information exchange from the North (this is discussed in more detail in chapter 5). Furthermore, the way that Latin American countries were being depicted by international news agencies discouraged economic and cultural exchange between Third World nations in the South. The ultimate purpose of the UNESCO discussions was to bring about a New World Information and Communication Order (NWICO). The resulting MacBride Report recommended more democratic national policies, including the fostering of South-to-South communication and a code of ethics for the mass media. It was in this context that the terms "access," "participation," and "self-management" were raised as indicators of democratic media. When the United States withdrew its membership and funding of the UNESCO commission in 1984, the discussion came to a halt (which to some confirmed the United States' unbending power). In the end, the ambitious NWICO plan was never realized and it has fallen from the vocabulary of communications movements. The debates surrounding NWICO have been superseded by new information rights debates—the most recent surrounding the World Summit on the Information Society.[1]

The UNESCO commission did bring a new awareness and interest in community-based media to academic, development agency, and advocacy circles. Proponents of NWICO had pointed to Bolivian miners' radio as an example of democratic community media.[2] Bolivian miners' radio dates back to the late 1940s. The stations—established by the unions for political purposes—became a primary means of resistance through decades of upheaval. In times of peace, miners used the stations to campaign for better working conditions, as well as education and cultural activities. The miners and their radio withstood numerous military attacks that resulted in loss of lives and the destruction of equipment. Their levels of access and participation were not particularly high compared to many contemporary models and, as with all community media, Bolivian miners' radio needs to be seen as specific to its time and place. However, the stations are a striking early example of self-organized media, and for this reason they came to signify the potential of community media.

The way the argument in support of community media was framed in the debates surrounding NWICO persisted for some time: the grassroots community media movement possessed the potential to overcome the imperialist threat of the mass media. Alternative media initiatives (both broadcast and print) were said to destabilize the one-to-many communication structures of the mass media through their participatory, two-way structure. *Passive* audience members could be transformed into *active* producers. The problem with this argument was that it was premised on a conception of popular media as monolithic and singular. Even critics of alternative media were applying the same paradigm, asserting that the promise of community media must be checked by the reality that small-scale media could not—and would never—compete with the mass media for audiences. For instance, a British study from 1984 argued that the alternative press would remain marginal as long as it continued to adopt nonhierarchical, collective structures "adopted for political, never for economic ends."[3] Community media, whether you were for or against it, was compared to the mass media. Its proponents saw it as an army of new noncommercial players who could break up the concentration of media power that was held in so few corporate hands; its detractors depicted it as an insignificant combatant against the pervasive force of commercial news and entertainment.

Although such intellectual constructions of community media still remain, they are essentially flawed. The basic argument might even seem irrelevant for many living in Western democracies who do not see the popular media as crudely repressive. How can we argue for the need for "revolutionary" media when we, as the audience, have the ability to make our own cultural choices? How do we account for our own capacity to take or leave the values, products, and cultures available in the media? There are many examples of mass media programming that challenge dominant cultural stereotypes and that may even be described as "alternative" in their vision of society.

While community media theorists were arguing for new structures of ownership and control, other media scholars were arguing that the mass media also possessed uniting, conciliatory qualities, giving it the ability to bring issues of social and political importance to the attention of large parts of the population simultaneously. For example, popular television can teach its voluntary, entertainment-seeking audience about identity and difference, sustaining and advancing citizenship—a type of "democratainment."[4] The textual analysis tradition of media studies has demonstrated the complexity of the cultural landscape and the capacity of readers to navigate that field. This has shown us that, even if power relationships are skewed in terms of few corporations at the expense of society, this does not preclude power at the individual level of the reader/viewer/listener. Audience theorists, too, have shown how audiences can adapt media content into a myriad of different uses and cultures.[5]

The shift in media studies towards a conception of the active audience demands that some aspects of the NWICO debate (at least that which was concerned with the audience being controlled by American content) be rethought. But, despite the fact that media theory has moved beyond imperialist notions of domination over the thoughts and tastes of the audience, the critical left remains "firmly couched within transmission models of communication," worrying over the imposition of the dominant culture upon the receiver.[6] This has only served to leave community media studies out of touch with important developments in the media studies field that incorporate more complex ideas of power, identity, and cultural change. That said, community media studies is now beginning to acknowledge the inadequacies of its own tradition and is developing new perspectives that are important to media studies as a whole.

Justifications for alternative, community, and radical media are now being disentangled "from the often axiomatic assumptions we have about audiences."[7] Alternative media is in fact an extension of the active audience (from active consumption to production),[8] a cultural interaction, and not an argument against popular media. One expansive study of radical media by its leading theorist, John Downing, describes the efforts of media makers who are challenging dominant ideological frameworks as "consciousness raising." Radical media is better understood via theories of *counterhegemony* (disruptions to dominant power) and *counter–public spheres* (a term to describe the myriad and diverse spaces where discussion and dissent occur) as well as new social movement theory, rather than as simply oppositional. These concepts explain how radical media mobilizes itself and responds to the wider social arena and take into account its many forms and viewpoints.

The "microsubversive strategies" of radical media are not necessarily the expressions of a public that is "seething with systematically masked discontent" but are a testing of limits—a pressure placed on moments of elite power—often through quite everyday activities and cultural forms.[9]

Therefore, even though community media may be dispersed and small-scale, a study of it can provide important insights into the wider research agenda of media studies. As media studies writer Nick Couldry, points out, "if we are concerned with the broader social process of mediation—characterised by an extremely uneven distribution of symbolic resources—then ignoring alternative media is not only arbitrary, but it misses the key point about them: that they are the weapons of the weak."[10] It does not make sense to ignore community media when the starting point of media studies is the way in which the media represents our own—or others'—reality, which in turn influences our status and the repercussions flowing from our actions (symbolic power). Ordinary people's efforts to put themselves within the media frame may be only a small contribution to the mediascape compared with the large amount of material generated by the media industry. However, this alone should not make it marginal as an object of study. The attempt to alter the dynamics of symbolic power is intensely interesting precisely because it is posed as a challenge, a disruption, or as a *tactic*.[11] This approach recognizes the oppositional quality of alternative media without placing it in a binary position in relation to the mainstream media. If we privilege "alternative media practices' wider concern with the politics of speech, rather than its positions on formal politics," it may spark "a debate on the conditions for effective democracy in mediated societies."[12] The move to see alternative media within a more complex understanding of power has been important within the reinvigoration of community media as an area of study. For instance, Chris Atton points out that the classification of fanzines (web- or print-based fan media) as "subcultural" runs the risk "of collapsing a range of class positions, social relations, political and cultural ends, and claims to solidarity and opposition into a social setting that is essentially structural."[13] Instead, new community media theory seeks to understand what is offered by alternative organizational models in their own right.

A South American media academic working in the Unites States has developed a unique and useful approach to community media. Clemencia Rodriguez writes that she was compelled to find "a new route to conceptualizing community media" upon realizing that her experiences of working within groups in Columbia, Texas, and Catalonia did not fit easily within the available theoretical frameworks.

Our theorizing uses categories too narrow to encompass the lived experiences of those involved with alternative media. Communication academics and media activists began looking at alternative media as a hopeful option to counterbalance the unequal distribution of communication resources that came with the growth of big media corporations. This origin has located the debate within rigid categories of power and binary conceptions of domination and subordination that elude the fluidity and complexity of alternative media as a social, political, and cultural phenomenon.[14]

By reframing alternative and community-based media as "citizens' media," Rodriguez seeks to move beyond previous academic discourses that position community media projects as linear and "conscious processes towards a common goal."[15] The fragmented, messy, and often contradictory existences and ambitions of alternative media are not indications of its failure but evidence that our previous assumptions about alternative media have been misplaced. Citizenship theory focuses on people's responsibilities, roles, loyalties, and differences, and how these factors can be accommodated for democratic outcomes. Community and alternative media can be seen as an articulation of citizenship, when citizenship is seen as the day-to-day endeavor to renegotiate and construct new levels of democracy and equality. Central to this conception of alternative media is an idea of citizenship that is inclusive of pluralism and yet able to account for different subject positions and social relations. Rather than citizenship being simply the minimum framework of liberalism or the all-encompassing preoccupation of civic republicanism, citizenship is seen as an "articulating principle" that allows for a plurality of specific allegiances while maintaining equality and liberty. Citizenship must "always be recreated and renegotiated" within this context.[16] Rodriguez's shift to "citizens' media" does not remove the themes that have always been the focus of alternative media: protest and dissent, collective organization and participation, culture and the media, viewing and producing. However, these themes are not strung together in order to create a singular project or a cohesive, rational goal for the project of democratic media, but are instead seen as multiple fronts upon which citizenship is being constantly negotiated through expressions of identity and cultural strategies.

The possibilities of these new conceptions of citizenship *enactment* or *expression* through community media are important in the context of this book. By opening up new, nonessentialist notions of participation, community media becomes much more interesting. Early understandings of community media imposed a false (and most likely impossible) ideal—neglecting the subtleties and complex dynamics of mainstream media uses as much as those of alternative media itself. This discourse closed off community media to other uses and led to depictions of its small-scale nature as an indication of failure, and its ordinariness as a lack of power. Neither scale nor aesthetics should preclude us from exploring the value and unique dynamics of community media.

Defining Community Media

Community media is generally defined as media that allows for access and participation. As this book is concerned with how community media has been constructed through policy and advocacy, it will also explore a number of "controls" that have been used to ensure that media calling itself community media is in fact that—such as nonprofit status and representativeness of a particular group. In community media studies literature, however, definitions have proved contentious. The term "community media," in its widest sense, includes a massive array of activities and outcomes, not all of which are small or nonprofit. The gay press and fan websites are just two examples of media that address a particular community but may not necessarily be nonprofit or identify themselves as "community media." With such a dispersed field, it is no wonder that studies of the media and democracy often concentrate on alternative media, rather than community media as a whole. I find this privileging of alternative media (as an object of study) somewhat problematic, as I will explain momentarily. However, it can provide some useful insights into what it is that community media does differently than the mainstream.

A large portion of the debate on alternative media is taken up with what alternative media is. Some define it according to production, distribution, and organization, and include highly personal/individual zines (self-published magazines) within an area usually defined by group activity. The alternative press in the United Kingdom, for instance, displays all of the diversity and experimentation of community-based media. For Atton, the way in which the publications are produced is their defining feature, an indication of their alternative status. One group describes itself as a "disorganization," happy with its lack of hierarchy and unpredictable ways of getting things done. The micropress Oxford Institute for Social Disengineering does not see its small audience as a problem, stating that many publications with a small circulation are better than one publication with a large circulation. Furthermore, publications are often printed with anti-copyright stipulations, encouraging others to photocopy and distribute at will. Some are published with blank pages so that readers can participate by adding something to their own copy. Collective practice is actively sought, as are ideas from people who are not generally seen as belonging to the intellectual elite; it's a form of "prefigurative politics"—the attempt to practice socialist principles in the present.

The alternative press demonstrates that community-based media possess a culture of media making that is very different from the professional media. They turn readers into writers, thereby bringing new ideas into the cultural sphere. This activity might be called *self-expression*. In some respects, self-expression is an individualistic concept that can seem at odds with the notion of community—as in group-based—media. However, these publications still recognize that the values and experiences of the self are shared with like-minded others. Therefore, the expression of personal ideas is a means for the community to see and understand itself better. The arrival of new technologies that allow for greater read/write participation and that are centered on the notion of self-expression (such as the Internet), raise questions as to the future of community-based media. These issues are explored at greater length in chapters 6 and 7.

Another way to define community media is by its regulatory constraints. Low-budget zines of minimal distribution work to a somewhat different rhythm to community radio and television. Although some low-power radio stations (such as those in the microradio movement in the United States, discussed in chapter 2) have tried to avoid licensing regimes, the majority of community radio and television enterprises require some resources and a license to operate. As a result, they have made it part of their cause to acquire support and are rarely self-financed in the way that zines are.[17] By comparison, radio and television are "shackled" by the constraints of finding sponsors or advertisers and "hampered by restrictions on access to broadcasting frequencies."[18] The alternative media and zine culture exist at a remote distance from the worries of media regulation. They could be seen as more "community" in that they avoid the problems that occur when communities must deal with laws and forces that operate to a different model than their own internal dynamics. However, community radio and television, by demanding that broadcasting be restructured to accommodate the public, make a more direct challenge to the status quo, even if their content and production methods are more conventional. They ask us to rethink the way in which media information is managed at the governmental level—a point I will return to shortly.

Clemencia Rodriguez has gone to lengths to elaborate on why some small-scale media can be considered "citizens' media"—empowering, progressive, and alternative—whereas others cannot. Reading a video produced as part of a citizens' media project by three Chicana girls, Rodriguez writes that the video opens "a path toward a rendition of the barrio grounded in the love of three girls for the place of their childhood."[19] The typical renditions of the barrio, characterized by sepia tones and violent scenes, are not found in the video, which is titled *Wild Fields*. Instead it conveys inconclusiveness— shown through diffused light—and flux, which is conveyed by a constantly moving camera. Citizens' media leaves behind "all legacies of pre-existing codes," plunging into "the in-betweens; before entities were coded as subject or object, dream or reality; before we were each assigned a value, which inevitably confines us all to a system of exchangeable units." It is these qualities that distinguish citizens' (or alternative) media from the "endeavours of skinheads and white supremacists, Christian fundamentalists and neo-Nazi groups which intend to tighten still further the order of Being's straight-jacket."[20]

Although I do not dispute the potential to differentiate types of community media on aesthetic or ethical grounds, in practice the decision to accept some types of community media over others is problematic. In chapter 2, these tensions are discussed in terms of freedom of speech models that employ first-come, first-served strategies, and access regimes that seek to institute programming in terms of community needs. My concern is not that some content is more desirable than other content. The issue that community media practitioners and policy makers face is whether or not structures exist that can steer community media in positive directions and whether that is necessary at all.

The problem with alternative media theory is that it focuses only on one aspect of community media activity. Its appeal is nicely summed up by cultural theorist George McKay in his work on DIY ("do it yourself") culture, a term which is frequently used to describe alternative, or activist, media: "DiY culture's a combination of inspiring action, narcissism, youthful arrogance, principle, ahistoricism, idealism, indulgence, creativity, plagiarism, as well as the rejection and embracing alike of technological innovation."[21] Even those who refute these assumptions (McKay amongst them) still ponder the basis of its appeal. The term "community media" carries less cheekiness and more confusion than "alternative media." Downing sees wider "community media" as a tricky field of study: "whichever way you cut it, the term persistently raises many more questions and dilemmas than it answers."[22] However, it is these questions and dilemmas that are my focus here. To unravel them requires looking at the good, the bad, and the ordinary. It also means delving into the contentious field of community within contemporary democratic theory.

Communitarianism vs. Liberalism

Community media will always defy generalization and be difficult to manage because communities themselves are such complex entities. The community sphere is generally considered to be a natural part of contemporary democracies and is seen to be a site for diversity and values that the market and government cannot achieve. The dispute over community is not whether it exists or whether it should exist, but whether communities should be encouraged or left to form and dissolve at their own will (and at the mercy of outside forces such as economics and law). Theories of community were prevalent in Enlightenment philosophy—discussed in the work of Smith, Hegel, and de Tocqueville. In the past two decades, the concept of community has experienced a theoretical revival.[23] Communitarianism is a political theory that investigates the limits of liberalism by exploring the value of communities and how community benefits may be enhanced. It has also been influential in a new type of politics that has emerged in recent years which has proved important in policy development around community media.

Community broadcasting sits at the intersection of the administratively controlled broadcasting environment (having to comply to license conditions and regulation) and the more random, messy, and "natural" configurations of the community sphere. In many respects, the institutionalization of community media is a means to manage something that has previously managed itself, and this creates a set of dilemmas that are unique to community media. There is constant tension between who should gain access, what level of editorial control stations should maintain, and how to determine whether stations are representative of the community their license was intended for. It is these qualities that make community media a unique object of study and why it is that community media not only *requires* but *brings with it* alternative policy approaches.

Community supporters claim that it is something inherently democratic while its critics see it as a dangerous concept (at least when taken to its extreme). Community media certainly has both progressive and regressive qualities. Supporters are often motivated by the idea that people in groups are capable of participating in, and defining, their society in a meaningful way through their shared collective interest. Is community media capable of *improving* the world in which we live? Does it matter? Should we devote resources to it, and if we do, what will be the long-term consequences? Once it is established, is it capable of serving all interests or should it just cater to those who decide to get involved? All of these questions have been at least partly addressed in the political science debates over communitarianism.

For those who attempt to defend community on normative grounds, community is inescapable. Community is a social web, or bonds that are shared. These bonds "carry a set of shared moral and social values,"[24] duties and responsibilities that are essential to social cohesion. The communitarian argument, which sees this as the primary organizing principle upon which social structures should be designed, has been criticized for relying on romantic notions of natural unity and for claiming to be progressive when it is, in fact, often based on conservative and nostalgic ideals. From this angle, the desire for unity through community can lead to the denial of difference by creating an opposition between what is considered to be "authentic" and "inauthentic" social life. Many who appeal to the ideal of community "tend to evoke an effective value" through their desire for social wholeness, unity, and meaning.[25] Insular communities border on fanaticism, devaluing that which is not within the community as "other." Community shelters, and closes off communication in these discussions. It negates the existing reality, detemporalizing social change, "providing no understanding of the move from here to there that would be rooted in an understanding of the contradictions and possibilities of existing society."[26] Proponents of community are also criticized for invoking nostalgic desires, promoting a return to the "warm, encompassing (and closed) communities of the premodern era."[27] One commentator has written of Australia's SBS radio (a nationally funded broadcaster, working under a charter of multiculturalism) that programs can become "avenues for the propagation of the 'imagined communities' of the immigrants—strange, limited, partial expressions of their experience."[28] Such tendencies also apply to community group broadcasting. Community can be progressive and radical, conservative and moralistic, nostalgic or revolutionary. In modern capitalist societies, diversity appears to be its only defining feature.

The debate about what community is, and what importance it should be given politically, was for some time played out as a rights debate between communitarians and liberals. The liberal argument asserts that individual rights must be the primary concern of political society, as through the protection of the individual's rights the good life is most likely to occur. Much of the liberal argument is reliant upon the "state of nature" or variations of it: a hypothetical position in which individuals are stripped of their memory of history, class, knowledge, or the place that they occupied within society. In these circumstances, any rational individual would choose a system of equality in which a set of basic rights were protected. No matter how she (or he—she does not know her gender) was to "end up" when her life attributes were returned, she would be guaranteed a level of safety and well-being. On this basis it is possible to arrive at a set of minimum rights that will ensure the best possible outcome for all. The liberal language of individual rights, it is argued, is sufficient for meeting group needs. Creating political institutions or legal rights that are structured or based around cultural interests may affect the kinds of cultural communities that people decide to form, or lead to the maintenance of ones that are no longer relevant.[29] Furthermore, individual liberty may be jeopardized if the interests of the individual become secondary to the rights of the group. A liberal framework is seen as paramount as groups are not fixed entities but are constantly forming and dissolving in response to political and institutional circumstances. In this portrait of liberal rights, community exists outside of the political realm; it is a matter of personal affiliation that political action would only distort to the favor of some over others.

Communitarians are dissatisfied with this argument and assert the primacy of the social over the individual. Our culture, ideas, material circumstances, and values do matter and it is through our interaction with others that society exists. Furthermore, a focus on individual rights overlooks the duties and values (civic virtue) that are fostered by community and that are necessary for a well-functioning society. This is where community media is placed. Communities are valued for the contribution they make, both culturally and in the provision of services that make democracy work better. The abstract self of liberal theory is unacceptable as "particularities can never be simply left behind or obliterated."[30] In its most adamant form, communitarianism asserts that the emphasis on individualism in liberal theory fosters an amoral, fragmented society. Liberalism promotes discontents such as isolation, the rat race, apathy, and divorce. In all, "the procedural republic cannot secure the liberty it promises, because it cannot sustain the kind of political community and civic engagement that liberty requires."[31] A moderate communitarian, Michael Walzer finds a contradiction within such arguments. Communitarians on the one hand argue that liberalism misrepresents our situation as we are inevitably part of a society, with ties to family, cultural groups, friends, work colleagues, and so on. But at the same time communitarians assert that society has lost the togetherness that it once possessed. These two communitarian arguments are "mutually inconsistent; they cannot both be true. Liberal separatism either represents or misrepresents the conditions of everyday life."[32] On the strand of thinking that sees society as having become fragmented "into the problematic coexistence of individuals," he contends that we may as well "assume that liberal politics is the best way to deal with the problems of decomposition."[33] In other words, if we are "a community of strangers" then the liberal justice approach is the most suitable system. Nonetheless, communitarianism does make an important contribution that is not incompatible with liberalism. It is possible that liberalism can prevent us from seeing the value of the historical path and from recognizing that we could know and treat each other better. Liberalism is the only means to ensure freedom but, within that, the notion of community can be a correction that enhances liberal values. It can never be a totalizing theory, but is a useful and necessary recurrent theme that reminds us what type of society we would like to live in.[34]

For many theorists of democracy, the hard opposition between liberalism and communitarianism is unnecessary. Iris Marion Young writes that "unlike reactionary appeals to community which consistently assert the subordination of individual aims and values to the collective, most radical theorists assert that community itself consists in the respect for and fulfilment of individual aims and capacities. The neat distinction between individualism and community thus generates a dialectic in which each is a condition for the other."[35] In many respects the two principles belong to the same political culture[36] and the usefulness of the debate lies in the reconciliation of the two schools of thought rather than the continued assertion of their fundamental polarities. The actual dialogue made possible by the two theories—our use of their universal norms for the sake of argument—is what allows us to dispute and to engage with the institutional realization of both individual rights and the social whole. Although this take on the matter is still essentially intersubjective—possibly closer to the communitarian critique as it starts from the social context—it does not dismiss the importance of the rights thesis. Rights are essential to ensure that free dialogue and engagement on political issues occurs:

> In short, rights do not only secure negative liberty, the autonomy of private, disconnected individuals. They also secure the autonomous (freed from state control) communicative interaction of individuals with one another in the public and private spheres of civil society, as well as a new relation of individuals to the public and the political spheres of society and state (including, of course, citizenship rights). . . . The rights to communication, to assembly, and association, among others, constitute the public and associational spheres of civil society as spheres of positive freedom within which agents can collectively debate issues of common concern, act in concert, assert new rights, and exercise influence on political (and potentially economic) society.[37]

It is this approach that carries the most weight in the context of this book. Rather than attempting to base an understanding of community broadcasting within a philosophically irrefutable notion of community, my aim is to focus upon the use of community as it is deployed to reach certain cultural and political ends. I locate this activity within the sphere of civil society. In the United States, civil society is central to a new politics that takes into account the role of community. In the United Kingdom, Australia, and parts of Europe, this has been mostly articulated through third way politics. Let's take a closer look at the new politics of community and the relationship of civil society to community media.

The Civil Society Debate

Civil society is a domain created by people through their associations, bonds, and allegiances separate from the state and the market, but tied to both. In Walzer's definition, civil society is "the space of uncoerced human association and also the set of relational networks—formed for the sake of family, faith, interest and ideology—that fill this space."[38] Some theorists place emphasis on the clubs and nonprofit groups that we voluntarily take part in— from bowling clubs and bridge to scouts and political parties.[39] Others include the more disparate networks of new social movements and Internet discussion groups.[40] Civil society is most easily explained as "relations of conscious association, of self-organisation and organised communication"[41] that are either institutions or near-institutions. In some respects, civil society is a way of speaking about community beyond the "natural" intercommunication between people—it is community as a sphere of social activity within liberal democracies, firmly positioned within the structures that make up modern politics. It is not far removed from the concept of community, which is why it has become popular to speak of the renewal of civil society as a political strategy to advance the cause of community and to argue against individual-centered politics.

The civil society debate has had a particular treatment in America. It is used to express insecurity towards America's future, in particular the country's moral and social outlook. An influential book by political scientist Robert Putnam, *Bowling Alone*, has come to epitomize this approach—although Putnam is far from alone in his views. As one commentator observed, the unprecedented media and popular attention that Putnam's work has attracted make it "impossible to argue that interest in the idea of civil society was somehow manufactured or ungenuine. Clearly the idea and the national mood worked in tandem."[42] Putnam's own account of the "national mood" is salient:

> In 1992 three quarters of the US workforce said that "the breakdown of community" and "selfishness" were "serious" or "extremely serious" problems in

America. In 1996 only 8 percent of all Americans said that "the honesty and integrity of the average American" were improving, as compared with 50 percent of us who thought we were becoming less trustworthy. Those of us who said that people had become less civil over the preceding ten years outnumbered those who thought people had become more civil, 80 percent to 12 percent. In several surveys in 1999 two-thirds of Americans said that America's civic life had weakened in recent years, that social and moral values were higher when they were growing up, and that our society was focused more on the individual than the community. More than 80 percent said that there should be more emphasis on community, even if that put more demands on individuals.[43]

The methodology behind such figures, as well as Putnam's broader observations on the drop in voluntarism and group membership, has been challenged on many counts.[44] But although trust may be difficult to measure, and other forms of civic engagement may exist that are not identified in *Bowling Alone*, Putnam does pick up on a mood worthy of consideration. The civil society debate is centered on an idea of a perceived decline in moral values and asserts that Americans have been "pulled apart from one another and from our communities over the last third of the century."[45] That participation in politics (voter turnout and party membership), in the institutions of civil society (its associations and clubs), as well as informal ties (social gatherings such as picnics and bowling), has sunk is said to have consequences for both democracy and the general happiness of citizens. How America ended up in this situation is difficult to discern in much of the civil society debate, except that failed social policy is seen to be part of it, with poverty, crime, family breakdown, and drug addiction symptomatic of political and social collapse. Others assert that voluntary activity is a necessary politicizing experience that raises participation in formal political processes. It is not simply that community organizations are viewed as one answer to social policy concerns, but that values such as trust, loyalty, and altruism are being threatened.

It is possibly the reluctance within American thought to depart from an individualist framework that has led to such reliance upon morality as a means to social advancement. If individual selfishness weakens pluralism to the point where people become "religious and cultural freeloaders, their lives enhanced by a community they do not actively support and by an identity they need not themselves cultivate,"[46] then what can be done? European-style associationalism (whereby large nonprofit associations direct public services) does not necessarily provide an easy answer in the American context, as in the European model rights are subordinated to association membership made compulsory by the state. It is, therefore, no surprise that much of the civil society debate has become a lament for the decline in the moral responsibility of individuals. Those who have sought to answer the problem have looked to the realm of civil society as a possible means to strengthen social bonds with only minimal state involvement. Their basis for making this claim is that interaction with others creates trust and responsibility, which will manifest itself in the wider political community to the benefit of all. The ultimate responsibility for social improvement is placed on individuals' personal qualities, with an acknowledgment that these values are formed through social relations.

One of the problems with this type of moralism is that it can paint an unrealistic portrait of what exists in the cultural sphere. Not only is Putnam suspicious of the media, seeing it as destructive of community, but also much of the civil society debate ignores the types of affiliation and activity that are not "desirable" in the cultural realm of middle-class America. As access stations (cable channels reserved for public, educational, and government use) demonstrate, so long as the free speech imperative remains, the speech that is likely to result is unpredictable. Television channels on which teenagers freely swear while playacting WWF wrestling can hardly be said to be promoting middle-class notions of good community. Community media in the United States has undertaken a virulent fight against indecency restrictions, indicating that "the undesirable" (or too desirable) is not likely to go away. Access television asks us to look at the world, good and bad, face on.

Putnam's conception of civil society and the notion of moral decline possibly even undermine democracy, threatening personal liberty and blocking social justice and solidarity—even though Putnam conceives of it doing the opposite.[47] The singular focus on voluntary associations as moral incubators is misguided on two counts: firstly, for ignoring the importance of political institutions and legal rights guarantees, and secondly, for overlooking the genesis of ideas and policy that occur through deliberation in civil society. The first point is important: it highlights the fact that rights protect and encourage freedom of association, diversity, expression, and so on—an important aspect of pluralism that supports America's culture of voluntarism as much as its individualism.[48] The second point is that Putnam must rely upon moral notions of trust and reciprocity in lieu of an adequate conception of deliberation and information exchange in civil society. Civil society theorist Jean Cohen is dissatisfied with the conclusion drawn by Putnam and others that horizontally structured rather than vertically structured associations create "good" social capital, thereby increasing political responsibility. She points out that this method is flawed as "we are never really told why only horizontal as distinct from vertical associative networks produce social capital." She continues:

> I suspect that the issue is handled this way because the most obvious argument cannot be made without considerably complicating the theoretical framework: namely, that perhaps what develops interactive abilities and democratic competence within an association is participation as an equal in the exchange of opinions and in collective deliberations over associational affairs—that is, voice in the association's internal public sphere. Hierarchical, authoritarian associations such as the Mafia can easily generate skill in strategic action; the Catholic Church can generate loyalty. But I suspect that only associations with internal publics structured by the relevant norms of discourse can develop the communicative competence and interactive abilities important to democracy.[49]

So although civil associations can have moral outcomes such as the fostering of toleration and trust, the focus needs to be on deliberation and the democratic qualities of groups. For, "if *all* the myriad associations of civil society were structured like the Mafia, I doubt that either democratic competence or even liberal tolerance among citizens would be widespread."[50] We need to question the assumption behind much civil society discourse that trust between individuals within groups must necessarily lead to trust in wider society. For instance, there is no reason to assume that participation in a choral society will translate into political engagement or the desire to create a good society. There is nothing to lead us to the conclusion that intragroup trust will ever be anything other than particularistic without the influence of other factors. It is what Cohen calls "voice," rather than values such as loyalty, trust, and virtue, that is most important in civil society. Such a focus on voice and deliberation requires an understanding of the public within civil society discussions. Without this, the civil society debate descends into talk of moral decline that has little to do with democratization. This point is important in relation to access television (chapter 2) as this media has been created on the belief that a public space for deliberation is essential to the vitality and strength of civil society.

Community Media in the Civil Society Context

The concept of civil society is capable of reconciling some of the contemporary debates around issues of democracy, participation, rights, and welfare. But for civil society to be capable of engaging with such issues, civil society cannot only exist in the private realm (as in the charity sector, family, etc., which often takes place outside of the political realm). The pluralist model,

---

Boston Neighborhood Network

Boston Neighborhood Network Television (BNN) is a public access television station established by Boston's cable franchise agreement in 1983. The station is aware that community groups, and not just individuals, require assistance in order to be able to participate in public access television. With resources stretched, many groups are not able to find volunteers or staff with the time to learn television production, which excludes many associations in the community who could potentially make use of the station.[a] Boston Neighborhood Network Television undertakes to encourage and facilitate media use by community groups out of a belief that the work of such groups is vital to the community. The solution for BNN is a channel called BNNLive, which is run as an automatic studio, requiring only two station volunteers and a fixed set that can be made available to groups within the community. Panel-style discussions can be broadcast without the groups needing to produce programs themselves. The move towards programs such as those on BNNLive suggests that some access stations see themselves as playing a part in the support and revival of civil society, placing a strong emphasis on the importance of associations. A look at the program schedule for BNNLive over a one-week period shows programs called the *Citywide Parent's Council, MA Association of Women Lawyers, The Greek Program, Arthritis Answers, Small Business Today,* and *Let's Talk About It* (by Citizens for Participation in Political Action). The program format may be basic, but it works for groups needing to get information out to their communities. Furthermore, the station is aware that with such associations on its side, it is unlikely that the city will renege on BNN in future contracts.

---

[a] Curtis Henderson, interviewed by Ellie Rennie, Boston, May 5, 2001.

---

for instance, depicts society as a collection of groups and the state as an organization of individual citizens, where "society and state, though they constantly interact, are formally distinct."[51] (See chapter 2 for further discussion.) This approach denies the possibilities presented by associational life, the public sphere, and new social movements as "spheres of positive freedom"[52] in which people learn difference and debate issues—activities that are political, transformative, engaging and participative. It could also be said that if civil society continues to be seen as nonpolitical, it will become even more marginal.[53] Prominent civil society theorist John Keane agrees that civil society should not be relegated to the realm of the "private" but understood as part of the political process. He sees democracy as a political system in which civil society and state institutions are both necessary. They are interdependent yet distinct, separate, and contiguous and a part of a system in which power (in the household, boardroom, or government office) is subject to public dispute, compromise, and agreement.[54] From a media studies position (which implicitly takes it as a given that nonstate activity is an important area of social life), this definition of civil society is the most useful and appropriate.

When the role of communication in civil society is taken into account, it causes us to question whether a healthy public sphere can be achieved through public service broadcasting alone: "A healthy democratic regime is one in which various types of public spheres are thriving, with no single one of them actually enjoying a monopoly in public disputes about the distribution of power."[55] Keane's view of the role of the media in civil society is one in which a plurality of groups express their solidarities and oppositions to each other, rather than seeking out an ideal, uncontaminated model of communication. He asks in the closing paragraphs of *Civil Society* whether "the future is likely to see a variety of contradictory trends, including not only new modes of domination but also unprecedented public battles to define and to control the spaces in which citizens appear."[56] He recognizes that in current civil society discussions, questions around the media and communication, and their role within civil society, are so far only "poorly formulated."

I take as a given that communicative action in some form "lies at the heart of both the theory and the practice of democracy."[57] The public sphere, defined by Jurgen Habermas as "the social space generated in communicative action,"[58] is implicit within the notion of civil society, as only an understanding of communication within public space can link civil society to democratic theory.[59] It is, therefore, a significant gap that so little work on civil society takes into account the role of the media, except to see it as destructive of face-to-face forums (for instance, Putnam's *Bowling Alone*). Community media, being a media that is produced by civil society groups, has a unique relationship to the types of citizen participation that occur through civil society engagement.

It is conceivable to include the commercial media in the civil society domain and draw a basic state–civil society distinction (as opposed to state–civil society–market). Although this is not the approach I take here, it has its merits. Keane includes the market in civil, justifying it on the grounds that the separation of civil society from the economy falsely renders civil society economically passive. Furthermore, it could be said that accounts that see civil society as distinct from the market tend to depict nonprofit alliances as "good" while the market is "bad"—a binary that is not necessarily a true representation of either. This recognition of the mutual dependency of civil society and the market is important: "Where there are no markets, civil societies find it impossible to survive. But the converse rule also applies: where there is no civil society there can be no markets."[60] Keane's observation of the falsity of an economy–civil society divide is pertinent.

The relationship of the two spheres is discussed in this book in terms of the tensions between community media and market participation. In particular, I refer to the anticommercialism associated with community media and how this may work to marginalize the sector and reinforce the interests and power of the commercial sector (chapter 3). However, I *do* see it as necessary to conceptually separate the market from civil society. In contemporary liberal democracies the economy is often seen as the only alternative to the welfare state. I am interested in a third approach, whereby the associations formed out of nonprofit motives are seen as legitimate participants in governance. In a structure where the power holders are just as likely (if not more) to be privately owned economic actors as bureaucratically organized governments, the nonprofit sector should be recognized as an identifiable alternative model. In the broadcasting realm, the nonprofit construction of community media is a deliberate measure to ensure that community interests are not overlooked or overcome as a result of economic incentives. This does not mean that community media should be banned from participating in the economy (which only serves to keep it impoverished and ineffectual), but that its organizational model should reflect community aims. At a purely empirical level, broadcasting is an administratively achieved space of defined interests, in which civil society has sought to define itself through something other than public and private media—and this self-definition suffices. I do not dispute the view that all media play a role in civil society; however, I am chiefly concerned with the media that civil society chooses to create as something distinct from market and state. In my definition, therefore, civil society is something that is associational and nonprofit, generated for itself and by itself rather than for or by the state or the market.

The concept of civil society and the debate around it is dealt with in this book in a range of contexts. Firstly, it is necessary to recognize that people's engagement in civil society is the reason why some of us set out to establish community media in the first place. Community media is created out of the belief that civil society requires communication platforms—the two are, in this respect, mutually dependent. This is seen in the campaigning efforts of aspiring community broadcasters around the world—the noncommercial pirates and the test transmissions that have lead to the establishment of community media. As has been observed in the European context, community broadcasting, in the majority of cases, was established as a result of continued pressure from community groups rather than by government-inspired directives (see chapter 3). Community media should therefore be seen as a means to the maintenance and extension of civil society by civil society itself.

Secondly, the concept of civil society is useful when discussing community media as it avoids making generalizations about its essential nature. Much writing on community media focuses only on the radically progressive aspects of programming and the production process. As a result, community media as a whole has attracted much less attention than has one of its components—alternative, or radical, media. Although these studies are important in that they examine what is unique about community expression, they do not account for the large amount of community media that is *not* radical or social change–focused (as discussed above). Using the notion of civil society expands the field to encompass all community media.

Thirdly, the concept of civil society as a contributor to the field of political action presents a range of policy options that deserve consideration in the broadcasting context. For instance, political scientist Paul Hirst writes of the failure of both left and right to institute effective social democracy. The politicization of property relations and the struggle for exclusive control of the one political space has resulted in the left-right opposition, both of which "strove to make their control of the state permanent and that policy irreversible."[61] Politics now consists also of campaigns of resistance (feminism, environmentalism, and antiracism) as well as campaigns led by cultural groups, pressure groups, support groups, and others. These movements arise from anywhere, often from intolerable situations and sometimes from everyday routine. They are not fixed, although they may be organized and long lasting. Politics was never entirely dominated by left and right, and it is the case that, more and more, nonstate, regional, and supranational players have the ability to influence policy. For Hirst, this denotes, or requires, a return to associationalism—governance of social affairs through civil society and voluntary organization. This does not involve the wholesale supplanting of existing institutions; rather it provides a vital supplement to them that enables their defects to be meliorated.[62] This rethinking of institutional arrangements is supportive of voluntary, nonprofit organizations. Within such a vision, community does not have to be marginal or defined by opposition, but is capable of offering new avenues for participation that work with an acceptance of the difference, diversity, and power structures of the contemporary world. Other relatively new political theories and movements are also contributing to what can only be seen as a revival of the idea of civil society. Included in this "search for new compromises between states and societies" in which "grand fictions about the primacy of state institutions are thus laid to rest"[63] are the third way attempts to "connect" government with community.[64] I also add "alternative development" to this group of "new" politics as it aims to construct a post-scarcity society through community participation (this is discussed in the media context in chapter 5).

None of these movements are without their problems—in fact their deployment in the communications field has already proved fraught with difficulties. They are included within the context of this book to demonstrate how community has been mobilized to achieve certain ends. In many respects, community media is already contributing alternative models of organization and information distribution (see chapter 6) which have gone largely unrecognized. The question remains how these "natural" formations may inform new policy possibilities in a rapidly changing communications arena. The debates currently occurring around civil society in popular and political theory provide a way into these issues.

This brings me to my final reason for considering community media in the civil society context. Civil society is separate from the state, but in many respects it requires a relationship with the state in order to exist. For community radio and television, the relationship with the state is made clear by the legislative frameworks and policy decisions that define how this somewhat dispersed and varied activity will be implemented. Theories that do not take into account the dependency of community media upon state structures and administrators risk overlooking the positive role that the state can play towards the development of community media.

Third Way

Community media is sometimes pursued as a means to achieve social change. For instance, it can bring skills to a particular community, helping community members to participate in the knowledge economy. This approach is related, at least in part, to the political trend known as the third way. Although the third way has been mostly associated with the politics of Tony Blair's New Labour in the United Kingdom, its reach is far wider. Bill Clinton in the United States and Paul Keating in Australia employed third way strategies in their respective attempts to unite economic reform with traditional left social policy in the 1990s. The most influential theorist of third way politics, Anthony Giddens, sees it as an overall political orientation which has developed out of left-of-center parties as a response to globalization, the knowledge economy, and "profound changes in people's everyday lives."[65] He therefore includes left-party policy developments within Scandinavian nations, Holland, France, and Italy since the late 1980s as part of the emergence of third way politics. The intellectual foundations of third way stem from the communitarian theory of Amatai Etzioni, whose concern for social cohesiveness and community appealed to Western leaders, possibly due to its rhetorical usefulness and the now familiar run of buzz words: "community," "engagement," and "social inclusion." No doubt Etzioni's communitarianism also resonated with the Christian values personally recognized by a number of these leaders (Blair in particular). Although the intellectual idea originated in the United States, the U.S. version of communitarianism could not be directly appropriated in countries such as Australia and the United Kingdom, where left parties maintained a stronger role for the state in the maintenance of the social good. Hence the third way's departure from civil society theory and associationalism, which both imply an eventual separation of the state from a strengthened community sphere.

The main assumptions of the third way, summarized from Giddens, are as follows:

- An unhindered market economy is at odds with social justice but socialism is not applicable to the current global system.
- Governments should take an activist role rather than encouraging top-heavy bureaucracies. Public-private partnerships may provide new solutions to social and economic issues.
- Governments must respond to political apathy, the fast-growing non-party of nonvoters.
- The state should not dominate markets or civil society, although it does need to regulate both.
- A new social contract is needed that links rights to responsibilities.
- The left's commitment to equality requires new strategies. For instance, investing in skills rather than reacting to the insufficiencies of the market through subsidy.
- Full employment is achievable by adapting to technological change rather than propping up ailing industries.
- There must be a connection between social and economic policy.
- Welfare should be reformed, particularly where it creates ingrained moral hazards or "perverse effects."
- Crime should be actively combated for safe and secure communities.
- Governments should be committed to ecological preservation.
- Capitalism should be responsive (shareholder capitalism).[66]

Although there is not room here to explore all of these points, a quick glance shows that community has been given a more central place than in other political approaches. For instance, the move away from centralized government and the simultaneous emphasis on skills creation and responsibility means a stronger role for civil society organizations in partnership with local governments. However, the third way has met with a great deal of criticism, not the least being that it is a complex, piecemeal, and pragmatic approach to policy formation that is not easily explained to the public at large. As one critic writes, "The attraction of free markets on the one hand and central planning on the other is the simplicity of the models—the central idea is easy enough to grasp, even if implementation is problematic. The third way, by contrast, involves a mass of contentious concepts and a wide variety of practices."[67] Conservatives have taken this further, seeing Blair's as a politics of permanent revisionism that opens the way to manipulation and rule by expediency.[68]

It has also been observed that the influence of communitarianism has been minimal within the operations of party politics, possibly because it provides very little in the way of real policy solutions. Most important, however, is the critique that communitarianism cannot succeed if structural inequality has not already been overcome.

> Communitarian discourse is inadequate if it ignores persistent poverty and structural inequality. The fear of anomie and desire for social cohesion is dependent on forging a moral consensus, which communitarians rightly see the market as singularly incapable of developing by itself, a dilemma still unresolved for New Labour. At a time when significant sections of British industry from cars to textiles have been hit by plant closures resulting in redundancy, following foreign-owned corporate decisions, the knock-on effect for the local community is devastating. The work community has a centrality in most people's lives which are becoming noticeably more stressful, as work and social/family life become squeezed by growing employer demands.[69]

Others point out that the emphasis on local government may not produce the desired results; it may instead encourage parochialism and put responsibility on low-level government that is easily made victim to cronyism. Critics believe that community engagement policy is turning members of Parliament into "untrained social workers."[70]

The applicability of third way politics to community media is discussed in chapter 5. For now, it is enough to recognize that the notion of community has become a contentious field, where political aspirations clash with entrenched issues of inequality and debates over the role of the state. Community media ideals, as a result, require revisiting. They no longer belong to an outdated ideology but are being deployed in various contexts—moral, developmental and even as part of economic agendas.

Understanding Community and Governance

British political scientist Nikolas Rose treats community as a "remaking of po-litical subjectivity"[71] that brings new options into the political field. This is also a useful way of thinking about the purpose and goal of community media, as it avoids positioning community as something static and knowable. Com-munity is not singular or uniform but is located in the diverse networks and allegiances of everyday life, at the point where such configurations meet with the strategies of government. The Western philosophical tradition of com-munity (beginning with Rousseau and Marx) "ended up giving us only vari-ous programs for the realisation of an essence of community," as Nancy has shown us.[72] That single-solution approach, which sought a totalizing account of community in order to justify a larger operational goal, is unconvincing in a post-communist world dealing with the contradictions of global capital and culture. Furthermore, it denies the inherent "incompleteness" of community: community is a process, a relationship; it is interaction and communication. Therefore, community is a space that claims to be outside of politics—even regarded by some as pre-political—that nonetheless requires political action to bring it about: "It is the objectification of a plane formed at the unstable and uncomfortable intersections between politics and that which should and must remain beyond its reach."[73] Community is uncalculated, formed through a sense of affinity and identification, a recognized essence, or a sense of be-longing. It also involves processes of group formation, mobilization, and pub-lic participation. When community is instituted as a third sector, and partic-ularly as a participant in a regulated broadcasting environment, it becomes an object of governance. Uncalculated communities are made operational via this transaction and become an instrument through which values and culture are directed. In this way, community media embodies the paradox of the third sector. It appears, on the one hand, as a space beyond politics, "a kind of nat-ural, extra-political zone of human relations."[74] However, it is also very much a concerted political style, one that supports and allows a type of government and its programs to work. Seen as a transaction of governance, it is possible to understand how interventions have shaped cultural forms, what interests have been supported or weakened, how community has functioned in the project of democracy, and in this case, how community has fared as a sector of the media.

The current political movements that rely upon notions of community are not without their difficulties and inconsistencies. Their usefulness lies in the recognition that politics is no longer a matter of two competing options (left and right).[75] Contemporary shifts towards community do not seek to find the truth of community, but see it as a means to new opportunities for political change. These debates and political movements are applicable and relevant here precisely because they attempt to explain the use of community within contemporary liberal democracies. Community media policy, in particular, needs to be seen in this context, as it is—with all broadcasting policy—"the product of social and political choices, not of accident or impersonal economic or technological forces alone."[76] Community media has mostly been seen as a means to counter or overcome existing systems rather than to complement them. The theoretical framework proposed here allows us to look instead at the possibilities and options that community brings to current media contexts.

Seeing community media as part of civil society places more emphasis upon management and institution, upon the position of groups within their broader context and as a product of a larger sphere of closely related activities and networks. It is also useful in understanding what community broadcasting is seen to *achieve*—what compromises are reached between government and citizens, what corrections to existing structures—and how it attempts to reshape communication. The tensions, contradictions, and possibilities of civil society can help explain how and why community media performs, and is treated, in a particular way.

The organizations of the third sector provide a means for citizens to learn responsibility and to collectively influence the workings of the state and the market through civil society. But, although ideas and issues are shared and deliberated within civil society, civil society is also partial, inconclusive, and not easily understood.[77] As a result, theories that uphold the democratic potential of community are in constant danger of generalization, of idealizing that which is arbitrary, and of proclaiming benefits that cannot be easily proven.[78] Walzer writes that civil society can be "[m]ore like working in an ethnic alliance or a feminist support group than canvassing in an election, more like shaping a co-op budget than deciding on national fiscal policy. But can any of these local and small-scale activities ever carry with them the honour of citizenship? Sometimes, certainly, they are narrowly conceived, partial and particularistic; they need political correction. The greater problem, however, is that they seem so ordinary. Living in civil society, one might think, is like speaking in prose."[79] The local and small-scale media discussed in this book are often overlooked because of their size or "ordinariness." But they are a part of the media that groups and individuals have fought hard to develop and maintain. They represent the public's deep and complex engagement with the media and with the structures and institutions that determine how the media is managed. Chapter 3 will investigate the aesthetics of community media and what it means to "speak in prose," using Walzer's analogy. But first it is necessary to understand two of the defining principles that underpin community media—the concepts of access and free speech.

Notes

1. See Sean O'Siochru and Bruce Girard, eds., *Communicating in the Information Society* (Geneva: United Nations Research Institute for Social Development, 2003).

2. Alan O'Connor, ed., *Community Radio in Bolivia: The Miners' Radio Stations* (Lewiston, N.Y.: Edwin Mellen Press, 2004); Clemencia Rodriguez, *Fissures in the Mediascape* (Cresskill, N.J.: Hampton Press, 2001).

3. Chris Atton, *Alternative Media* (Thousand Oaks: Sage, 2002), 36.

4. John Hartley, *Uses of Television* (London: Routledge, 1999).

5. Ien Ang, *Living Room Wars: Rethinking Media Audiences for a Postmodern World* (London: Routledge, 1996); Karen Ross and Virginia Nightingale, *Media and Audiences: New Perspectives* (Maidenhead, U.K.: Open University Press, 2003).

6. Ang, *Living Room Wars*, 165.

7. John Downing, *Radical Media: Rebellious Communication and Social Movements* (Thousand Oaks: Sage, 2001), 9.

8. Downing, *Radical Media*, 3.

9. Downing, *Radical Media*, 16.

10. Nick Couldry, "Mediation and Alternative Media, or Relocating the Centre of Media and Communication Studies," *Media International Australia*, no. 103 (2002): 27.

11. Michel de Certeau, *The Practice of Everyday Life* (Berkeley: University of California Press, 1984).

12. Couldry, "Mediation and Alternative Media," 26.

13. Atton, *Alternative Media*, 57.

14. Rodriguez, *Fissures in the Mediascape*, 3–4.

15. Rodriguez, *Fissures in the Mediascape*, 22.

16. Chantal Mouffe, "Democratic Politics Today," in *Dimensions of Radical Democracy*, ed. Chantal Mouffe (London: Verso, 1992), 14.

17. Atton, *Alternative Media*, 142–43.

18. Atton, *Alternative Media*, 142.

19. Clemencia Rodriguez, "Citizens' Media and the Voice of the Angel Poet," *Media International Australia*, no. 103 (2002): 85.

20. Rodriguez, "Citizens' Media and the Voice of the Angel Poet," 85.

21. George McKay, *DiY Culture: Party & Protest in Nineties Britain* (London: Verso, 1998), 2.

22. Downing, *Radical Media*, 39.

23. Will Kymlicka, *Contemporary Political Philosophy*, 2nd ed. (Oxford: Oxford University Press, 2002).

24. Amitai Etzioni, "Old Chestnuts and New Spurs," in *New Communitarian Thinking*, ed. Amitai Etzioni (Charlottesville: University Press of Virginia, 1995), 19.

25. Iris Marion Young, "The Ideal of Community and the Politics of Difference," in *Feminism/Postmodernism*, ed. Linda J. Nicholson (New York: Routledge, 1990), 302.

26. Young, "The Ideal of Community and the Politics of Difference," 302.

27. E. J. Dionne Jr., "Introduction: Why Civil Society? Why Now?" in *Community Works: The Revival of Civil Society in America*, ed. E. J. Dionne Jr. (Washington, D.C.: Brookings, 1998), 6.

28. Andrew Jakubowicz, "Speaking in Tongues: Multicultural Media and the Constitution of the Socially Homogeneous Australian," in *Australian Communications and the Public Sphere*, ed. Helen Wilson (Melbourne: Macmillan, 1989), 111.

29. See Chandran Kukathas, "Are There Any Cultural Rights?" in *Political Theory* 20, no. 1 (1992): 105–39.

30. Alisdair MacIntyre, *After Virtue*, 2nd ed. (Notre Dame, Ind.: Notre Dame University Press, 1984), 219.

31. Michael J. Sandel, *Democracy's Discontent: America in Search of a Public Philosophy* (Cambridge, Mass.: Harvard University Press, 1996), 24.

32. Michael Walzer, "The Communitarian Critique of Liberalism," in *New Communitarian Thinking*, ed. Etzioni, 57.

33. Walzer, "The Communitarian Critique of Liberalism," 55.

34. Kymlicka, *Contemporary Political Philosophy*.

35. Young, "The Ideal of Community and the Politics of Difference," 307.

36. Jean L. Cohen and Andrew Arato, *Civil Society and Political Theory* (Cambridge, Mass.: MIT Press, 1992), 20.

37. Cohen and Arato, *Civil Society and Political Theory*, 22–23.

38. Michael Walzer, "The Idea of Civil Society: A Path Towards Social Reconstruction," in *Community Works*, ed. Dionne, 129.

39. Robert Putnam, *Bowling Alone: The Collapse and Revival of American Community* (New York: Simon & Schuster, 2000).

40. Jean L. Cohen, "American Civil Society Talk," in *Civil Society, Democracy and Civic Renewal*, ed. Robert K. Fullinwider (Lanham, Md.: Rowman & Littlefield, 1999); Robert Huesca, "Conceptual Contributions of New Social Movements to Development Communication Research," *Communication Theory* 11, no. 4 (2001).

41. Cohen and Arato, *Civil Society and Political Theory*, x.

42. Alan Wolfe, "Is Civil Society Obsolete? Revisiting Predictions of the Decline of Civil Society in *Whose Keeper?*" in *Community Works*, ed. Dionne, 18.

43. Putnam, *Bowling Alone*, 25.

44. William A. Galston and Peter Levine, "America's Civic Condition: A Glance at the Evidence," in *Community Works*, ed. Dionne; William M. Sullivan, "Making Civil Society Work: Democracy as a Problem of Civic Cooperation," in *Civil Society, Democracy and Civic Renewal*, ed. Fullinwider.

45. Putnam, *Bowling Alone*, 27.

46. Michael Walzer, "Pluralism: A Political Perspective," in *The Rights of Minority Cultures*, ed. Will Kymlicka (New York: Oxford University Press, 1995), 139–54.

47. Cohen, "American Civil Society Talk."

48. Sidney Verba, Kay Lehman Schlozman, and Henry E. Brady, *Voice and Equality: Civic Voluntarism in American Politics* (Cambridge, Mass.: Harvard University Press, 1995).

49. Cohen, "American Civil Society Talk," 63.

50. Cohen, "American Civil Society Talk," 63.

51. Walzer, "Pluralism: A Political Perspective," 148.

52. Cohen and Arato, *Civil Society and Political Theory*, 23.

53. Paul Q. Hirst, "Democracy and Civil Society," in *Reinventing Democracy*, ed. Paul Q. Hirst and S. Kibilnan (Oxford: Blackwell, 1996).

54. John Keane, *Civil Society: Old Images, New Visions* (Cambridge: Polity Press, 1998).

55. Keane, *Civil Society: Old Images, New Visions*, 186.

56. Keane, *Civil Society: Old Images, New Visions*, 189.

57. Nicholas Garnham, "The Media and the Public Sphere," in *Communicating Politics*, ed. P. Golding, G. Murdock, and P. Schlesinger (Leicester: Leicester University Press, 1986), 37.

58. Jurgen Habermas, *Between Facts and Norms: Contributions to a Discourse Theory of Law and Democracy*, trans. William Rehg (Cambridge Mass.: MIT Press, 1996), 360.

59. Cohen, "American Civil Society Talk."

60. Keane, *Civil Society: Old Images, New Visions*, 19.

61. Paul Q. Hirst, *Associative Democracy: New Forms of Economic and Social Governance* (Cambridge: Polity Press, 1994), 8.

62. Hirst, *Associative Democracy*, 12.

63. John Keane, *The Media and Democracy* (Cambridge: Polity Press, 1991), 35.

64. Anthony Giddens, *Beyond Left and Right* (Cambridge: Polity Press, 1994); Anthony Giddens, *The Third Way and Its Critics* (Cambridge: Polity Press, 2000).

65. Anthony Giddens, ed., *The Global Third Way Debate* (Malden, Mass.: Polity Press, 2001), 3.

66. Giddens, ed., *The Global Third Way Debate*.

67. Robert Leach, *Political Ideology in Britain* (Basingstoke: Palgrave, 2002), 221.

68. Otto Newman and Richard de Zoysa, *The Promise of the Third Way: Globalisation and Social Justice* (Basingstoke: Palgrave, 2001), 117.

69. Newman and Zoysa, *The Promise of the Third Way*, 143.

70. Newman and Zoysa, *The Promise of the Third Way*, 116.

71. Nikolas Rose, *Powers of Freedom: Reframing Political Thought* (Cambridge: Cambridge University Press, 1999), 176.

72. Jean-Luc Nancy, *The Inoperative Community* (Minneapolis: University of Minnesota Press, 1991), 12.

73. Rose, *Powers of Freedom*, 182.

74. Rose, *Powers of Freedom*, 167.

75. Hirst, *Associative Democracy*.

76. Thomas Streeter, *Selling the Air: A Critique of the Policy of Commercial Broadcasting in the United States* (Chicago: University of Chicago Press, 1996), 6.

77. Michael Walzer, "Citizenship," in *Political Innovation and Conceptual Change*, ed. Terence Ball, James Farr, and Russell L. Hanson (Cambridge: Cambridge University Press, 1989).

78. Will Kymlicka and Wayne Norman, "Return of the Citizen: A Survey of Recent Work on Citizenship Theory," *Ethics*, no. 104 (1994): 363.

79. Michael Walzer, "The Civil Society Argument," in *Dimensions of Radical Democracy*, ed. Mouffe, 106.

CHAPTER TWO

Access and Free Speech

In 1968, in the slums of Montreal, a local organization known as the Saint Jacques Citizens' Committee took to the streets with portable cameras, interviewing residents and later discussing their footage at public meetings. The project, organized by Dorothy Todd Hénaut and Bonnie Klein, was part of Challenge for Change, a National Film Board of Canada initiative designed to provoke social change through the use of film. In their report on the Montreal project, Hénaut and Klein expressed hopes that one day citizens' groups would be able to make programs for local television outlets. At the same time, in Virginia the first community access channel had just begun cablecasting.[1]

Basic to the Challenge for Change approach was "the concept of the filmmaker as an organizer, activist, stimulator, catalyst, or whatever he might choose to call himself, as distinct from his usual role."[2] The idea that the filmmaker could, through the use of technology, shape social relations in ways different from predominant mass media formats became the first justification for community broadcasting and cablecasting. At its heart was the concept of access—access to distribution of community-produced programs via broadcast or cable technology. It was this that led a group called Town Talk to establish community access to cable television at the crucial time of license renewal in Thunder Bay, Ontario, in 1970—a strategy that has persisted in North America, and one that I will return to. Challenge for Change provided equipment and training to the Thunder Bay group, and programming consisting of locally produced programs, live studio segments, and

47

phone-ins. However, despite the substantial following that the programs attracted, the community television group was not able to withstand its opponents: "Local authorities were opposed to the presence of video crews at certain meetings. Some government officials in Ottawa charged that the project was controlled by radicals. The local cable company, backed by the national association of the Canadian cable industry, opposed giving up control of programming and finances to a citizens' group. The company asserted greater control by requiring submission of programs three weeks in advance and an end to phone-ins."[3] Power dynamics such as these—editorial control by the cable company, as well as government support for industry over the establishment of a public space—are recurrent themes in the history of community television and radio. These forces caused the end of the Thunder Bay experiment before the year was out. However, community broadcasting did develop in Canada, and it is now seen by many as the birthplace of the community broadcasting movement in the First World.

The Canadian experience provided a fundamental argument for the establishment of community broadcasting and cablecasting. Public access television became equated with the American commitment to free speech—a principle that is confronted every day through the use of access television by local communities and individuals. Some authors choose to distinguish between "access" and "community media," with the latter being locally produced and more coordinated.[4] In fact, the term "access" has a number of meanings when used in relation to community media. It is used to describe a community-run television station (access television, sometimes called "public access television"), as well as the access policy principle upon which these stations are founded, namely, the public's right to broadcast on cable channels. It may also refer to the first-come, first-served programming policy employed by many access stations (discussed below), or access to production facilities. Although access television in the United States can look very different from community television in Europe, they work from a similar philosophy. In both cases, the negotiation of access, localism, and community building often defines a station's success in terms of its ability to fulfill community needs. The American reevaluation of access provides a useful means of discussing the dominant values behind both approaches.

Both access and free speech need to be seen within the wider context of broadcasting in the United States. This has been described by media policy expert Thomas Streeter as a system of "corporate liberalism"—not in a purely theoretical sense, but in terms of the guiding belief and vision that informs policy and government decisions. This is a "messier, cruder" form of liberalism than that conceived of by the Enlightenment thinkers, and is somewhat paradoxical in its implementation. Corporate liberalism involves bureaucratic structures ("corporations" as in agencies and institutions) working to create the market, to make it work; it is therefore, "a dynamic response to complex social contradictions and conditions, conditions that include various forms of resistance to corporate control."[5] Even seemingly nonmarket notions, such as the public interest, are a means to create harmony between competing forces in society, resulting in a compromise that ultimately falls in favor of private interests. Access is part of this agenda. Although access policies and campaigns draw attention to the unequal distribution of power and resources in broadcasting, they are also a demand for access to a resource that someone else owns or controls, therefore presupposing the legitimacy of that ownership. Furthermore, it should be seen as an administratively achieved means to appease interests with an objective of neutrality: "The granting of access is thus easily interpreted as one of technocratic corporate liberal adjustments useful for maintaining smooth relations between corporations and the consuming public."[6] This chapter does not attempt to prove or contest the dominant liberal philosophy but to uncover the contradictions and tensions within it.

The administrative and legal treatment of access television in America demonstrates that the access principle is a marginal concession within a system that largely serves private interests. However, access television also deals with social forces that exist outside of the market—with communities and issues that do not fit easily inside the framework within which they operate. This chapter looks at these tensions, moving beyond the claims to access and free speech and towards the attempt to construct civil society through access television. This involves a change in the notion of access, based on a more complex idea of empowerment rather than the earlier (minimalist) individual rights–based conceptions. In the final sections of this chapter, access television's attempt at democratic media is compared to both American community radio and Canadian community radio and television.

The Problem of Access

George Stoney, a New York academic, worked as a guest executive producer for Challenge for Change from 1968 to 1970. Upon his return to the United States, he set up the Alternative Media Center at New York University with Canadian documentary producer Red Burns. The center's objectives included media education, the encouragement of communication for diverse groups, and greater public control of the media. One significant achievement of the Alternative Media Center was an intern program, through which people were trained to work at cable companies around the country.

Several interns went on to establish the first access facilities and channels and soon became involved in lobbying the Federal Communications Commission (FCC) for the provision of access channels. Out of this came the sector's umbrella membership organization, the National Federation of Local Cable Programmers (NFLCP), which has since been renamed the Alliance for Community Media.

In 1970, two cable franchises were awarded for the borough of Manhattan, with two public access channels and two government channels written into the contract at the last minute. One company provided the community with a studio with a camera, a playback deck, and a director free of charge. The Alternative Media Center made videos that documented neighborhood characters and opinions from their location on Bleeker Street, Greenwich Village. The videos were screened in shop windows, apartment lobbies, and from the back of Stoney's station wagon, as few people had cable television in the 1970s.[7] But other radical video groups also began to appear, and, in 1971, two Manhattan access channels were screening five or six hours of content a day.

Community media made its way onto cable television systems beyond Manhattan through these early advocacy and production efforts. Thousands of local channels are now devoted to public access (which exists on 16.5 percent of all cable television systems), educational access (12.9 percent), and government access (10.7 percent)—a triad known as PEG. Cable access television is the quintessential American platform of community media. It is a medium that is seen by some as controversial and profane, by others as ordinary and superfluous, and by the cable companies as an imposition. Those working in cable access defend it vigorously on the grounds of pluralist democracy, free expression, and community and individual development. It makes for difficult television terrain, and yet is a uniquely American cultural phenomenon. Although other countries have since instituted similar models of public access television (Germany's Offener Kanal is strikingly similar to the U.S. access prototype), public access is in many respects a showcase of a nonprofit pluralist domain and is saturated with American political principles.

To be clear from the start, no one believes that the original ideal of public access has been fully realized, including its most devoted supporters.[8] The program schedules of public access television are enough evidence that radical democratic talk is not all that congregates within the access space. Religious and spiritual groups dominate many channels (although not all). Tapes are not previewed prior to screening, as this is considered adverse to the free speech intent, resulting in a hotchpotch of programs with varying production values. Programs with quirky titles such as *The Purple Hamster Show* can be seen scheduled alongside *The Jesus Show* and *Atheist Alliance Presents* on San Francisco's public access channel, CityVisions.[9] Zane Blaney, the station manager, admits that much of it is "niche" viewing, but adds that "hotspots" that attract a significant number of viewers can also be found.

George Stoney commented on the problematic content of access television in 2001 and called for a reconsideration of its first-come, first-served structure: "As early as 1972, when Red Burns and I worked with Nicholas Johnson, the lone 'green' member of the FCC, to craft the language for the provision of access in cable franchises, the concept of 'first come, first served' was fundamental to ensuring that all users would be treated equally. . . . Now, almost three decades later, we have a wealth of experience to help us reconsider the challenges and shortcomings in implementing this concept."[10] But public access television remains fundamentally centered around the idea of access and it is unlikely to give up its founding philosophy. The difficulties that the stations have faced over the years, not the least the question of whether anyone is watching, have, however, caused some of its initial structures to be questioned as Stoney now believes they must be. Access television is rethinking its values and purpose.

The radical beginnings of access television in North America have not disappeared. Paper Tiger, for instance, started with a series on New York's Manhattan Neighborhood Network (MNN) in 1981 in which media theorists and critics (the first being Herb Schiller) discussed excerpts from media publications. Its programs—many deliberately rough-edged with hand-drawn graphic cards and visible booms—now number over four hundred. They include programs on the antiglobalization protest movement, the Zapatistas, and union issues, and get distributed from their offices in Soho to the activist community worldwide through alternative media networks.[11] The Deep Dish network, conceived by Paper Tiger, gathers and distributes social change television (via satellite dish) to access stations wishing to screen their series throughout the United States. With other cooperatives and groups such as Free Speech TV, the Committee for Labor Access (CLA), Not Channel Zero, and Downtown Community Television, alternative media is alive and definitely kicking on public access television. Paper Tiger continues to screen its programs on MNN and even receives grants from the station in order to continue producing. Radical media did not disappear from public access; it was simply joined by the less radical, the religious, the local, the extreme right, and interested individuals.

The democratic nature of radical media can be studied in its own right. That is a different task to understanding the forum of public access television as a created space, for all its diversity, problems, and battles. Access television's progressive potential has been marred by a lack of resources, "by the bias of localism and by a lack of ties to larger spheres of discussion and debate."[12] Alternative/radical media has, as a result, carved out its own identity separate from access television and has moved beyond the local to become a masterful promoter of itself and its global community. All of this activity largely exists outside of the structure of access that is being considered here, although an available distribution platform has been important for its endurance. However, efforts are growing to improve the image of access television and to reconstruct it as a site for community building, for the renewal of civil society. It is these aspects, rather than radical media content, that I am concerned with. In order to get to the heart of these issues, the policy and legal aspects of access television first need to be outlined, in particular the institutional dilemmas and their relationship to the philosophical underpinnings of access.

Cable Franchise Agreements and the Problem of Property Rights

In terms of policy, the history and current position of community television in the United States is inextricable from, and subservient to, that of the cable television industry. It is a contractual relationship that has created significant tensions, resulting in over three decades of legal sagas.

Cable television had a humble start. It was first used as a subscriber service to relay broadcast signals into homes with inadequate over-the-air transmission as early as 1948. Antennas were assembled by local technicians (one antenna sat in an old bus on a hill) in order to receive and amplify broadcast signals, which were then piped via cables into homes.[13]

Cable television therefore emerged not because of a straightforward technical need (radio frequency repeaters could have been set up by networks), but because there was no economic incentive or obligation for the networks to serve small communities. These limited remote area systems, originally known in America as community antenna television (CATV), grew from seventy in number to over eight hundred in the decade of 1952–1962.[14] With such expansion, as well as improvements in cable technology (which gave it the potential for more channels than free-to-air television), the cable industry began to look towards providing programming beyond basic retransmission. The National Association of Broadcasters became concerned that this new technology, with its local and somewhat hobbyist character, had the capacity to infringe upon their mass market. They were right to be concerned.

The relationship between community television advocates and the cable industry was one of cooperation and mutual benefit during the 1960s, when the cable industry was seeking to gain the favor of the government and reg-ulators. In 1968, the first U.S. public access channel began operation in Dale City, Virginia. It was run by the Junior Chamber of Commerce along with a council of community representatives; it cablecast for two years without ad-vertising. The FCC saw a public interest attraction in such enterprises and in 1969 (leading up to the 1972 cable rules) required large cable systems to originate their own programming and to experiment with community ac-cess.[15] As a result, the cable industry made no attempt to curb the efforts of the Alternative Media Center when it was formed in 1971. But the discourse of localism, as well as technocratic claims that depicted cable technology as a social cure-all, had set in motion a national cable policy that was to ulti-mately work against both visions. One result was a policy that focused on lo-cal broadcast outlets, missing the national character of the broadcast sys-tem.[16] The model of cable television that developed, whereby cable franchises are administered through local authorities, meant that access tel-evision was to develop as a diverse, uneven, and tenuous phenomenon, lack-ing a national policy commitment.

The FCC's first major intervention into the cable industry came in 1966, when it banned signal importation into the nation's one hundred largest markets. This freeze, which favored the networks, remained until 1972, dur-ing which time the commission conducted a review of cable television to-wards the consideration of its first comprehensive plan for the industry. Over that time, policy rhetoric and lobbying efforts transformed "community an-tenna television" into the more impressive-sounding "cable" technology. This important discursive shift was pushed by a progressive libertarian agenda from the Rand Corporation, the American Civil Liberties Union, the electronic industry, city governments, and eventually the FCC itself. For Brenda Maddox, writing in 1974, cable television had real democratic po-tential: "it begins with something that was once despised—a crude makeshift way of bringing television to remote areas—and sees it transformed over the opposition of powerful enemies into the cure for the ills of modern urban American society."[17] The 1972 FCC cable report and order exposed the com-mission's change of heart towards cable, allowing and encouraging the in-dustry to expand for the benefit of the public. One of the consequences of the report, apart from asserting the FCC's capacity to regulate the cable in-dustry, was that it gave local governments the ability to negotiate franchise agreements with the companies. In addition, for the only time in U.S. his-tory, access television became a federal policy goal, with cable systems in the top one hundred markets required to reserve three separate channels for pub-lic, educational, and government access. In 1976, this was revised to services with thirty-five hundred subscribers or more, with cable providers being allowed to combine PEG onto one channel where there was inadequate demand or channel capacity. But the Supreme Court invalidated the public access requirement once and for all in 1979, when Midwest Video Corporation successfully argued that the requirements infringed on their editorial prerogatives and overstepped the FCC's authority. The ruling, however, left the First Amendment issue unresolved and did not prevent congressionally or municipally mandated access.

In 1977, a federal appeals court ruling permitted Home Box Office (HBO) to bid for programming, which also meant that they could distribute films and sporting events via cable, in direct competition with the commercial networks.[18] That decision, along with the possibility of cheap networking via satellite technology, led to the transformation of cable into the multibillion dollar industry that it is today. The supposed public forum of access television continued to be written into municipal franchise agreements, with the number of stations surpassing two thousand by the 1990s. As cable companies competed for franchises, communities lobbied their city governments for channel capacity, facilities, and, in many cases, a percentage of the subscriber revenue. In one example of the power of municipal government control, twenty-four access channels were negotiated in the Dallas–Fort Worth area.[19] Bunnie Riedell, former executive director of the Alliance for Community Media, believes that franchise arrangements have proven to be beneficial for access television as the agreements have produced a wide range of management and governance models. Furthermore, as the stations are established via a contractual agreement between local authorities and private companies, they cannot be easily eradicated through federal legislation.[20] Riedell's view reflects the liberal idea that political interference—the arbitrary whims of politicians—can be transcended by recourse to the law. The flip side to this arrangement is that, policy-wise, access television is now less of a defined public forum than a potential legal battleground.

The FCC's requirements relating to public access channels and its operating rules could not be enforced after the Midwest Video Corporation case. However, the rules are indicative of the model of public access that has been constructed through local authorities ever since. The operating rules specified that access was to be first-come, first-served and nondiscriminatory; without advertising, lottery information, or indecent matter; and that records must be kept of individuals and groups who have requested access time.[21] Access television was to be implemented first and foremost on the basis of speech rights. In her book on access television, Linda Fuller writes that, "philosophically, the concept of public access has its roots in John Stuart

Mill's social libertarian theory; politically, in First Amendment guarantees of free speech; legally, in FCC and Supreme Court mandates for localism and viewer rights."[22] The outcomes of free speech rulings are closely followed by the sector as they define how far "first-come, first-served" policies can be altered. As the primary justification for access television, it would seem logical that the liberal rights framework would provide its security, but this has been far from the case. The legal history of public access shows that the relationship of access to First Amendment rights remains unspecified.[23] Moreover, public access channels have not been recognized legally as public forums and remain vulnerable to constitutional challenges by the cable companies themselves. These challenges to the legitimacy of public access have themselves relied upon First Amendment rights, asserting that public access television is an infringement on the cable company's ability to control its own resource.

In 1984, Congress developed a national policy for cable television, which codified the ability of the franchising authority to require PEG channels, facilities, and equipment. The act forbade cable operators from exercising editorial control over the channels but stipulated that they could not be found liable as a result of access content. It also placed limits on the amount of intervention available to franchise authorities and capped the franchise fee at 5 percent of subscriber revenue. The act did not prevent the establishment of monopolies at the local level, thereby effectively protecting industry despite being couched in the language of deregulation.[24] Some lower court decisions upheld the implied (but not explicit) status of PEG channels as public forums. For instance, a case involving the Ku Klux Klan and Kansas City found that neither the government nor the cable operator had a right to censor content. In other cases, however, it was found that the government had no compelling interest in mandating public access.[25] In 1992, a new move by Congress undermined the public forum status of public access channels to an even greater degree. The Cable Television Consumer Protection Act made cable operators liable for obscene programming on access channels, effectively restoring the cable operator's editorial control—and hence their property rights—over the channels. The Alliance for Community Media challenged the indecency rules before the U.S Court of Appeals for the District of Columbia Circuit on the basis that the channels were public forums in which programmers had First Amendment rights. They were unsuccessful. During the trial, the FCC countered that the cable operator's rights were being restored rather than those of access programmers being taken away.

That public access has been found to potentially violate First Amendment rights of the cable operator demonstrates how the liberal rights framework has had highly contested, contradictory outcomes for access television. The cable television structure, in which government-sanctioned cable monopolies have a greater claim to First Amendment rights than other parties, has dealt "an argument for the public protection of private censorship."[26] That public power has been used "to establish a private monopoly by way of an exclusive cable franchise"[27] is an example of why First Amendment rights can only be understood through property rights—whether a space can be considered a public forum or private property. There is no consensus amongst judges as to how access challenges should be dealt with in terms of its claim to public forum status and the competing property claims of cable companies. Public access has been seen by some as analogous to the granting of public easements on private property—a bargain with local government "to provide a right of access to the cable system in exchange for the use of public rights-of-way."[28] But for others, access channels are deemed to be unconstitutional infringements of the private property of the cable operator. Although free speech is still seen as a means to debate, even dissent, in practice it functions in favor of industry relations and can insulate industry from political accountability.[29]

In the opinion of communications law academic Laura Stein, only an empowering, rather than a defensive, approach to speech rights will protect public access television. She believes the state can play a positive role in providing forums for democratic speech and asserts that there is ample precedent in both "law and policy to support the legitimacy of government action that safeguards democratic speech."[30] However, without nationally legislated public cable-channel capacity, judicial battles fought at the whim of the cable industry are likely to persist.[31] As one legal brief summarized "the good news is that the First Amendment is alive and well, and the bad news is that it is usually difficult (or impossible) to predict how the First Amendment will be applied to specific situations."[32] Expecting courts to unanimously embrace an empowering speech regime seems a distant hope under a dominant American public philosophy that equates liberalism foremost with property rights but disguises the implicit power relations of property behind a natural rights framework. These issues will be addressed again in chapter 6, in relation to the communications commons debates. For now, it is enough to see that access has been an easily undermined phenomenon in the United States and that no universal conception or dedication to access as a public space exists.

Access and First-Come, First-Served: Reassessing Rights

Access is an avenue through which Americans engage with and contest ideas of free speech and pluralism. It is not simply a theoretical principle that is

Davis Community Television

When I visited the university town of Davis, California, in 2001, a Republican student group had invited a speaker who "promotes the idea that we don't need to do any more apologizing for what he calls the 'damn slave thing'" to speak at a gathering. Black student campaign groups demanded that the speaker's advertisement be pulled from the student newspaper, then attended the event in order to stage a walkout. The station manager at Davis Community Television, Kari Peterson, decided to devote an episode of their program *Get the Word Out* to the topic. The station's dilemma on that day was how to choose a host for the program without appearing to take sides—but that was only a particular instance in what Peterson saw as a bigger issue. This seemingly routine problem was recounted to me in order to highlight the everyday problems that access television stations confront in terms of the negotiation and management of free speech. By creating a program to discuss issues of community concern (in this instance racism), Davis Community Television was pushing the boundaries of access in a profound way. The station was deliberately intervening into the "first-come, first-served" policy of access by choosing to showcase certain issues and encouraging access by groups that might not otherwise participate.

Davis Community Television once followed a strict access mandate, seeing itself as "completely hands-off," according to Peterson. "We provided a soapbox and . . . our job was to facilitate others' use of the equipment. . . . [M]y job was to open the door in the morning." Peterson explained, however, that the people who came through that door were mostly people "with a lot of time on their hands, some fringe element, individuals, people for whom video is a passion." In order to encourage others within the community to use the station, Davis Community Television devised a number of generic programs that would be run by volunteers and interns at the station with supervision and training conducted by staff. The idea behind the programs was that people within the community would be able to speak on issues relevant to them or their organization without having to go through the long and difficult processes of training, production, and postproduction. It was a move away from the producer-driven ethos that has traditionally characterized community television. Peterson explained it as "making community speech easier," but also as the facilitation of dialogue within the community: "Our mission has evolved to become about serving our community, much more of a community development mission. It has to do with strengthening the community by empowering people of diverse viewpoints to speak, but the other part of the equation is to ensure that people are hearing what they have to say."[a]

---

[a] Kari Peterson, interviewed by Ellie Rennie, Davis, 2001.

called on to justify requests for electronic public forums, but the questioning, creation, and trial of American political values on a daily basis. Simply "opening the door in the morning" reflects a first-come, first-served philosophy, whereby individuals are not discriminated against but granted equal rights of access. It negates the idea that some groups should be privileged over others, even if that might balance out the representation of different groups within that locality. The fervency with which this policy has been discussed and implemented in the past through public access television in the United States, and which continues today in many stations, demonstrates the working, or active, presence of philosophical ideals within community media. As Downing writes, "[T]he First Amendment, the right to free public speech, is not a settled American achievement, nor is it an arid desert for professional lawyers. It is a contested area, which has everything to do with our always fragile, threatened rights to communicate about toxic waste dumps, policy violence, City Hall corruption, and the scandals of our schools, teen pregnancy and a whole long list besides. If access TV is not seen as the best guarantor of what our First Amendment rights are in contested situations in our localities, then its purpose is cloudy and its future very obscure."[33] The U.S. tradition of public access was built with a straightforward interpretation of the First Amendment as its defining principle. If everyone has an equal right to produce and distribute his or her viewpoint through public access, then the resulting marketplace of ideas will enhance America's pluralist democracy. The normative liberal doctrines were embedded within this model—it provided a framework based upon rights with only minimal restrictions imposed in the allocation of resources (time slots, equipment use). However, observations and accusations that democracy was difficult to find within the plethora of "vanity video" style programs that were submitted began to be voiced in the 1980s. Theorists held that behind these calls was a reassessment of the notion of free speech itself—more speech did not necessarily equate with better speech. It was a challenge to the predominant contemporary liberal doctrine that the mere provision of access rights would yield a better system for all.[34] It is pluralist in that personal alliances are considered a matter of individual choice, and difference is considered a matter of toleration. Public access, in this way, has been a defined but thinly managed space of individual expression with community (as in group) media occurring as a derivative activity, or by-product.

At a day-to-day level, the free speech principle has been important in overcoming potential conflicts that could arise in the attempt to prioritize community interests. Through his interview research with volunteer producers in the mid-1990s, John Higgins came to the conclusion that the free speech dogma was a strategy that "allowed individual producers to endure ideological differences that otherwise might be personally intolerable."[35] The value of free speech was that it could work as an accepted rule that everyone had to follow. Toleration was realized not so much through idealistic notions of constructive dialogue, but through compliance to a legalistic rights policy. In one instance, a volunteer insists that he will not work on any program "that's contrary to Christ," although he admits that he did help one such producer to get his car started: "his choke broke down and I helped him with his starter [laughing]. Crawled right up under it and helped him with it, but I'm not gonna help him with his program."[36] As this short story indicates, cooperation and toleration have resulted from the pluralist approach even if only to a limited degree.

The Alliance for Community Media published a special issue of its quarterly *Community Media Review* entitled "Rethinking Access Philosophy" in 2002. In it, the notions of "first-come, first-served," free speech, and the relationship of theory to practice are confronted by both scholars and practitioners. This collection is one of the few texts that unites community media theory with the concerns and observations of practitioners. It demonstrates plainly that community broadcasting in the United States not only needs to be seen within the context of American pluralism, but that it is intimately caught up in the complex project of advancing community concerns within a liberal, individualist framework. Higgins writes in his contribution that "the critiques from within public access, developed in a laboratory of daily practice, represent positive steps to move beyond simple assumptions of democracy and power, toward a more integrated view of access within a complex society framework."[37] In this way, access television is attempting to balance liberal principles with nonmarket life. Measures such as those taken by Davis Community Television are efforts to bring civil society into view, negotiating the needs of groups without abandoning a commitment to individual freedom.

American community media theorists have discussed this shift in terms of competing claims over speech rights. They have not departed from the rights discourse so much as redefined its boundaries in relation to the access story. This is seen to be a move away from current "one-dimensional" interpretations of free speech that pursue strictly individual and equal rights regardless of social context and a return to early American interpretations of free speech. This means an emphasis on individual rights as a means to wider social freedom and benefit for all. It is also as a move towards more recent critical interpretations of free speech that highlight issues around ideas of "truth" and power—factors that are purposefully erased in liberal theories in order to assume that the best outcome for all is met. As with the communitarian critique of liberalism, the critical approach holds that the liberal premise is misleading as individuals cannot be separated from the society and circumstances in which they live. To do so risks the entrenchment of inequality, as those with less power and resources are unlikely to compete fairly with those who have more. The premises of freedom of expression in American liberal theory go beyond the individual's freedom of expression, suggesting a need to balance individual freedom against larger social goals such as rights of access to the media and a right to hear.[38] Stein's discussion on the legal grounds of public access follows this line of thought, taking participatory democratic theory as a means to understand the full role of public access and that "speech rights must be interpreted in light of the real conditions affecting democratic speech."[39]

These critiques are not a departure from liberalism, or the access commitment to speech rights, but more of a departure from a particular market-oriented individualism that has emerged out of liberalism in recent decades. As other writers have also asserted, the stylized contrast between liberalism and communitarianism was less defined in classical liberal theory than it is in the dominant liberal position of current American politics. Although the Enlightenment thinkers, in particular John Locke and John Stuart Mill, were captured by ideas of reason and empiricism—a rationalism that was important in overcoming previously justified hierarchies and oppression—they did not abandon moral traditionalism. Despite their secularism, they remained dedicated to ideas of truth. The point is that the corrective notions of access do not depart from liberal philosophy, but only dispute the modern-day American manifestation of it. Individual rights remain central to understanding access television; however, the end result—the ultimate social goal—requires intervention in terms of channel capacity and direction in the creation of more watchable channels. Contemporary liberalism, as one political philosopher has noted, is "vastly more secular and arguably more materialistic than earlier liberalism. It is much more agonistic regarding what constitutes the good life and human virtue. And, to make a point which is particularly pertinent to the concerns of communitarianism, it has transformed and radicalized the whole conception of political individualism."[40]

For the defenders of access television, it is important to be mindful of social benefit. If anything, the problematic aspects of public access television tell of the fragmentation that results from a hands-off approach to community. Where critics of access were skeptical of its relevance to democratic process, its supporters responded that, yes, "civic life is a cultural process that must be nurtured."[41] If public access is left to its own devices—or to the whims of the cable companies—then new thought needs to be given to American values and public philosophy. And with it, to new practices of civil society support and communication. It is worth remembering that "most often, when individual men and women insist on 'being themselves,' they are in fact defending a self they share with others."[42]

Access and the Civil Society Debate

Boston Neighborhood Network (see chapter 1) and Davis Community Television are both rethinking their access policies. Manhattan Neighborhood Network has also turned one of their channels into what they call a "curated" channel, with programs (not necessarily live) selected for their relevance to the Manhattan community. This approach—encouraging associations—is premised on the idea that speech rights and America's general "public philosophy" are ill equipped to deal with "the erosion of community."[43] The idea that "if the locality is to take access television as a serious matter, as a communication lifeline, then it cannot be simply left to its groups to find their way to the door"[44] is a call for renewed civic engagement. The restructuring of access to provide for the participation of associations and the deliberation of community concerns is therefore underpinned by the idea that civil society can make an important contribution that cannot be met through strict adherence to a neutral rights policy. Although the connection is not made between access television and the civil society debate in the literature, the parallel exists.[45] What is the point of considering civil society arguments in the light of community radio and television? To ignore the role of community media within civil society—its potential and realized status as a means to information distribution for a myriad of civil society organizations—is to underestimate its importance. It is also the case that there is a movement within some access stations to reaffirm its centrality to civil society groups and to expand these networks. There is, therefore, an undeniably deliberate engagement with notions of civil society extension and renewal. Seeing access television only in terms of an uncomplicated, minimalist notion of speech rights denies this role.

Access television is therefore devoted to the sometimes contradictory principles of individual rights and community building—promoting local issues, concerns, groups, and personalities, but refusing to sit in judgment of what should be considered right and wrong within that pluralist, sometimes fragmented, realm. When the moral role is necessarily abandoned (but the community engagement role acknowledged), all that can be said about access stations is that they are distributors of information and network builders.

Their claim to community building comes not through the promotion of values or the selection of communities that are deemed "good" for society, but through their provision of a channel through which communities can potentially reach out to their members or others beyond their immediate group.

Community Radio

Community radio has had a difficult history in the Unites States. As radio is licensed federally via the FCC, community radio has not been able to pursue support at the municipal level in the way that cable access television has done. Given the policy hurdles it has faced, the persistence of community radio broadcasters is astounding.

The world's first amateur radio organization was formed in 1906, led by an eleven-year-old from New York City who lobbied Congress to preserve the rights of amateur broadcasting. Writes historian and journalist Jesse Walker, "It was a strange moment in history, a time when the defence of popular access to the airwaves could fall to a few boys on the cusp of adolescence. Stranger still, such boys were the radio innovators of the day, discovering uses for a technology the establishment had assumed would be employed only for point-to-point communication, ideally by licensed professionals."[46] The early ham radio movement was not inspired by political principles so much as enthusiasts' desire to practice their hobby. But they did rally together to preserve the public's right to the airwaves, which makes them an important part of the history of community radio in America. The reason it seems so strange that eleven-year-old boys could stand up for public access has to do with the long and difficult battle for "free" radio that has occurred since. Walker tells a story of how pacifists, right-wing extremists, Boy Scouts, high school rebels, stoners, priests, rock stars, and Chairman Kennard of the FCC have all struggled for that cause. Although there have been some successes, U.S. community radio has experienced countless setbacks. As Pete triDish of Prometheus (a low-power radio advocacy group) has pointed out, even Chairman Kennard "was completely deluded about his ability to make even the most modest changes in favor of democratic reform of the media."[47]

The *Titanic* hit an iceberg in 1912, bringing the burgeoning ham radio movement down with it. False reports and pranks circulated by amateur radio broadcasters during the disaster caused public outrage at the state of emergency communications services. When the U.S. government developed its Radio Act of 1912 the ham radio enthusiasts were relegated to a piece of unwanted spectrum and not allowed to broadcast more than two hundred meters. In response, they formed the Hiram Percy Maxim's American Radio

Relay League to promote a national ham network. By 1920, a quarter of a million hams monitored fifteen thousand stations. Government retaliated. While many amateurs were called to use their communication skills to assist in World War I, stations were repeatedly shut down by the Navy throughout the war.

At the conclusion of the war, radio experienced another boom as both hams and educational stations resumed their activities. During the early and mid-1920s, "commercial broadcasting remained a controversial experiment" while nonprofit and amateur radio flourished.[48] One enthusiast, Lewis Hill, built his first transmitter at the age of six. He was later to become the pioneer of community radio in the United States.

Between 1922 and 1925, the then secretary of commerce, Herbert Hoover, held a series of conferences on radio, out of a concern that the 1912 act was insufficient to deal with the massive growth. As a result of that conference, which involved hams, the education sector, and the radio industry, three principles were put into place: "the airwaves belonged to the public, the federal government should regulate broadcasting to establish order on the broadcast spectrum, and privately owned stations could broadcast in the public interest."[49] This was to be the basis for the American model of broadcasting: the "trusteeship model," whereby private interests were charged with maintaining the public good. It was also the rationale that resulted in the decline of nonprofit radio. Educational stations were allocated less-desirable frequencies and made to share them with local commercial stations. The number of education channels dropped from ninety-four in 1927 to forty-nine in 1931.

By 1946, Lewis Hill was grown up and ready to do something about the state of radio. He started an organization that he called Pacifica, which stood for the organization's location on the West Coast as well as Hill's own pacifist beliefs. Hill had been a conscientious objector in WWII; he had refused to serve in the military, alarmed by the restriction of individual liberty enacted via the government's war policies. Hill's libertarian ideals extended to a belief in freedom of communication that would underpin his community radio efforts. For a time he worked as a radio announcer and night news editor at a commercial station, but he left in protest over "the rip-and-read news format of the commercial station and its one-sided coverage of domestic and international affairs."[50] Hill's plan for a new style of radio took a few attempts, but he eventually managed to persuade the authorities to grant him a nonprofit license for an FM radio station in the San Francisco Bay area. Hill originally intended to support the nonprofit station with advertising, but the FCC indicated that this might jeopardize his proposal. He also sought an

AM license, as radios at the time were not made to receive FM broadcasts. The fact that the FM band was still an experimental domain was probably, in the end, what got him a license at all. In 1938 the FCC had reserved twenty out of one hundred available FM channels for noncommercial use, and the license to Pacifica was the first that did not go to an educational or religious organization.

The station that Hill and half a dozen others founded, KPFA, began broadcasting in 1949. The station would have three objectives, cultural, journalistic, and social: to provide an outlet for the musical, literary, and theatrical talent of the local community; to engage in comprehensive news coverage using a wide variety of sources; and "to engage in any activity that shall contribute to the lasting understanding between nations and between the individuals of all nations, races, creeds and colors."[51] As he was not able to undertake sponsorship in the form of advertising, Hill instead promoted the idea of listener support, selling cheap FM receivers with subscriptions and building a dedicated listenership. Hill promoted the station in different ways depending on who he was talking to—the FCC received one philosophy while the people who worked at the station or for the philanthropic funds received others. The three objectives that KPFA became known for did not explicitly mention the anarchist and pacifist goals, probably as they were formulated for the purposes of reporting to "the biggest liberal megafund of its time"—the Ford Foundation.[52] Nonetheless, Hill's articulation of Pacifica's mandate has guided the community media movement ever since.

The history of KPFA is well documented elsewhere.[53] The important thing is that KPFA was entirely different from anything else on air at the time. It sought out programming to advance the women's movement and catered to minority ethnic groups. It also provided a space where political issues could be debated from all angles. The station's dedication to diverse points of view meant that it encountered serious resistance from right-wing coalitions. A small proportion of programming from the Communist Party (CPUSA) caused immense displeasure in some circles, and brought an influx of complaints to the FCC. Downing writes that when the Senate subcommittee asked why three CPUSA members had been allowed to broadcast,

> The station manager pointed out that in the same month, KPFA had also given the microphone to a Los Angeles broker, an academic from the Center for the Study of Democratic Institutions, a Unitarian minister, the former chair of a Democratic Party club, a public relations specialist, the president of the Los Angeles chapter of the America Federation of Scientists, and, not least, Casper Weinberger, then chair of the Central California Republican Party

committee (later to be Secretary of Defence in the Reagan administration). They might have added that other conservatives, such as William F. Buckley, had been regular contributors at an earlier time.[54]

This dedication to freedom of expression was to become a central principle of many future community radio and television projects. Pacifica expanded from KPFA in Berkeley to KPFK in Los Angeles, WBAI in New York City, KPFT in Houston, and WPFW in Washington, D.C. It then began distributing a news service to other noncommercial stations via the Pacifica network.

However, KPFA also experienced many periods of financial uncertainty and was forced to go off air for a period in 1950–1951 to raise funds. The Ford Foundation played an important role in keeping it (and other) stations on air. They gave Pacifica a three-year grant of $150,000, which allowed the station to upgrade its space and equipment and engage in promotional activity. However, the grant money came at a price. The Ford Foundation's Fund for Adult Education (FAE) held a 50 percent lien on Pacifica's property. They also had the right to review the grant in the event of significant changes in structure or operations. In general, private philanthropies, often linked to a business, had a considerable influence over the development of noncommercial radio.[55]

The organizational structure of KPFA was one of its most radical aspects. Staff members were paid equally and the station was operated on a collective basis. Unfortunately, this was also one of the key factors that contributed to KPFA's many periods of turmoil. In 1952, a group of staff members revolted against a perceived centralization of power in the hands of Hill and two other founders. This was the first in a succession of "palace revolutions . . . that entailed debilitating emergency meetings, bitter personal and ideological conflict, firings and resignations, reinstatements and reorganization plans."[56] The strife also jeopardized their funding from the Ford Foundation, which withheld its support in the third year. The ensuing restructuring took its toll on Hill, whose health deteriorated. He became involved in a personal dispute and ordered that some staff members be fired. The following day, at the age of thirty-eight, Lewis Hill committed suicide. The station began to change and by the 1990s Pacifica had lost its community identity—a decline that has been attributed to an overcontrolling board, secrecy, and loss of direction at the local level.

Other community and education stations followed KPFA's lead onto the FM band. Lorenzo Milam obtained an FM license for Seattle and began broadcasting in 1962 under the call sign KRAB. He then set up other innovative stations throughout the country, differentiating them from the commercial stations, which he called "toads," and the educational ones, known as "bores." Some extremely interesting and antiestablishment commercial stations also made it onto the FM dial over that period, as most mainstream networks were still focused on AM. The FM stations didn't all make money and many of them gave up trying to sell advertising. But they were important in the history of U.S. radio, representing as much freedom and diversity as the nonprofit stations, even though they held commercial licenses. As the networks grew, these stations largely became conformist or were bought out by other, less innovative, broadcasters.

In 1975, a group of fifteen stations and applicants formed the National Federation of Community Broadcasters (NFCB). Membership remains open to any station that:

- Is incorporated as a not-for-profit
- Is governed by a group broadly representative of the community it serves
- Has stated and demonstrated commitment to the participation of women and Third World people in all aspects of its organization and operation
- Has a stated and demonstrated commitment to access by the general public to the airwaves
- Provides or seeks to provide a service to the general public and not to any single group, organization, or institution
- Seeks to reflect a diverse range of culture and opinion found in its community through its broadcast operations.

The establishment of the NFCB demonstrated that community radio was becoming a united force. However, this changed with the introduction of public service radio. Public broadcasting (PBS) was President Johnson's attempt to strengthen noncommercial broadcasting at the national level. A financing structure was implemented whereby stations could apply for money from the public purse if they could prove that they met certain criteria. The financing structure proved prohibitive for small college stations and low-budget alternative stations. But even those that could apply were not necessarily better off, and many believe that public radio had an adverse effect on community radio overall. Walker writes, "community stations that previously got by on listener pledges and local underwriting might be eligible for thousands more—*if* they hire more staff, increase their broadcast hours, seek more funds, and, under later rules, make their programming more mainstream in the pursuit of higher ratings."[57]

The impact of public broadcasting on community radio did not stop there. As the smaller ten-watt stations were cheap to establish, they had multiplied and were taking up spectrum that public broadcasting stations felt they could make better use of. The NFCB joined the campaign *against* small community stations in the name of spectrum efficiency. The small, un-funded stations—a large number of which were being run out of clubs and schools—were seen as in the way of a stronger community radio sector and as occupying licenses that could be put to better use. The FCC ruled that they would no longer award licenses to stations of ten watts or less. Existing low-power stations had to relocate to commercial spectrum or upgrade to one hundred watts. Ten-watt stations were no longer protected from larger stations' signals. As it happened, a number of the small (Class D) stations upgraded to one hundred watts before the deadline, causing further cluttering of the spectrum. In the end, public radio never took off as the Corporation for Public Broadcasting would have liked (compare the PBS to the BBC). Many station boards proved susceptible to corporate interests at the expense of community involvement. The requirements enforced upon the community stations brought about a type of professionalism that pushed out many of the more radical radio announcers. The American version of community radio suffered as a result.

But community radio was not over. In the late 1980s a movement called "microradio" surfaced, and by 1997 there were as many as a thousand of these unlicensed stations on the air. They stood up to the FCC to varying degrees—some in deliberate opposition, others in stubborn disregard. Once again, American radio was a surprising domain where a turn of the dial could produce some strange and diverse results. In many towns, the only local station would be an illegal enterprise run out of someone's garage or flat.

Walker cites a number of reasons why the microradio movement took off so suddenly. Equipment was better and cheaper than it had ever been before. Consolidation of commercial radio in the 1990s had resulted in narrow formats and predictable programming. Community radio had begun relying on Washington for money which it then had to fight for under the Reagan administration. Many stations turned to commercial underwriters for help. The Class D option (the early reservation of FM spectrum for educational and community use) had been closed down so that people could not start their own stations and the price of existing licenses had soared. Religious chains were eager to expand and took a lot of the now rare noncommercial frequencies available. Added to this, some well-known pirates emerged that captured the imagination of other would-be broadcasters. Other forms of DIY media, such as zines, began to thrive, restimulating interest in radio.[58]

Stephen Dunifer was an important pioneer of microradio. In 1991, during the Gulf War, Pacifica was just about a lost cause. Dunifer started Free Radio Berkeley, choosing on one occasion to place his transmitter in front of the KPFA offices to show that community radio had found new life. The radio station was mostly transmitted from different locations in the hills, the equipment carried in packs or transported in the back of an old car. After a run-in where the local police demonstrated that shutting down illegal radio stations was not high on their list of priorities, the station moved into an apartment. The FCC—which *did* consider shutting down radio stations a priority—fined Dunifer $20,000 for unlicensed broadcasting, a figure that was twenty times the levy that the law allowed. Dunifer found himself legal representation to contest the charge. When it went to court, however, Judge Claudia Wilken refused to grant the injunction, saying that the ban on microradio was unconstitutional. Wilken did eventually side with the government, but not until 1998—by which time Free Radio Berkeley had turned microradio into a national movement.

It was partly the threat posed by the pirate radio broadcasters that caused FCC Chairman Kennard to begin a rule-making inquiry into nonprofit low-power radio (LPFM) licenses in 1998. Kennard's original plan would have created three new classes, one operating at a maximum of one thousand watts, one at one hundred, and one at ten. But only the first would be primary and the others secondary, meaning they could be bumped by other stations. A business could own as many as five stations. The microradio movement was not happy and the National Lawyers Guild, Prometheus Project, and the Micro Empowerment Coalition set about lobbying for the licenses to be granted to nonprofits only.

Not surprisingly, the LPFM license attracted substantial resistance from both the commercial and public broadcasters, who claimed that the LPFM signals would interfere with their existing signals.[59] This resistance was taken to Congress, where a bill was passed that effectively limited the number and power of LPFM stations, and precluded the possibility for higher-powered transmitters in urban areas. The Radio Broadcasting Act 2000 also prevented former pirate broadcasters from applying for licenses (this was later found to contravene First Amendment rights). However, the act did not entirely restrict this new, and encouraging, community broadcasting development.

This condensed history is intended to show how the development of community radio in America has been divided between those who have sought formal legislative structures, adequate technical guidelines and capacity, and public funding—and those who have endorsed deregulation, spontaneous and unlicensed transmission, and a degree of anarchy in the running of community stations. Walker believes that if there is to be deregulation then it should be *real* deregulation. For him, that means abolishing the FCC which is "captive of the industries it regulates,"[60] and allowing those who use spectrum to have title to it as long as they use it. The government would stop hoarding spectrum for future licenses and throw it open to the public—either auctioning it or allowing new users to "homestead" it. This is similar to the model of access discussed in chapter 6 in relation to new technologies. It is a radical departure from the tradition of corporate liberalism that has defined American broadcasting to date. But this microradio platform (if microradio *has* a singular philosophy then it would be something close to this) is also something quite different from what other community broadcasters have fought for. It is a more random, uncontrolled idea of community media than KPFA and others pursued. But it also came about because the other model encountered too many difficulties, both internal and external. Microradio proves that, in America at least, when community radio cannot be made to happen by the normal routes, it will somehow find a way. Although LPFM provides some legal means for small community stations, it may not be enough to appease radio enthusiasts in the long run.

Digital Broadcasting and LPTV

Low-power television stations (LPTV) were created in 1982 as a means to enhance diversity and to encourage local programming. These licenses were created with secondary spectrum priority to ensure that they would not interfere with existing or new full-service stations. There are some twenty-two hundred licensed LPTV stations in approximately one thousand communities. They are recognized by the FCC as providing "a wide variety of programs to ethnic, racial and interest communities with the larger area," as well as local news, weather, and public affairs programming.[61] The stations are not necessarily community stations, many supplying retransmitted signals from the networks, or are used within schools for educational purposes. However, according to the FCC, LPTV services have significantly increased the diversity of broadcasting ownership. They therefore represent access to broadcast spectrum rather than community broadcasting per se.

As LPTV stations could easily be displaced (due to their secondary status), their ability to raise necessary capital has always been difficult. Now, with the introduction of digital television, the prospect of LPTV stations being pushed out of the picture has become a reality. In order for full-power stations to complete the transition from analogue to digital, the FCC has provided them with a second channel for the conversion period. In assigning digital television channels, the FCC maintained the secondary status of LPTV and was "compelled to establish [digital television] allotments that . . . [would] displace a number of LPTV stations."[62] The Community Broadcasters Protection Act sought to rectify this situation by providing LPTV with Class A, or primary, status. However, according to the criteria, LPTV stations can't win Class A status if their signals overlap with the digital-coverage areas planned by existing full-power broadcasters. The number of aspiring low-power television licensees far exceeds the number of licenses available.[63]

Digital broadcasting has not helped community radio either. The in-band on-channel (IBOC) plan provides full-power stations with spectrum around their current channel rather than a new channel allocation for digital broadcasting. When the simulcast period is over, the stations will be permitted to occupy the entire bandwidth they have used during the simulcast period rather than relinquishing their old channel to new broadcasters. Exposing the real issues behind spectrum planning, Prometheus Radio has written that this system means that more digital signals will occupy a given bandwidth (creating more potential for interference) than Kennard's plans for LPFM would have. "In the digital age, this is akin to elephants blaming mice for crowding them off the savannah."[64]

Canada

Canadian community media has experienced periods of relative stability, but it has also been subject to changes in legislation that have caused major disruptions to its progress. Canada's model for community television is unique in that it was once funded through an obligation imposed upon cable companies. However, this obligation was removed by the regulator in 1997, a situation that was eventually rectified in 2002. Although somewhat complicated, the resulting policy is the closest thing to a cross-platform community media policy in the world, and is worth examining for that reason.

Cable companies were permitted to discontinue community channels as a result of policy change in 1997. However, if they did so, the companies would have to pay a full 5 percent of their subscriber revenue to the Canadian production fund. If they maintained their community channels, then this would be reduced to between 2 percent and 3.5 percent. The community access channels were retained by many as a result, but they became increasingly professionalized and cable companies began to disregard the CRTC's guidelines. Many reduced, or ceased completely, their stations' access and training components. A station just outside of Montreal, TVC de Châteauguay, reported that their access had decreased from six hours a day to three minutes every

Télévision Communautaire des Bois-Francs

Télévision Communautaire des Bois-Francs (TVCBF) is located in Victoriaville, Quebec. The station began in 1974 as a video access center, established independently from the local cable company. Its board is elected by its membership, which is open to both groups and individuals within the community. In 1985 the private company Videotron bought the local cable franchise from the existing operator and contracted TVCBF to manage all local programming for Victoriaville's local community channel. TVCBF now functions as a community access channel, training and mobilizing volunteers and producing local programming. Sixteen thousand people in Victoriaville receive television via cable, and ratings have indicated that 20 percent of these viewers watch TVCBF on a regular basis, mostly for its local information programming. The Victoriaville community is committed to the channel. This has been demonstrated in recent years through the community's fight to keep the station community run.

When I visited in 2001, there was an atmosphere of anxiety at the station. Prior to 1997, cable companies were required to provide a community channel and to give 5 percent of their subscriber revenue to fund community programming. In 1994, TVCBF discovered that the cable company was not meeting this obligation. Between 1985 and 1991, Videotron was paying TVCBF $10,000 per annum. In 1991 this figure increased to $15,000; however, it was discovered that the figure should have been closer to $90,000. When TVCBF took their complaint to the Canadian Radio-television and Telecommunications Commission (CRTC), Videotron were made to pay the group not 5 percent of their revenue, but 9 percent. As a result, TVCBF's funding leapt from $15,000 a year to $150,000 a year between 1992 and 1998. When the obligation to host community television was removed in 1997, Videotron decreased their funding of TVCBF to $50,000 a year, leaving the group to make up the rest through community fundraising, their Bingo program (which brings in $30,000 a year), and grants. Videotron's attempt to prevent TVCBF from running the channel failed in Victoriaville only due to community mobilization and protest. However, Videotron had succeeded in closing down ten other community-run channels in the Montreal area, replacing them with their own content.[a]

---

[a] Isabelle Voyer, interviewed by Ellie Rennie, Victoriaville, 2001.

three weeks. Access consisted only of a segment on a program that showcases highlights of community programming throughout the region.[65] Possible reasons included the increased ownership concentration of cable franchises and cable operators moving towards networked systems and programming, as well as the cable companies' preference for professional programming.

Canada was considered to be the leader in community television prior to the 1997 changes. Cathy Edwards, documentary maker and former community television volunteer, described Canada as "second to none in the world prior to 1997 in providing a public space on television for individuals and community groups to express their concerns and to exchange information."[66] In response to the lack of access, community television advocate Jan Pachul submitted an application for an LPTV license in the area of Toronto. Although LPTV community licenses existed at that time for remote areas of Canada, there was no policy for such licenses in metropolitan areas. The CRTC rejected the application as it was outside existing license conditions. StarRay TV became a pirate television station—and Pachul an embittered adversary of the CRTC.[67] However, the CRTC did issue a review of community radio and television policy, encompassing cable television, digital services, and low-power television and radio.

The resulting policy, released in October 2002, makes a strong commitment to both access and localism.[68] Under the policy, cable companies still have the ability to run community channels and receive a reduction in their contributions to the Canadian production fund. However, they must abide by a number of rules, including a minimum of 60 percent community programming produced either by the licensee or by members of the community from the licensed area, which must be given scheduling priority. Furthermore, the licensees must devote a minimum of 30 percent of their programming aired to access programming or 50 percent where demand exists (free of charge). Where one or more local nonprofit community television corporations exist in an area—groups such as TVCPF and TVC de Châteauguay—then 20 percent of programming aired must be made available for access programs from such groups. Where there is more than one group, then a minimum of four hours of access must be granted to each group per week. Consultation with the community via advisory boards and/or feedback from volunteers is required, and the channels must reflect "the multicultural and Aboriginal reality of their communities." In terms of the financing of the community channels, cable systems with less than twenty thousand subscribers may elect to allocate the full 5 percent of their contribution to the Canadian production fund to local expression. Only limited sponsorship is permitted, although advertising is allowed where no other local services (radio or television) exist, presumably because there is no danger of them infringing on the markets of existing services. An important addition to the legislation is that where the cable operator does not provide a community channel, nonprofit community groups may apply for a community programming service license. This is to be arranged as a mandatory carriage arrangement (they will be required to cablecast the community content) where the operator does not operate a community channel.

In regards to low-power television, new rules replace the former remote licenses. Low-power television can be established either on a for-profit or non-profit basis where spectrum exists, but it would have second-class status to full-power stations—meaning that it can be required to cease operation or change its assigned channel if it interferes with a regular channel's signal. Low-power television may broadcast up to twelve minutes of advertising in the hour; however, it must be local advertising. Low-power radio can also be run on a nonprofit or for-profit basis, but the commission states that "the ownership of multiple low-power radio licenses and cross-ownership between low-power radio and low-power television will generally be discouraged."[69]

The policy does take into account the problems experienced by community television groups in Quebec. Groups around the Montreal area have resumed broadcasting their programs, as have other groups throughout the country. TVC de Châteauguay gets four hours per week, as they share the access time with other groups in their area. The legislation still gives priority to the private cable operator, in that where they choose to run the community channel themselves they may do so, as long as they provide the access quota and associated requirements. Only where the cable operator chooses not to run the station can groups such as TVCBF apply for an independent license. Some opportunities exist for sponsorship, and the cable operator is required to spend money derived from sponsorship on the channel. However, the CRTC, not wishing to deprive the Canadian production fund of the 5 percent of cable subscriber revenue, has stipulated that only smaller licensees can elect to put that money towards the community channel. The independent community groups cannot apply to the Canadian production fund. Furthermore, there is no requirement that the cable operator provide a portion of their revenue to the maintenance of these groups. The financial position of groups therefore remains tenuous. Finally, as there is no requirement that the community channel be carried on satellite, the community content is lost to a potentially large audience. In Montreal, when the Videotron technicians went on strike, as many as 15 percent of their customers moved to satellite. Although the Canadian legislation is forward thinking for its multi-platform approach (cable, digital cable, and low-power radio and television), as with most other places, satellite remains the sticking point.

Conclusion

The policy history of community media in North America is more complex than simply one step forward, two steps back. The battles for access have been fought on different fronts, largely in the absence of a federally mandated community media set-aside. It is not only a history of conflicting political agendas, but also of the unresolved position of community media principles within the wider broadcasting framework. This chapter has shown how community media requires a more complex investigation into access than speech-rights theory provides. Once community media's role within civil society is understood, more productive models arise. Chapter 6 looks at new articulations of access that seek to move beyond the idea of access to an otherwise controlled space and towards an "information commons." The concept of community building, introduced in this chapter, will be further discussed in chapter 5. First, however, some other policy values that have shaped community radio and television require attention, namely those of quality and noncommercialism.

Notes

1. Ralph Engelman, *The Origins of Public Access Cable Television* (Columbia, S.C.: Journalism Monographs, no. 123, 1990).

2. Engelman, *The Origins of Public Access Cable Television.*

3. Engelman, *The Origins of Public Access Cable Television,* 15.

4. Nicholas W. Jankowski, ed., *Community Media in the Information Age* (Cresskill, N.J.: Hampton Press, 2002).

5. Thomas Streeter, *Selling the Air: A Critique of the Policy of Commercial Broadcasting in the United States* (Chicago: University of Chicago Press, 1996), 40.

6. Streeter, *Selling the Air,* 195.

7. Laura R. Linder, *Public Access Television: America's Electronic Soapbox* (Westport: Praeger, 1999).

8. See, for example, Patricia Aufderheide, *The Daily Planet: A Critique on the Capitalist Culture Beat* (Minneapolis: University of Minnesota Press, 2000).

9. CityVisions, April 2001 program schedule.

10. George Stoney, "The Essential George Stoney," *Community Media Review* 24, no. 2 (2001): 29.

11. DeeDee Halleck, "Paper Tiger & Deep Dish: A Brief History," *Community Media Review* 24, no. 2 (2001).

12. Laura Stein, "Access Television and the Grass Roots," in *Radical Media: Rebellious Communication and Social Movements,* ed. John Downing (Thousand Oaks: Sage, 2001), 321.

13. Thomas Streeter, "Technocracy and Television: Discourse, Policy, Politics and the Making of Cable Television" (doctoral thesis, University of Illinois, Urbana-Champaign, 1986).

14. Ralph Engelman, *Public Radio and Television in America: A Political History* (Thousand Oaks: Sage, 1996), 236.

15. Laura Stein, "Can the First Amendment Protect Public Space on U.S. Media Systems? The Case of Public Access Television" (paper presented at the International Communications Association meeting, Washington, D.C., May 2001).

16. Streeter, "Technocracy and Television."

17. Maddox in Streeter, "Technocracy and Television," 97.

18. Andrew Calabrese and Janet Wasko, "All Wired Up and No Place to Go: The Search for Public Space in U.S. Cable Development," *Gazette* 49 (1992).

19. Linder, *Public Access Television*, 9.

20. Bunnie Riedell, interviewed by Ellie Rennie, Washington, D.C., May 21, 2001.

21. Linda K. Fuller, *Community Television in the United States: A Sourcebook on Public, Educational, and Governmental Access* (Westport, Conn.: Greenwood, 1994), 20.

22. Fuller, *Community Television in the United States*, 4.

23. Stein, "Can the First Amendment Protect Public Space on U.S. Media Systems?"

24. Streeter, *Selling the Air*.

25. Stein, "Can the First Amendment Protect Public Space on U.S. Media Systems?"

26. Calabrese and Wasko, "All Wired Up and No Place to Go," 140.

27. Calabrese and Wasko, "All Wired Up and No Place to Go," 140.

28. Stein, "Can the First Amendment Protect Public Space on U.S. Media Systems?" 20.

29. Streeter, *Selling the Air*, 193.

30. Stein, "Can the First Amendment Protect Public Space on U.S. Media Systems?" 34.

31. Aufderheide, *The Daily Planet*.

32. James N. Horwood and Allison L. Driver, "Public Policy Update: Court Decisions and FCC Rulings," Spiegel & McDiarmid 2002, at www.spiegelmcd.com/pubs/jnh_public_policya.htm (accessed October 14, 2002).

33. John Downing, "Community Access Television: Past, Present and Future," *Community Television Review* (August 1991): 8.

34. Aufderheide, *The Daily Planet*; and Downing, "Community Access Television." See also Laura Stein, "Democratic 'Talk,' Access Television and Participatory Political Communication" (paper presented at the twelfth EURICOM Colloquium on Communication and Culture, "Communication, Citizenship and Social Policy," University of Colorado at Boulder, 1997).

35. John Higgins, "Which First Amendment Are You Talking About?" *Community Media Review* 25, no. 2 (2002): 13.

36. Higgins, "Which First Amendment Are You Talking About?" 13. See also John Higgins, "Community Television and the Vision of Media Literacy, Social Action, and Empowerment," *Journal of Broadcasting & Electronic Media* 43, no. 4 (1999).

37. Higgins, "Which First Amendment Are You Talking About?" 12.

38. Calabrese and Wasko, "All Wired Up and No Place to Go."

39. Stein, "Can the First Amendment Protect Public Space on U.S. Media Systems?" 33.

40. Thomas A. Spragens, "Communitarian Liberalism," in *New Communitarian Thinking*, ed. Amitai Etzioni (Charlottesville: University Press of Virginia, 1995), 43.

41. Aufderheide, *The Daily Planet*, 134.

42. Michael Walzer, "Pluralism: A Political Perspective," in *The Rights of Minority Cultures*, ed. Will Kymlicka (New York: Oxford University Press, 1995), 146.

43. Michael J. Sandel, *Democracy's Discontent: America in Search of a Public Philosophy* (Cambridge, Mass.: Harvard University Press, 1996), 3.

44. Downing, "Community Access Television," 8.

45. I acknowledge an engaging discussion about the civil society debate with Rob McCausland of BNN in May 2001.

46. Jesse Walker, *Rebels on the Air: An Alternative History of Radio in America* (New York: New York University Press, 2001), 13.

47. Pete triDish in Walker, *Rebels on the Air*, 264.

48. Engelman, *Public Radio and Television in America*, 19.

49. Engelman, *Public Radio and Television in America*, 19.

50. Engelman, *Public Radio and Television in America*, 44.

51. Engelman, *Public Radio and Television in America*, 46.

52. Walker, *Rebels on the Air*, 50.

53. John Downing, *Radical Media: Rebellious Communication and Social Movements* (Thousand Oaks: Sage, 2001); Engelman, *Public Radio and Television in America*.

54. Downing, *Radical Media*, 330.

55. Engelman, *Public Radio and Television in America*, 51.

56. Engelman, *Public Radio and Television in America*, 53.

57. Walker, *Rebels on the Air*, 143.

58. Walker, *Rebels on the Air*, 214–15.

59. Prometheus Radio Project, "Low Power Signal: Special Interest Noise," Prometheus Radio Project, May 2000, at www.prometheusradio.org/artnoise.shtml (accessed March 23 2003).

60. Walker, *Rebels on the Air*, 267.

61. FCC, Order of Proposed Rulemaking: In the Matter of Establishment of a Class A Television Service, RM 9260 (January 13, 2000), 2.

62. FCC, RM 9260, 3.

63. Bill McConnell, "TV's Terrestrial Imperative," *Broadcasting & Cable* 130, no. 7 (2000).

64. Prometheus Radio Project, *The Next Full Giveaway: Digital Radio*, October 2000, www. prometheusradio.org/artdigital.shtml (accessed March 12, 2003).

65. André Desrochers, interviewed by Ellie Rennie, Montreal, May 16, 2001.

66. Catherine Edwards, "Response to Public Notice CRTC 2000-127," unpublished paper (Calgary, 2001).

67. See StarRay TV, at www.srtv.on.ca (accessed July 1, 2002).

68. CRTC Broadcasting Public Notice 2002-61.

69. CRTC Broadcasting Public Notice 2002-61, paragraph 152.

CHAPTER THREE

Quality and the Public Interest

The era in which radical and not-so-radical independent stations [in France] challenged the state's monopoly on radio broadcasting ran from March 1977 through summer 1985. . . . An exquisite touch was when one rebel station (known in the movement as "the pirate's pirate"), actually succeeded in broadcasting for 4 months from right inside the very headquarters where the jamming signals were emitted, operated by a technician totally disillusioned with his work as a jammer.

—John Downing

Community television in Europe emerged out of, and in response to, a broadcasting environment characterized by public service broadcasting monopolies. Although the policy and institutional structures of individual nations differed significantly during the monopoly era, broadcasting on the whole was essentially closed to competition after the initial experiments of the 1920s. Nations allocated broadcasting spectrum to semipublic institutions, giving them exclusive permission to broadcast. These broadcasters were not necessarily single institutions or "national" in their reach: Belgium and Switzerland both had separate broadcasters for different language groups. Britain allocated spectrum to commercial consortia in addition to its national service, while the Netherlands licensed broadcasters according to the "pillars" of ideological associations that structured civil society. German broadcasting was (and remains) organized at the state, rather than federal, level. Despite these differences, it is generally the case that as European viewers and listeners tuned in to a limited number of channels, TV's mass media found a mass audience for four decades.

Eli Noam, in his history of European broadcasting, writes that the success of these institutions, with their politically and culturally influential programming, made the public service broadcasting structure seem "the natural order of things, as if exclusivity over a major form of information provision in open societies were not highly unusual."[1] When change eventually arrived in the 1970s and 1980s, the strength of this belief surfaced, with defenders of the status quo in government and intellectual arenas appearing in force. Public service broadcasting was therefore the measure by which other forms of broadcasting would be compared. As a result of this climate, community broadcasting would be judged on the basis of quality, under the threat of privatization. Community broadcasting in Europe, therefore, needs to be seen within a different context than community media in North America. Noncommercial television and radio in countries without a dominating public broadcaster (United States, Canada, and, to some extent, Australia) must confront a different set of issues than in countries where they have arisen "from criticism of a monopolistic public service system that was considered out of touch."[2]

At the heart of the tensions surrounding the decentralization of broadcasting discussed here—piracy, the cable experiments, and the establishment of community broadcasting—is the ongoing theme of the relationship between civil society and the state. The complex question of whether community broadcasters are made stronger through state assistance or best left to their own devices is the fundamental difference between the European and North American models. Where the U.S. tradition sees civil society as necessarily separate from the state, and potentially distorted by state involvement, the European tradition sees civil society as dependent upon, and made stronger through, the state's assistance. In the final section of this chapter, I shall discuss some of these issues in relation to the changing structures of civil society in Europe.

Others who have attempted to draw conclusions on the state of European broadcasting have written of the problem of generalization. This is certainly an issue in respect to community broadcasting, where vast differences are found within countries as well as between them. The examples in this chapter are therefore simply illustrations of themes and are not meant to represent the continent as a whole. However, international developments since the emergence of community broadcasting have meant that stations throughout Europe have faced a common set of issues, even where models have varied greatly. A number of concurrent forces, of which pressures by citizen groups for participation was just one, caused decentralization of broadcasting in Europe.[3] The opposition political parties in countries where state control was most stringent (such as France and Italy) sought representation in the media. Economic interests advocated decentralization in order to enter the broadcast market. Within the public broadcasting corporations themselves, staff had been seeking greater freedom from centralized control. And, at the same time, the electronic sector was being promoted as an area of national economic development in many countries, leading to high-tech policy and the installation (rollout) of cable infrastructure.

In their introduction to the only comprehensive volume on European community media, Nicholas Jankowski, Ole Prehn, and James Stappers wrote: "Many general trends in media developments seem impervious to national borders: satellite television and the impact of foreign programming on national and local culture, commercialisation of radio and television programming at all levels of the media system, and the tension between desire for community involvement in programming and a trend toward more professional production standards. These and other similarities are strikingly evident among local radio and television stations across Europe."[4] Beyond changes in media, Europe itself was transforming. New levels of secularization, the arrival of new immigrant communities, the formation of the European Community (formerly the EEC), and an emerging post-communist era for the East set a dramatic backdrop for the arrival of small-scale media. The various European models of community broadcasting that emerged have been surveyed in Jankowski, Prehn, and Stapper's collection *The People's Voice* and elsewhere.[5] This chapter builds upon this work to consider the broader tensions that shaped community broadcasting in Europe and to consider the new force now confronting the sector.

Sailing the Airwaves: Community Broadcasting's Pirate Beginnings

The initial disruptions to public broadcasting's privileged status came from the sea—signals beamed into countries from unlicensed stations located on ships off the coast of Scandinavia. In 1958, the first commercially run "pirate" radio station, Radio Mercur, transmitted into Denmark, setting a trend which later spread to the Netherlands, Belgium, and Britain.[6] Radio Mercur (1958–1962) earned an alleged six million kroner. The station was shut down by the authorities, only to be purchased (ship and all) by a new pirate, Radio Syd (1962–1966), which broadcast into Sweden. Although sometimes lucrative, pirate stations were also leaky boats for investors. Laws were passed in Sweden, Belgium, and Denmark from 1962 onwards to outlaw the stations, some with strict penalties—including the seizure of assets.[7] Although the Netherlands did not create antipiracy laws until 1974, the stations were still clandestine enterprises wherever they existed, defying national borders and operating with ambiguous ownership structures and an overall disregard for copyright and wavelength agreements.[8]

The stations gave audiences what was absent from public service broadcasting at that time, namely, American-style popular entertainment. But the pirates were seen as a legal problem rather than an indication of audience dissatisfaction with existing media. Political parties and licensed broadcasters raised concerns about the potential for the pirates to interfere with emergency signals. They also warned that the stations were likely to encourage listeners to get involved in fascism, communism, or recreational drug use.

Although the commercial pirates seem far removed from community media, their antiestablishment attitude makes them, to some extent, a precursor of community radio.[9] Both were movements "from below," and a challenge to the established order. But where the commercial pirates did not possess the moral legitimacy required to gain legal status, the same could not be said for the second wave of pirates—this time established out of noncommercial motives.[10]

In Italy, where the monopoly broadcaster was under tight political control, clandestine, left-wing, local stations run by trade unions and social movement groups began to appear, known as "radio libres." In the town of Biella, near Turin, cable pirate Tele Biella had distributed programs to one hundred subscribers, informing them of alternatives to the political status quo. Tele Biella set an example by questioning the legal foundations of monopoly broadcasting. When it was shut down, Tele Biella fought the decision in the Constitutional Court. The case demonstrated to others that change was possible. In 1974 Radio Bologna per l'Accesso Pubblico began broadcasting, demanding the decentralization of broadcasting. "Run by a cooperative of workers, students, and communication experts, the station's reach, with a 20km radius, was local, but its effect was national and sensational. Coming from the heartland of regional support for the Italian Communist Party (PCI), the broadcast was an explicit criticism of RAI, the Italian state broadcasting organisation, and an appeal to Parliament and public opinion for reform."[11] Hundreds of stations followed the Bologna example, and although the authorities attempted to stop them, legal appeals were upheld. In July 1976, RAI's monopoly was declared constitutionally invalid at the local level and more stations flooded the airwaves. By June 1978 there were 2275 stations, giving Italy record numbers in terms of radio stations per head. A great number of these stations were commercial, and many others were linked to the political right. Lack of regulation had stations resorting to all kinds of tactics to keep their space on the airwaves; those with the strongest financial backing and highest power survived. The movement for community media had, in this case, led the way for commercial broadcasting.

In France, the Ecology Party had a role to play in the development of community radio. The pioneer of community radio in France, Antoine Lefébure, surreptitiously set up his transmitter in a television studio. During a discussion program on television TF1, Brice Lalonde of the Ecologists produced a radio which announced the launch of Radio Vert—publicizing the station to a national audience.[12] Although the government repeatedly jammed their signals, Lefébure and his colleagues formed the Association pour la Libération des Ondes (ALO) and by 1978 twenty groups possessed their own transmitters. Free radio won the support of the Socialist party, and when it came into power the new government set up a committee to license local radio (RLP). Both the president and the prime minister were initially opposed to advertising, and an amnesty was granted on the condition that stations undertook to not carry advertisements, to not set up networks, to transmit with limited power, and to be constituted as nonprofit associations. Out of this, thirteen hundred stations were licensed; as financial problems set in, however, a number began to broadcast advertising. In 1984 Mitterrand announced he would permit advertising, beginning a process of commercialization. By the end of 1985, sixteen hundred stations had been licensed as RLPs.

As these first attempts at decentralized radio in Italy and France demonstrate, pirate stations, whether commercial or community, were a challenge to the control of the airwaves by top-down public institutions/corporations. Dissatisfaction from the viewing public, the initiatives of hobbyists, and political frustration from underrepresented groups had aspiring broadcasters going to great lengths to break into a controlled technical space. That some secured audiences large enough to attract advertising revenue is an indication of the public's desire for an alternative.

This prehistory of European community broadcasting makes an easily romanticized story—pirate broadcasters sailing, and selling, the airwaves. But piracy is an activity that does not just belong to an idealized past. Where constraints on broadcasting exist, people will find a means to transmission. And where piracy is found today, its rivals are no longer associated exclusively with public broadcasting; broadcasters from the commercial sector strike also, out of a need to protect their markets. Piracy is a tactic of the weak,[13] an intervention by those who seek to find gaps in the strategic spaces of regulated broadcast spectrum. It exists outside of the defined spaces of community broadcasting, and yet it often works through the same networks and movements. In some countries, the pirates have made it clear that it is no longer acceptable for arguments of spectrum scarcity to be maintained— at least where signals do not interfere with those bands set aside for legal broadcast use.[14]

Community broadcasters continue to use similar strategies. In the early 1990s, a community television campaigner in the United Kingdom found a loophole in the U.K.'s broadcasting legislation and requested that the regulator find available spectrum for text-based services, which did not require a license. In this way, community media pioneer Dave Rushton discovered how much spectrum, and where, was not in use—information he used in the campaign for local television.[15] In terms of use of electronic space, piracy and community broadcasting both work on a similar principle. However, where community broadcasting seeks a delineated commons—a campsite for anyone to make use of—piracy pitches itself where it can, with little regard for who controls that space or who happened to be there first.

This history also demonstrates how community and commercial media came to be in the same boat, as it were, during the transitional period of the 1970s. As both were seen as a threat to the status quo, interesting alliances formed between the two not-yet-recognized sectors. Coming up against the powerful public service advocates, this did not always work to the advantage of the community sector in terms of the way community broadcasting was perceived. A look at the initial experiments in community television (which preceded community radio in most countries) demonstrates the changing relationship of community broadcasting to both the public and private sectors.

A Blurred Vision:
The European Community Television Experiments

Histories of the early community broadcasting trials yield two recurrent themes: decentralization, in terms of the breakdown of the monopoly systems, and amateurism as a threat to existing standards. Neither of these issues can be dealt with without reference to the changing position of public service broadcasting in terms of its assumed "rightful" control of broadcasting and notions of aesthetic quality. With the European community television trials taking place within systems which were, at that time, dominated by public service broadcasting, the predominant values were those which were being perpetuated by the incumbents. When the first European community broadcasting trials took place in the 1970s, North American cable community television had already been established. It was looked to as a model but was recognized as operating in very different circumstances. In 1978, a media academic well known for his work on community media, Peter Lewis, warned that it was important to take into account what alternative media "was an alternative to." Localism was a feature of North American broadcasting and viewers were "accustomed to seeing low-budget local programs." He further pointed out that "there is no long tradition, at least in the USA, of public service programming, or of public service local radio in either country."[16] Community broadcasting in Europe, from the start, sat uneasily between the private and public sectors—it was noncommercial but still far from the established public institution model; it was supported by industry but only to the extent that it would open the way for mass commercial media. Furthermore, the community producers were reliant upon the commercial cable providers in order to fulfill their ideals of participatory media, while the cable companies saw local television as a means to win government favor. The community television experiments were described at the time as the "alliance of the mercenaries and the missionaries."[17]

The first round of noncommercial community television experiments began in England (1972), followed by the Netherlands (1974), Denmark (1974), French-speaking Belgium (1976), and Sweden (1979), with Germany (1984) to follow. The degree of private involvement in the experiments differed across nations, but the tension between community television and the potential privatization of broadcasting was common throughout. In the United Kingdom, the privately owned company Greenwich Cablevision successfully lobbied the minister of posts and telecommunications to allow programs of local origination on its cable system, which until then had been restricted to relaying existing broadcast services. Greenwich Cablevision and five other licensees were permitted to participate in similar experiments on the condition that the licensees would exist without public money, that they would provide local, community-oriented programming, and would maintain a high degree of quality. Advertising, sponsorship, and the screening of films were all prohibited.[18] In the 1970s, the cable companies were expecting the Conservative government to develop legislation that would permit pay TV services. The provision of community television channels was described by one Cable Television Association member as a means to "set a precedent—the first time that someone other than the broadcasters was entrusted with communicating with people in their homes."[19] Richard Dunn of the Swindon Viewpoint station also believed that "part of the agenda was pay television, that whilst the community television experiments were experiments in community television, perhaps the government might sympathetically look on pay television in the future if companies like EMI were successful in providing community television services."[20]

Another commercial interest was the electronic hardware industry, which was looking to expand its market by promoting the idea of video production to ordinary people. The Sony Portapak—a heavy, nonbroadcast quality video camera that was developed out of the U.S. military budget—was put to use in the cable community television trials.[21] It is now an infamous relic of those first cable programs—outdone by countless generations of video cameras— but at the time it was an important tool for community broadcasters as it was relatively affordable and easy to use. The people at Swindon Viewpoint saw it as their goal to enable local people "to borrow equipment, light weight port-a-packs [sic], the old Sony port-a-packs, which people could borrow free to learn how to use television cameras and recording equipment to make their own programs, to edit themselves."[22]

Such alliances found their harshest critics to be working within media studies. The British school of critical cultural studies, in particular, read community media with suspicion due to the involvement of private interests. This is an academic tradition firmly grounded in Marxism but with a concern for culture as well as economics, in particular the nexus of the two. The legacy of Marxism within this strand of cultural studies manifested as a belief in "progressive" tendencies (and their opposite), the primacy of production over consumption and an emphasis on ownership and control.[23] Although on the surface these features would seem supportive of the community broadcasting project, commentary remained strongly divided between the leftist advocates and the leftist critics. For the latter, community broadcasting was too weak to be revolutionary; it did not presume the primacy of the state (or public service media) as the vehicle through which change must occur, and it was opportunistic in its financial structures.

In an article titled "The Myths of Video," media theorist Nicholas Garnham portrays the Portapak as being unsuitable for Europe, which, in his opinion, should be above the U.S.-style "technical fix."[24] Garnham criticizes the amateurish quality of community video and video art, seeing film as the superior format for broadcasting. For him, community participation is a myth promoted by industry to sell Portapaks to "video freaks" and to open up the cable market. He writes: "The claim for community video still, however, retains a lingering and dangerous propaganda force in the field of cable television. The major economic interests behind the manufacture of electronic hardware are also involved in a concerted, long-term push to develop cable as a means of breaking the public control of broadcasting. The aim is to gain access to certain specialised and profitable segments of the audience to the detriment of that European tradition whereby broadcasting has a duty to serve the whole community."[25] Another well-known media theorist, Graham Murdock, also writes of the hidden commercial agenda in the community television experiments: "From the point of view of the companies involved, then, the present cable experiments fulfil two principal functions. Firstly, they act as public relations exercises aimed at establishing the present operators as capable of running a domestic television station responsibly, and persuading the government to allow cable to precede on a commercial basis. Secondly, they provide convenient opportunities for electronics manufacturers to develop and test 'hardware' facilities. They are, in fact, one component in these companies' overall 'Research and Development' programs."[26] Elsewhere, the community broadcasting experiments received substantial government investment but were still viewed as a step towards the entry of private interests into broadcasting. In Denmark, pressure for community broadcasting came from citizens' groups with the first local cable television experiments beginning in 1973 for a four-year trial.[27] In 1981, due to inconclusive evidence concerning the first trial, a new experiment was initiated. Despite the fact that the experiments were subsidized and advertising was prohibited, a significant amount of money was invested by the private sector into local television. Even in Denmark, with its history of state-assisted associationalism, private interests pursued community broadcasting in anticipation of liberalization. Where the government contributed the equivalent of 1.6 million euros for the duration of the second-round experiments, it is estimated that a total to the equivalent of 23 million euros were spent on local TV in 1985 alone.[28] By 1986, 108 radio and 42 television licenses had been granted with some local programs out-rating those of the national broadcaster Danmarks Radio (at the time the only other broadcaster). Again there were indications that community broadcasting was not as people had expected it to be. Although the first round of Danish experiments had not been broad enough for a decision on local cable broadcasting to be made, the report on the experiments did find that programming had not met political expectations. The content that resulted was "soft" rather than focused on local political agendas. From the start, "the political centre had one idea while the program-producing periphery predominantly had a different one."[29]

Academic commentators were suspicious of the community television trials, seeing them as a means for cable companies to progress their own interests through the sale of Portapaks and the rolling out of cable, as research and development exercises to test commercial enterprises, and as, eventually, a means for cable companies to change policy in their favor. Commercial investment was seen as an underhanded business that negated any moral grounds that the community stations made claim to. What is striking about this critique is that an arrangement that allowed for unprecedented community involvement in broadcasting was seen as outright privatization when it could just as easily have been viewed as a "publicization" of private interests.[30] It is unlikely that these judgments would hold today, when the political climate favors "partnerships" between business and community (largely in spite of the persistence of critical Marxism and neo-Marxism within cultural studies). That commercial interests can help assist community participation and access to equipment, or that community broadcasting provides research and development for the commercial sector is no longer seen to be covert and improper.

The U.K. experiments floundered after 1979, when the returned Labour government made it clear that pay TV was not likely to eventuate in the near future. Two stations survived for a time beyond this date: Swindon Viewpoint, which was granted money from the lottery fund, and Channel 40 in Milton Keynes, which was funded by the post office. These stations eventually closed down, and only recently did the U.K. government develop legislation for community broadcasting services. This time around, local commercial television preceded community television, with over sixty local television licenses originally awarded. The licenses were mostly bought by a company called the Local Broadcasting Group, which later folded under financial pressure. Only a handful of local television stations remain.[31]

In the other countries that undertook community television experiments, permanent frameworks for both television and radio have since been developed, although not without significant hurdles and delays. Researcher Ed Hollander contends that community broadcasting policy did not result from the experiments but from continued campaigning by groups after the experimental period was over (with the exception of Neighbourhood Radio in Sweden). He writes that the cautiousness of European governments can be attributed to their "concern for possible commercialization of cable communication facilities. Allowing use of the cable by any nonpublic broadcasting organization might create a precedent, it was thought, for other, less idealistic uses of the cable."[32] In the follow-up edition to *The People's Voice*, titled *Community Media in the Information Age*, Jankowski is much more optimistic. He writes that in Western Europe, "local and regional stations have achieved legitimation in national media policies; restrictions on modes of transmission have been lifted; stable financing has—in a number of select countries—been attained; training has expanded."[33] With the threat of decentralization now a reality, the caution and fear over the introduction of community media seems to have finally passed.

Values

During the community television experiments, Peter Lewis posed a challenge to the dominant values in European broadcasting. He observed that despite expectations, a large amount of the community content produced in the United Kingdom was not news or investigatory documentary. However, "underlying even the nostalgia of a local history program, or the angling demonstration or the coverage of a church fete, is a challenge to the notion of impartiality." Community radio and television challenge the dominant value of impartiality in reporting, a phenomenon "with which the professionals in broadcasting will have to come to terms. It is not that the monasteries of broadcasting face dissolution; only that the monks within them must realise that people outside *can* learn to read and write and that not all manuscripts have to be illuminated."[34]

The value judgments made on the basis of quality that dominated the writing on the European community broadcasting experiments have remained a feature of academic and policy discussions ever since. So familiar is this critique that it is rarely questioned or debated. Participation in broadcasting by ordinary citizens is equated with amateurism, and amateurism is treated apprehensively within the broadcasting arena—in television in particular. Community broadcasters and their programs are judged in terms of transmission quality, journalistic standards, and artistic/technical merit, all of which have the capacity to impede or enhance the viewing or listening experience. However, these standards are also related to assumptions and expectations about the control of broadcasting, including who will make *best* use of the airwaves, aesthetically and morally. In the European context, the public service broadcasters had the advantage of quality, while amateurism and commercialism were in many respects seen as the antithesis of it. Although critics bemoan the lack of quality in community media, the notion of quality in government-funded public service broadcasting has been thoroughly contested, and with it the justifications upon which public service broadcasting rests.[35] With the position of the public broadcasters shifting—their once unquestioned command of cultural space having now been challenged—the status of community television in respect to notions of quality also deserves revisiting.

Media studies research has shown that a discourse of value has supported public service television (meaning "the institutional and discursive processes that work to rank, distinguish, and attribute status to certain cultural forms and practices and the audiences that recognise and enjoy these"[36]). Quality is not deployed in respect to one cultural or taste-group's appreciation, but as a totalizing value that implies an intrinsic good or aesthetic superiority. The public service broadcasters are held to produce the *best* television, a value that works to disguise the cultural interests that are in fact being served. By universalizing concepts of what good television is, the interests that are being met are also universalized. As a result, difference is excluded. Televisual forms and practices outside of this (community television for instance) are also seen "as fundamentally 'other' and inferior."[37]

The discussion of the European community television experiments centered on whether community-made programs were "good enough" for distribution to the general public. In belittling community content, television production was elevated to a talent beyond the learning ability of most people: "With very few exceptions, the majority of program makers show very little understanding of the video medium. This may not seem surprising: after all, most have never used video equipment before, and have little knowledge of the standard conventions of television production. But even those volunteers who continue to make programs are not encouraged to give much thought to the medium they are using. Most have the same attitude as the typical home movie-maker."[38] It is fair to say that a lack of production quality will discourage audiences from viewing. But this was not the case across the continent. For instance, the stations in Denmark that survived the experimental period displayed a high level of professionalism and developed a distinct station profile.[39] Since the experimental period, it has been a common issue within stations to improve the technical standards of programming, although this is constantly in tension with the principle of access and freedom of expression. This is the case even in the "purest" of community television stations, Berlin's Offener Kanal. The cable television station survives entirely on money derived from the TV license fee (1 million Deutschmarks in 2001) and runs with a strict ethic of access (videos are not previewed prior to broadcast so as not to imply judgment of content). However, in recent times the station has begun to address its scheduling, sought to upgrade its equipment, and revised its training programs in order to create more "watchable" television (see also the discussion of Salto, below).[40] But beyond the obvious issues of technical standards, community media is seen as the territory of niche interests, localism, and amateurism. All of these characteristics sit in stark contrast to the traditional notion of quality in public service broadcasting and its unifying notion of "the public."

The rethinking of public service broadcasting came through an acceptance of the popular media as an important site of cultural learning. The cultural advantage that public service broadcasting maintained for so long had rested upon its independence from private interests; commercial interests would not be able to jeopardize public service broadcasting's ability to convey objectivity and "truth." Commercial media, despite its ability to attract audiences, was seen as less suitable, less informative, and to some extent tasteless. The pleasure gained through viewing commercial media was therefore cast as less valuable than the information gained through watching or listening to the public service broadcasters. The notion that the "sublimation of pleasure" was necessary in order to gain moral superiority began to be challenged.[41] Public service broadcasting came to be seen as the "disciplining" of the tastes of the popular class in order to claim a privileged status in the public sphere—what has been called "democracy as defeat."[42]

Apart from the theoretical considerations, there were other chinks in the armor of public service television in terms of its place in national political orders. The relationships of state-society-citizenry were changing; party allegiances were weakening; and secularization and/or depillarization, as well as "an overall ethos of consumerist hedonism," was suffusing Europe. This meant that the services offered began to appear "old fashioned and their traditional clients appear a declining constituency."[43] Furthermore, the public service broadcasters met with criticism from those with "alternative" views about the role of the broadcasters, demanding more public accountability and diversity and attacking the complicity of the broadcasters with dominant political forces. As a result, the appeal of the liberal-utopian vision of infinite communication channels grew. This did not so much signify the death of the public service broadcasters as much as a loss of the principles upon which public service broadcasting once rested. In many respects, these values precluded the variety of roles that public service broadcasting performs, including multicultural services and the nurturing of new talent. One suggestion is that public service broadcasting should be seen in the context of the media ecology within which it exists, rather than automatically assigned a privileged position due to some preconceived association with quality, democracy, and citizenship.[44]

The commercial media have their supporters who have justified their status as rightful occupants of the cultural sphere against the dominant European values. The concern that community broadcasting paves the way for commercial interests is no longer plausible due to the now decentralized European broadcasting environment. Regulatory distinctions have been developed in many First World countries that distinguish for-profit from nonprofit local media, making the association even less relevant. But where the value assumptions of both the public and commercial sectors have been rethought, the position of community broadcasting within this decentralized broadcasting framework remains unexplored.

Quality and Community Media

Little research has been done into audience reception of community media, in terms of how viewers engage with its content. Some textual analysis of community programming has shown that community content does not necessarily conform to the formats of more professional programming.[45] Due to this lack of existing research, it is difficult to make qualified conclusions about alternative values perceived in relation to community broadcasting.

One study commissioned by Denmark's Ministry of Culture does, however, provide some valuable insights into notions of quality in community broadcasting. The study, conducted by researchers Per Jauert and Ole Prehn, focused upon changes in the funding arrangement for local television in Denmark. Following the experimental period, local radio and television became a permanent feature of Danish broadcasting in 1985 and 1987 respectively. Advertising was permitted by 1988, and a support fund was set up whereby funds levied off profit-making stations would provide support to local radio where it was needed. It became apparent that the stations were developing into for-profit and nonprofit sectors, but that "legislation was basically organised according to non-commercial principles,"[46] for instance a ban on networking and limited transmission areas. In 1994, a decision was made to create new license categories, resulting in 82 commercial and 174 noncommercial local radio licensees, and 23 commercial and 30 noncommercial television licensees.[47] A new system of state subsidy for the noncommercial stations was developed, in part derived from the public's contribution to the TV license fee (previously reserved for the national broadcaster Danmarks Radio) and a tax on the now networked commercial local television stations. The nonprofit television sector received a total of 6.7 million euros in subsidy in 2001, distributed according to the amount of broadcasting time each station was producing. As "quantity became the chief concern rather than quality," this system was changed to an application process based on a merit system for priority programs.[48] In late 2001 the subsidy was reduced to 5.3 million euros per annum for the 2002–2006 period (despite a large increase in the number of licensees), partly due to the tax on the networked local stations being lifted. Jauert and Prehn see the reduction as a "political signal that the non-commercial stations have the lowest priority in media policy."[49] With the shift to a "beauty contest" funding model, one of the main focuses of the study was to assess the quality of community programs. Recognizing the disputed nature of quality in the broadcasting context, Jauert and Prehn used interview and focus group research to assess the extent to which quality was considered a dominant value for both viewers and producers. They found that:

The participants emphasise the nearness and thoroughness of the broadcasts and in particular the special, lingering tempo as some of the most prominent qualities of many of the local broadcasts. The slow tempo also gives people the opportunity to finish speaking, which for several participants is almost a relief compared to the fifteen-second democracy of "the big media" news programs. The "amateurish charm" exists and is appreciated, that is, the broadcasts are not judged primarily based on their technical or journalistic correctness, but rather on their ability to evoke or express participation and nearness.[50]

The focus groups condemned community television programming when it attempted to imitate genres that they were "unable to fulfil." Community television that sought to replicate the content of commercial and public service broadcasting was seen as simply second-rate, rather than appealing to the viewer's own sense of community identification. It was therefore shown that community television viewers do not tolerate poor quality, or that they should. Rather, the Denmark study demonstrates how different sets of values are at work alongside the dominant and assumed values around quality.

Jauert and Prehn identify "proximity, relevance and a sense of participation and sincerity" as values that are associated with community media.[51] These values have remained secondary to the value of quality that has traditionally defined public service broadcasting. However, these values are significant as they demonstrate that audiences engage with community media differently than they engage with either commercial or public service broadcasters. This identification is tied to the viewers' own sense of familiarity with their local community or a community of interest, as well as to an awareness of how the material is produced. It is an insight into someone's viewpoint, the story of an ordinary participant. In other words, it is not judged in the same way that qualified and professional renditions would be, but on its own terms.

One of the consequences of the changing role of public service broadcasting has been a new conception of the public interest. New values of diversity, multiple viewpoints, and participation through new technologies are being coopted into the function of public service broadcasting. For the community sector, such values have always been present. Steve Buckley, former general manager of the Community Media Association in the United Kingdom, has written, in response to the BBC's new localization and interactive efforts, that "in the fast moving, free-thinking world of the Internet, community media is an idea coming of age and the BBC wants to be part of it."[52] One possible consequence is that new forms of partnership could be formed between the public and community sectors, beyond the calls (typical of Europe) for a portion of the TV license fee where it exists. There is still a strong devotion to public service broadcasting in the United Kingdom. Local television has struggled to survive and many who want community media to work feel that the BBC has a role to play in its survival. A report on local and community television discusses the 2004 review of the BBC's charter and suggests that a part of the license fee should be used for community media use: "This would not be top-slicing, instead the BBC would be encouraged to further develop its local strategy by entrusting local groups with individual subsidies, as well as enfolding them within legally binding partnerships. These contracts would require adequate protections to prevent the BBC exploiting, or appearing to exploit, community groups."[53] The report looks positively on the BBCi experiments in local interactive television in the town of Hull, which included *Video Diaries*, interactive drama, local news, and information. The BBC's *Capture Wales* is also a good example of how community participation can, with the right structures and guidance, create content with high narrative and production values.[54] But although the proposal for sixty local BBC services (each with ten minutes of local content updated each hour) signifies a new interest in community, the report warns that the idea currently offers "more questions than answers," particularly in regard to the screening of local content not originated by the BBC. Although these trends are positive in terms of the redefinition of the role of public service broadcasting, partnerships with public service broadcasters may not be the best way forward for community media. In the United States, funding offered via public service broadcasting meant the decline of community radio as community stations became increasingly professionalized and susceptible to corporate interests. Groups were restructured in order to meet the criteria set out by those distributing funding, which had consequences for programming and participation (see chapter 2). Even though public service broadcasting appears to be redefining itself according to community needs, these issues require further investigation in regards to their impact upon community media.

Civil Society

In the Netherlands, civil society associations have been more involved in the broadcasting system than they have been in any other country. The Netherlands stands as a unique example of associationalism in broadcasting, where civil society has been privileged over market and government agencies in radio and television. This model was the result of the once "pillarized" society of the Netherlands, and it can only be viewed as having occurred within that history. But despite the particular social structure from which it arose, broadcasting in the Netherlands displays problems for associationalism as a guiding institutional arrangement. This public system, based upon community, ideology, and voluntary association, was ultimately challenged in the same way as the systems in other European countries in the 1970s. Amsterdam's cable community broadcaster, Salto, is the product of public dissatisfaction and alienation from organized civil society. It therefore demonstrates the transformation and fragmentation of civil society, and broadcasting's contribution to this shift.

The four pillars of Catholicism, Protestantism, socialism, and liberalism that dominated the social landscape in the Netherlands during the twentieth century meant that the country was largely organized through nonprofit associations (or "corporations"). Each pillar ran its own schools, unions, clubs, and media, producing approximately 15 percent of Dutch GNP in the 1980s, an output greater than that of the central and local governments combined.[55] In 1967, a new broadcasting act opened the way for groups other than those organized by the four pillars to broadcast. With sufficient members, groups were allocated time slots based on a sliding scale. The larger the group, the greater the number of hours per week that group would be granted. Furthermore, groups were required by the act to prove that they contributed to the diversity of broadcasting, thereby ensuring that existing broadcasters were not duplicated, or their interests threatened.[56]

The model of diversity that was employed in the Netherlands broadcasting system reflected historical differences based on religious and political affiliation. It differed from other public broadcasting systems in that it made no claim to represent a unified national community. As one critic describes it, "the *idea* does mainly relate to an '*external*' and *exclusive* diversity in which different 'voices' and outlooks have their own separate channels, rather than to the more commonly encountered 'internal' diversity, according to which all tastes are catered for by channels serving large, heterogenous audiences."[57] In this way, broadcasting in the Netherlands was seen either as exceptionally pluralistic or as enshrined segregation.[58]

Within discussions around associative democracy, some theoretical considerations have been raised regarding the European "corporatist" style of governance. The primary concern is that civil society involvement in the provision of public services can exclude groups outside of the nominated associations from any significant participation. The applicability of these concerns to broadcasting is that they raise the important issue of how organized forms of civil society should be regulated to participate in the broadcasting landscape, as well as the potential exclusions that result from such forms of participation. How power is distributed within civil society is a major concern: "In today's polity, the most powerful organised interests look no more like the textbook's

Salto

In the Netherlands, piracy—both commercial and noncommercial—was an indication that the broadcasting system based upon the four pillars had begun to lose relevance. Amsterdam's community broadcaster, Salto, originated out of pirate radio and television. When cable television was first introduced to Amsterdam in 1978, anarchist groups began hacking into the cable system and broadcasting experimental programming and pornography at night. Despite a broadcasting structure designed according to the pillars of civil society and based upon affiliation and membership, groups such as the squatter movement sought out their own means to production and representation.

When a legal framework was developed for community broadcasting, Salto was awarded the license and the anarchist groups became regular programmers (for instance *Staats tv-Rabotnik*). The community broadcasting law in the Netherlands stipulates only one license within a designated area, with the licensee able to broadcast on any platform and across a number of channels (the exact number is negotiated politically). Beginning with one radio and one television station in 1984, Salto now has three television channels and six radio channels, four of which have both cable and terrestrial transmission frequencies. One of the television channels is devoted to AT5, which was a local news channel owned by a private publisher. When the owner found the station to be unprofitable, the city bought the channel. It then "gave" it to Salto, so as "not to be seen as having municipal/state broadcasting"[a]—reflecting the nation's long-standing skepticism towards state control.

Salto itself has attempted to develop a more open structure, whereby individuals—and not just legal entities, such as incorporated associations/foundations—can broadcast programs. According to station manager Erik van der Schaft, Salto's original board of sixty people caused "paralysis in terms of governance," with "everybody having their say about God knows what." This unworkable model—a mixture of access and corporatism—has now been dismantled, with the board reduced to less than fifteen and policy development delegated to the station manager. Individuals not aligned with an association can now submit programming proposals; the programs are only broadcast when they are deemed technically suitable for broadcast by the station. According to van der Schaft, the changes have been implemented in order to attract more creative programming:

> Before, the truly creative people were scared away by all the bureaucracy and the ones who were left behind were the ones who knew their way around our social and welfare system: people who know how to get subsidies and know how to work the system to their advantage. I feel we've lost a lot of talent that way and now we're trying to bring them in. Especially younger people—why try to get them to set up a

foundation when they can just make programs? It's a bit more difficult for us in terms of trying to get the money they owe us and what have you, but I feel that is a risk we have to take.

---

[a] Erik van der Schaft, interviewed by Ellie Rennie, Amsterdam, March 28, 2001.

citizen-initiated concerns than General Motors looks like a ma and pa store."[59] The "ma and pa" scale civil society groups excluded from corporatist models include the "weaker" or more transient groups, such as single-issue alliances, the networks of new social movements that defy formal organization, and groups concerned with local issues or issues of culture and identity.

The Salto example indicates the breakdown of the corporatist model, particularly its relevance for younger people living in Amsterdam. A community station reliant upon such a structure risks irrelevance for the proportion of the population who do not wish—or know how—to "work the system to their advantage," as van der Schaft puts it. Rather than seeing such a change as the demise of civil society, Salto has sought to adapt to this change and to find new means to include programmers who exist outside of the formal group structures. The desire to attract better programming is also a concern, taking into consideration that in the context of Salto, this means increased innovation and difference rather than high quality. But even behind this motivation is the sense that, without change, new spaces, ideas, and alliances within civil society will be alienated. Being "community," for van der Schaft, does not have to mean being old-fashioned, corporatist, or bureaucratic.

Europe, in this chapter, has been used to discuss the changing values that surround all sectors of the media yet which have not been translated, updated, and applied to the workings of community broadcasting. Where public service and commercial broadcasting have received such attention, the valorization of quality and the preeminence of the singular cultural voice have been called into question. The following chapters concentrate on where community is finding itself within the new structure.

Notes

1. Eli Noam, *Television in Europe* (Oxford: Oxford University Press, 1991), 4.
2. Hans J. Kleinsteuber and Urte Sonnenberg, "Beyond Public Service and Private Profit: International Experience with Non-Commercial Local Radio," *European Journal of Communication* 5 (1990): 97.

3. See Jay G. Blumler, ed., *Television and the Public Interest: Vulnerable Values in West European Broadcasting* (London: Sage, 1992); J. Harrison and L. M. Woods, "Defining European Public Service Broadcasting," *European Journal of Communication* 16, no. 4 (2001); and Wolfgang Hoffman-Reim, "Trends in the Development of Broadcasting Law in Western Europe," *European Journal of Communication* 7 (1992).

4. Nick Jankowski, Ole Prehn, and James Stappers, eds., *The People's Voice: Local Radio and Television in Europe* (London: John Libbey, 1992), 1.

5. See Nicholas W. Jankowski, ed., *Community Media in the Information Age* (Cresskill, N.J.: Hampton Press, 2002); Kleinsteuber and Sonnenberg, "Beyond Public Service and Private Profit"; Peter M. Lewis and Jerry Booth, *The Invisible Medium: Public, Commercial and Community Radio* (Basingstoke: Macmillan, 1989); and Patrick Vittet-Philippe and Philip Crookes, eds., *Local Radio and Regional Development in Europe* (Manchester: European Institute for the Media, 1986).

6. Robert Chapman, *Selling the Sixties: The Pirates and Pop Music Radio* (London: Routledge, 1992), 28.

7. Nico van Eijk, "Legal and Policy Aspects of Community Broadcasting," in *The People's Voice*, ed. Jankowski, Prehn, and Stappers.

8. Chapman, *Selling the Sixties*.

9. Ole Prehn, "From Small Scale Utopianism to Large Scale Pragmatism: Trends and Prospects for Community Oriented Local Radio and Television," in *The People's Voice*, ed. Jankowski, Prehn, and Stappers, 250.

10. Noam, *Television in Europe*.

11. Lewis and Booth, *The Invisible Medium*, 140.

12. Lewis and Booth, *The Invisible Medium*, 148.

13. Nick Couldry, *The Place of Media Power: Pilgrims and Witnesses of the Media Age* (London: Routledge, 2000); Michel de Certeau, *The Practice of Everyday Life* (Berkeley: University of California Press, 1984).

14. Lowe Hedman, "Sweden: Neighbourhood Radio," in *The People's Voice*, ed. Jankowski, Prehn, and Stappers.

15. Dave Rushton, interviewed by Ellie Rennie, Edinburgh, March 4, 2001.

16. Peter M. Lewis, *Community Television and Cable in Britain* (London: British Film Institute, 1978), 10.

17. Lewis, *Community Television and Cable in Britain*, 16.

18. Lewis, *Community Television and Cable in Britain*.

19. R. M. Denny in Lewis, *Community Television and Cable in Britain*, 17.

20. Richard Dunn in Tony Dowmunt, "Swindon Viewpoint, Aberdeen Cable, Cable Authority and the Grapevine Channel," in *Local Television Revisited: Essays on Local Television 1982–1993*, ed. Dave Rushton (Edinburgh: Institute for Local Television, 1990/1994), 22.

21. Nicholas Garnham, "The Myths of Video," in *Capitalism and Communication: Global Culture and the Economics of Information*, ed. Nicholas Garnham (London: Sage, 1990).

22. Dunn in Dowmunt, "Swindon Viewpoint, Aberdeen Cable, Cable Authority and the Grapevine Channel," 22.

23. John Hartley, *A Short History of Cultural Studies* (London: Sage, 2003); Graeme Turner, *British Cultural Studies: An Introduction*, 2nd ed. (London: Routledge, 1996).

24. Garnham, "The Myths of Video," 64.

25. Garnham, "The Myths of Video," 68.

26. Graham Murdock in Andrew Bibby, Cathy Denford, and Jerry Cross, *Local Television: Piped Dreams?* (Milton Keynes: Redwing Press, 1979).

27. Vibeke G. Petersen, Ole Prehn, and Erik N. Svendsen, "Denmark: Breaking 60 Years of Broadcasting Monopoly," in *The People's Voice*, ed. Jankowski, Prehn, and Stappers.

28. Per Jauert and Ole Prehn, "State Subsidies—Added Value?" (paper presented at the annual meeting of the International Association of Media and Communication Research, Barcelona, July 2002).

29. Jauert and Prehn, "State Subsidies—Added Value?" 4.

30. See Paul Q. Hirst, "Can Associationalism Come Back?" in *Associative Democracy: The Real Third Way*, ed. Hirst and Bader (London: Frank Cass, 2001), 24.

31. See Chris Hewson, *Local and Community Television in the United Kingdom: A New Beginning?* (Sheffield: Community Media Association, 2005).

32. Ed Hollander, "The Emergence of Small Scale Media," in *The People's Voice*, ed. Jankowski, Prehn, and Stappers, 13.

33. Jankowski, ed., *Community Media in the Information Age*, 4.

34. Lewis, *Community Television and Cable in Britain*, 74.

35. See John Hartley, *Uses of Television* (London: Routledge, 1999); Gay Hawkins, "Public Service Broadcasting in Australia," in *Communication, Citizenship, and Social Policy: Rethinking the Limits of the Welfare State*, ed. Andrew Calabrese and Jean-Claude Burgelman (Lanham, Md.: Rowman & Littlefield, 1999); and John Keane, *The Media and Democracy* (Cambridge: Polity Press, 1991).

36. Hawkins, "Public Service Broadcasting in Australia," 176.

37. Hawkins, "Public Service Broadcasting in Australia," 178.

38. Bibby, Denford, and Cross, *Local Television: Piped Dreams?* 28.

39. Petersen, Prehn, and Svendsen, "Denmark: Breaking 60 Years of Broadcasting Monopoly."

40. Jurgen Linke, interviewed by Ellie Rennie, Berlin, April 3, 2001.

41. Hawkins, "Public Service Broadcasting in Australia," 177.

42. Hartley, *Uses of Television*, 119.

43. Jay G. Blumler, "Public Service Broadcasting before the Commercial Deluge," in *Television and the Public Interest: Vulnerable Values in West European Broadcasting*, ed. Jay G. Blumler (London: Sage, 1992), 15.

44. Liz Jacka, "'Democracy as Defeat' the Impotence of Arguments for Public Service Broadcasting," *Television and New Media* 4, no. 2 (2003): 188.

45. Eric Michaels, *The Aboriginal Invention of Television in Central Australia 1982–1986* (Canberra: Australian Institute of Aboriginal Studies, 1986).

46. Jauert and Prehn, "State Subsidies—Added Value?" 1.

47. As licensees share frequencies, this does not represent community channels so much as "program actors" that often share channels with commercial providers. Jauert and Prehn, "State Subsidies—Added Value?" 7.

48. Jauert and Prehn, "State Subsidies—Added Value?" 6.

49. Jauert and Prehn, "State Subsidies—Added Value?" 11.

50. Jauert and Prehn, "State Subsidies—Added Value?" 25.

51. Jauert and Prehn, "State Subsidies—Added Value?" 26.

52. Steve Buckley, "If I Had a Little Money . . . ," Community Media Association, 2000, at www.commedia.org.uk (accessed December 3, 2001).

53. Hewson, *Local and Community Television in the United Kingdom*, 58.

54. See Ellie Rennie, "The Story So Far: Digital Storytelling, Narrative and the New Literacy" (paper presented at the Image Text and Sound Conference, RMIT University, Melbourne, September 2004).

55. Estelle James, *The Private Provision of Public Services: A Comparison of Sweden and Holland* (New Haven: Institute for Social and Policy Studies, Yale University, 1982), 34.

56. Noam, *Television in Europe*.

57. Denis McQuail, "The Netherlands: Freedom and Diversity under Multichannel Conditions," in *Television and the Public Interest*, ed. Blumler, 101.

58. Noam, *Television in Europe*.

59. Jane Mansbridge, "A Deliberative Perspective on Neocorporatism," in *Associations and Democracy*, ed. Erik Olin Wright (London: Verso, 1995), 134.

CHAPTER FOUR

Diversity

It is often said that community media would be great if only it were given half a chance. This is entirely understandable as, in many parts of the world, community media exists under political conditions that are either indifferent or hostile to its development. Australia's community broadcasting sector, on the other hand, is over three decades old. Since 1992 it has been enshrined in federal legislation and identified as the "third tier" of the broadcasting system, alongside public and commercial media. It therefore provides a good example of the kinds of issues that community media faces once it has achieved a reasonable level of permanency and acceptance from both the public and government. This chapter will cover a number of smaller themes, such as funding and localism, that are more day-to-day than the philosophical issues of access, quality, and development. However, if there is one thing that defines Australian community media it is that it can't easily be defined. This is partly due to the country's multicultural citizenry and robust (but under-recognized) civil society sphere, which offers a range of voices and interests. More generally, the principle of access means that when community media reaches the level of stability that it has achieved in Australia, it becomes incredibly varied. But diversity can also result in confusion; it makes it difficult to identify specifically what is occurring in the community media sector, and thereby makes its benefits and achievements hard to identify. As the media landscape changes to include more and more voices (via new technologies), it raises new issues for cultural policy. The Australian experience of diversity via community media is an interesting example of the challenge that cultural policy as a whole now faces.

The Emergence of the Third Sector of Broadcasting

From the start, momentum for community broadcasting in Australia was checked by a broadcasting structure that sought to accommodate and appease the interests of both public service and commercial broadcasting. Early community radio advocates expressed their concern at the lack of public debate around broadcasting policy.[1] As campaigner Max Keogh put it, this apathy was due not only to Australians' "infamous apathy to public affairs" but also to the apparent stability of the dual broadcasting arrangement that disguised other issues. Where the U.K. system was defined by a dominant public service broadcaster and the U.S. by its commercialism, Australia's combination of public and private meant that there was little discussion on the impediments to growth inherent within this arrangement. The closure of experimental FM broadcasts in 1961 caused Keogh, Trevor Jarvie, Brian Cabena, and others at the Music Broadcasting Society to take action. Keogh claimed that "to the public FM might just as well have been a time of day between AM and PM. In the past ten years it has been kept just as much in the dark."[2] Keogh was later to become involved in the establishment of 2MBS-FM, a Sydney classical music community station that was one of Australia's first FM radio licensees.[3]

Throughout its history, community broadcasting in Australia has been measured against the commercial and public service broadcasters. In 1978, the Public Broadcasting Association of Australia (PBAA, now the Community Broadcasting Association of Australia, known as CBAA) decided that community programming should be "complementary and supplementary and not seek to compete with existing services."[4] This definition was then pursued to the extreme by the commercial broadcasting lobby, which argued that community radio should not be allowed to broadcast classical, light, or popular music, or news, sports, or listener phone-in (or "talkback") programs. Although the Australian Broadcasting Tribunal (ABT) deemed that request excessive, they did make "complementary and supplementary" programming a requirement on community broadcasters. This, of course, was impossible to police, and "the most significant effect it had was the way it informed [community] broadcasters' understanding of themselves."[5] It enforced their subordination to the established media. The Australian community radio sector has always been comprised of diverse interests and groups, although some have been more dominant than others in the policy circles through which legislative change eventuates. In the early years, the educational and fine music advocates of community media liaised with government on the possibilities for community radio to the exclusion of more radical interests. Even that politically moderate group met with resistance. The then regulator, the Australian Broadcasting and Control Board (ABCB, now the Australian Communications and Media Authority, known as AMCA) argued against the establishment of community broadcasting entirely, claiming that there were no available frequencies for new broadcasters and that, in any case, community broadcasting would be a waste of spectrum. As a result, the first community radio stations were not issued licenses under broadcasting legislation by the ABCB, but were granted spectrum as "experimental" and "education" stations by the postmaster general under the Wireless and Telegraphy Act.[6] The University of Adelaide and two fine music stations in Melbourne and Sydney received these first licenses.

It took a great deal of ingenuity and lobbying from aspirant broadcasters (and supportive politicians) before "limited commercial" licenses were administered by the broadcasting regulator in 1978. The formation of the Public Broadcasting Association of Australia in 1974 was an important move, turning the informal advocate's network into a representative body that government could negotiate with. Both sides of politics ended up contributing to the legislative design for community radio. Liberal Minister Tony Staley went to extraordinary lengths to convince the Liberal party to permit the licenses, as Minister Cass from the Labor party had before him.

Community radio continued to grow through the 1970s and 80s. When the Broadcasting Services Act 1992 (BSA) was passed by Parliament, it contained provisions for a new community broadcasting license, making the sector a permanent fixture within the national media framework. Community television trials began in the mid-1990s and were licensed under the community broadcasting category in 2004. The Community Broadcasting Association of Australia continues to provide member stations with advice on attaining and running stations, and acts as the sector's policy development and lobby force. The Community Broadcasting Foundation administers government grants and core funding. Legislatively, community broadcasters are described as "not operated for profit or as part of a profit-making enterprise" and as being "provided for community purposes." Community broadcasting principles of access and participation are upheld in the Broadcasting Services Act and licensees are required to encourage members of the community to participate in the operation of the stations as well as the provision and selection of programming.[7]

Community radio currently attracts more than twenty thousand volunteers on a regular basis, contributing approximately $AU2.79 million in unpaid work hours each week.[8] In 2005 there were 355 community broadcasters and 46 aspirant stations, compared with 264 operational commercial radio stations. Sixty percent of the full licensees are located in metropolitan areas, and over ten percent of community broadcasting stations provide the only available radio service in their area. The community radio sector is now comprised of not only fine music groups, educational groups, and political groups, but also ethnic groups, Indigenous broadcasters, geographical communities, the gay community, religious communities, and, most recently, youth radio. So how does this large and diverse group of stations fare? In 1995, Australian media expert Albert Moran wrote: "Simply, the sector lacks the political power of both public service radio and commercial radio. While the sector has been sanctioned and offered some support by the state, it has also been under-resourced in terms of material needs such as equipment and funding and ignored in public debate, analysis and polemic."[9] Since 1996 there has been the justifiable perception in broadcasting-industry and government circles that the community broadcasting sector's political stocks have been on the rise. The community radio sector has doubled in size and, although it is not always prominent in "public debate, analysis and polemic," it has received vastly increased levels of direct government support and gained considerable recognition as a lobbying force. Community television has managed to survive against considerable odds. Localism, funding (including identification with a noncommercial ethic), and the role of community broadcasting within the wider media environment continue to preoccupy, as well as define, the sector. It is these concerns that I will focus on in this chapter. First, a closer look at the stations themselves.

Education Stations

Tertiary institutions played an important role in the emergence of Australian community radio. In 1968, the University of New South Wales was granted permission to conduct low-power radio broadcasting of course material. A staff member at the University of Adelaide, Jim Warburton, had observed similar uses of radio at the University of Indianapolis in the United States and put forward a proposal that his university begin using radio to transmit course work. The idea—which has captured the imagination of many an academic since—was to use radio as a form of outreach, extending university knowledge to the community at large. Although the university was reluctant at first, an offer of $AU100,000 from an anonymous donor put the proposal back on the table.[10] The first experimental radio license was awarded, and community radio began to seem possible. However, the station was limited to broadcasting educational content and was only allowed to promote their courses to existing students. Music was strictly prohibited. Eventually, the station was allowed to broadcast music and was encouraged to experiment with public access.

Twelve experimental tertiary licenses were issued in 1975, all linked to universities in some way with the exception of 2WEB in Bourke, which was set up with state education money directed at regional areas. Despite this promising start, the relationship between universities and stations was to become tenuous and difficult. The stations broadcast increasingly diverse content; many took on the access mandate and positioned themselves as alternative (often radical) sources of information, commentary, and music. To this day their programming remains predominantly alternative and access-driven. A number of universities with media studies courses still continue to make use of the stations for training purposes, however, distance education never became a primary function (see below).

Fine Music Stations

Two fine music stations were licensed at the same time as 5UV in Adelaide. These were 3MBS in Melbourne and 2MBS in Sydney; they were run by the Music Broadcasting Society, which had successfully lobbied government to allow it to broadcast on the FM bands. In 1976, the Australian Broadcasting Corporation (a national, public service broadcaster) established its own classical network. Community fine-music lovers in Canberra, Adelaide, and Perth settled for programs on other community stations, with 5UV and 6UV (university stations in Adelaide and Perth respectively) broadcasting up to thirty hours a week of fine music. In 1991 a network of fine music stations was established. Fine music stations gradually broadened their programming to include jazz, blues, folk, and nostalgia.

Radio for the Print Handicapped

Radio for the Print Handicapped (RPH) began as segments on previously licensed community stations in Melbourne. Its pioneers recognized the value radio could have to those who were vision impaired and set out to provide this group with information and descriptions that their audience might otherwise have missed. Their distinctive programming includes readings of the day's newspapers and descriptions of visual events, such as Christmas displays. The stations were licensed separately in 1978 on spectrum reserved for marine band licenses, which was accessible with a modification to the radio receiver. In 1988, the government increased the number of FM licenses, which meant that RPH could take over AM positions on the dial. The audience includes many sighted listeners who enjoy the pace and texture of having news and fiction read aloud. But it also serves those who cannot read because of illiteracy or learning/comprehension difficulties.

Ethnic Radio

In the 1970s, Prime Minister Gough Whitlam was looking for a way to inform the community about his new health care plan; he decided that broadcasting in languages other than English was needed in order to get his message across to migrant communities. Two stations, 2EA and 3EA, established for this purpose, were initially operated through the Federal Department of the Media. However, they were run with a high degree of community participation and it was expected that they would form part of a nonprofit association of ethnic broadcasters. In 1977, the Fraser government established the Special Broadcasting Service (SBS), a public broadcaster operating under a charter of multiculturalism. Ethnic community stations continue to operate and receive an allocated budget from the government in recognition of their value. Today community radio broadcasts in over seventy-five different languages.

Geographic Community Stations

Licenses that cater to geographic communities are difficult to describe collectively and are often discussed in terms of localism. Prior to community radio, towns such as Bourke were without television and only received radio from towns hundreds of miles away. Ian Cole, one of the Bourke station's founders describes the situation: "We listened to the ABC service off the Cumnock Radio Tower near Orange," he says. "All the programs came from Orange or Sydney. At night time, we listened to 2SM off the skip, the ionosphere. The station was some 500 miles or 800 kilometres away. Country music listeners would listen to 2PK at Parkes, which was also a long way away. We couldn't get it during the day but we could get it off the skip at night." When the Bourke community radio license was awarded, the station filled its programming slots with whatever it could get its hands on. Country music was scheduled around Japanese lessons and Deutsche Welle world news from Germany. The station that was built to provide local services to the bush was also one of the most cosmopolitan in the country.[11]

Some geographic-based stations appear cautious compared to other community radio stations. Programming schedules can resemble mainstream media, with playlists and professional-sounding DJs. In recent years, Christian broadcasters have also become a prominent subsector. They are cross-denominational and well-resourced, and have formed their own umbrella organization called Radio Rhema. Jim Beatson of the CBAA offers a neat description of their role and character: "Soft sell evangelism is mixed with a recognition that modern man must share domestic chores, support community projects, feel concern about loss of jobs in the rural and industrial sectors with a hankering for an era before overseas companies came to dominate the local economic landscape. Although evangelical by inclination, to date they have not promoted a U.S.-styled fundamentalist agenda."[12]

Radical Stations

The radical/alternative stations have proved to be some of the more consistent and well organized in the sector. One such station is 4ZZZ in Brisbane (which began as 4ZZ), born out of the student counterculture of the 1960s. At that time Brisbane was culturally and politically conservative. Gerrymandering of electorates meant that the Country Party stayed in power, with a majority of conservative members of Parliament from isolated regional areas. Their policies included censorship of books and music, the banning of public protests, and the creation of laws that singled out Aboriginal people for detention without trial, forced removal, and seizure of assets.[13] But although the conservative state government kept a tight reign on civil liberties, radio was governed at the federal level, and a group of forward-thinking students realized that alternative radio might stand a chance of surviving. When the progressive Labor party came into power, the students saw their chance.

The 4ZZ license was among the first awarded with a charter to broadcast rock 'n' roll, Australian music, and dissenting viewpoints—it never set out to be "complementary and supplementary." From the start 4ZZ argued that audiences in general were dissatisfied with the mainstream media fare. On December 8, 1975, it began its first broadcast with The Who's "Won't Get Fooled Again." 4ZZZ is now considered the pioneer of rock music radio in Australia. But it also provided an important, although somewhat dishevelled news service, which exists to this day. In the 1970s, 4ZZZ covered "environmental affairs, Aboriginal land rights, strikes, prisoners' rights, abuse of state power, corruption and women's rights."[14] For Australia's "Deep North," this was radical stuff indeed.

One of the station's founders, Kevin Hayes, describes its lasting contribution: "When I think that ZZZ has survived for twenty five years and has been passed from hand to hand in that time and it still lives, I think it's a fabulous thing. It's guardians [sic] are still getting born. When John Woods first played that record, 'Won't get fooled again,' we felt that we had achieved something which was almost un-do-able. It made me feel we could do what we wanted to do, not just play by the rules."[15] Today, the community radio sector plays an important role in the promotion of Australian music, particularly unsigned or up-and-coming bands.

SYN FM and JOY FM

The Student Youth Network (SYN FM) is run by and for people between the ages of twelve and twenty-five. As station manager Bryce Ives points out, the age restriction has had its benefits and drawbacks. For one thing, having to ask people to retire at the age of twenty-six and go and do their own thing has meant a constant loss of talent and expertise from the station. Finding program sponsorship for a cashless audience demographic has not been easy either. However, giving young, often school-age, volunteers responsibility in the running of the station has definitely been worth it. Programming at SYN FM is unusual and high-energy, showing that young people are not afraid to take risks when it comes to creative output. The station has also branched into television, producing programs for Channel 31, and publishes its own magazine four times a year.

Australia's only gay and lesbian radio station, JOY FM, is also located in Melbourne. The station began with a temporary license, opting to share airtime with other aspirant broadcasters Muslim Radio and Kool'n Deadly (an Indigenous station that has since been separately licensed). JOY was awarded a full-time license in 2001, partly thanks to the hundreds of letters that supporters sent during the license process. The license is not citywide, but the station can be picked up in the outer suburbs if the weather is good (station staff members joke that the government wouldn't give the queers a license to go too far). JOY is diverse, with programming directed at the multicultural queer audience, as well as transgender people and those living with HIV. One of the station's more successful programs discusses the issue of "coming out." On the program, gay men and women talk about how they came to accept their sexuality.

Indigenous Radio and Television

Indigenous media making has been immensely successful. Policy for Indigenous media, however, has always been hard won and less than comprehensive. Part of the problem is that Indigenous media has been managed by a number of different agencies, including the Department of Communications, IT and the Arts (DCITA), the Aboriginal and Torres Strait Islander Commission (ATSIC—abolished by the Howard government in 2004), the Department of Aboriginal Affairs, and the Department of Education, Training and Youth Affairs (DETYA). Aboriginal media associations, such as the Australian Indigenous Communication Association (AICA, previously the National Indigenous Media Association of Australia), have played a vital role by acting as representative bodies that government agencies can negotiate with.

Indigenous media is not restricted to community media. However, the community license has been important in the development of Indigenous media services in Australia. Apart from some reports of Aboriginal announcers on commercial radio in the 1960s, the first Aboriginal program is generally considered to have been aired on 5UV in Adelaide in 1972. Regular programs were to follow on community-run radio stations in Melbourne, Canberra, and Tasmania by the mid-1970s and the Northern Territory by the 1980s.

Calls for Indigenous radio and television stations came as a response to the introduction of satellite broadcasting in the mid-1980s. The government saw satellite as a means to bring metropolitan television services to the bush—and assumed that this was what populations in remote areas desired. The AUSSAT satellite was launched as a government-owned company in 1981. However, it proved to be excessively expensive, and the intention to allow part-time rental to local communities fizzled as prices soared. Four remote commercial television services were eventually licensed, with a recommendation that these provide free windows for Aboriginal programming. With the exception of the Aboriginal-owned Imparja channel, this has not occurred.

Indigenous communities were worried about the cultural impact of satellite television. Freda Glynn of the Central Australia Aboriginal Media Association commented at the time: "People sitting out bush are suddenly going to see things that they've never seen before. On a daily basis, for twenty-four hours. Effectively, what's going to happen is [that] the oldest living culture in the world is going to be destroyed simply because of a box."[16] In 1984 the Department of Aboriginal Affairs commissioned a report which was intended to address this concern.[17] It recommended the introduction of satellite television and radio reception and rebroadcasting facilities for remote Aboriginal communities as a means for them to control their own media. All of the report's recommendations were accepted, and the DAA was given the task of administering a new system called Broadcasting for Remote Aboriginal Communities Service (BRACS). The original BRACS units were simple: "A satellite reception dish, a decoder, a transmitter, a mast and an aerial, a radio studio including a microphone, an FM/AM tuner, a cassette deck, 2 VCRs, speakers, a camera recorder, a TV monitor, a control panel (not a mixing desk), a remote TV control unit, a cassette tape recorder and a video camera."[18] There are now over 105 BRACS facilities in remote communities, as well as over 25 community radio stations in regional and urban areas. A National Indigenous Radio Service provides bed programming for stations that do not have the staffing or resources to present their own twenty-four–hour programming, and includes a national news service. In 2005, the Australian government conducted a review into the viability of creating digitally transmitted Indigenous television service. Despite significant community support for the establishment of a dedicated Indigenous television channel, the government decided to allocate funds ($48.5 million over five years) for Indigenous programming only. As a result, programs will be broadcast on an existing station (Imparja in central Australia and either community television or cable TV in metropolitan areas).

Community Television

With the support of the Australia Council, ten independent video access centers and two resource centers were established in 1974, which provided communities with access to video production equipment and training. As great as this was, it meant that the resources concentrated into production were out of proportion to the available broadcast opportunities.[19] The access centers hence became the sites out of which community television campaign groups were formed. The first proposal for community television—a mobile low-power service to link the access centers in Melbourne and Sydney—came in 1976. However, the government opted to defer its decision to fund the initiative. It would be almost two decades until a full community television service would finally get off the ground. Throughout this period, successive governments retained a generally supportive attitude towards the development of community television but remained reluctant to commit resources to its development. Although the coalition parties made promises to introduce community television by 1981 (Prime Minister Fraser even wrote a letter to the PBAA to inform the organization that he intended to call for license applications), no such efforts were made.[20]

The metropolitan producers had watched with interest as pirate television stations were established by Indigenous communities in remote areas—the Pitjanjarra in Ernabella, South Australia, and the Walpiri of Yuendumu, a township on the edge of central Australia's Tanami desert.[21] When the BSA 1992 was introduced, the original BRACS services (which had progressed from "pirate" status to "limited licenses") became fully licensed community broadcasters.[22] Although Indigenous broadcasting was to take a legislative path that differed from the path the metropolitan stations followed (see below), these first stations were a significant development in the campaign for community television. Other efforts were also made to secure community channels on cable television. That idea was thwarted by the government's reluctance to impose carriage arrangements on the financially fragile cable sector, despite the persistence of community television campaigns since the 1970s. In 1982, community television broadcasts were screened on SBS television on two weekends, coordinated by the Open Channel video access center in Melbourne.[23] In the years 1986 to 1988, community television groups sought incorporated association status with the intention of transmitting low-power signals to their local neighborhoods. RMITV, a founding member of MCT31, which continues to run out of RMIT University, conducted the first test transmission permitted under the Radiocommunications Act in 1987. This was followed by subsequent tests established with the Australian Broadcasting Tribunal's approval.

Successive governments cited spectrum scarcity and the expense of television broadcasting in rejecting petitions for community television beyond the test transmissions. As it had consistently been stated by government agencies that community television would not receive direct government funding, the community television test transmission groups instead focused their attention on securing spectrum and permanent licenses; they intended to finance the stations by other means.[24] It was not until 1992 that the government decided that the sixth high-power television channel should be used for community purposes until a final decision was made on who would occupy it.[25] As there was no commitment from the government at this time to ensure permanent spectrum allocation for community television, the stations began broadcasting on temporary licenses, under what was to be known as the "community television trial." Community television services began broadcasting in Melbourne in 1994, followed by Sydney, Brisbane, Adelaide, Lismore, and Perth. Attempts were also made to launch stations in Hobart and Bendigo, but the licenses were withdrawn by the Australian Broadcasting Authority (ABA) as the groups failed to fully launch their services within the allocated time frame. In May 1999, the minister revoked the use of the sixth channel in areas other than those holding existing broadcast licenses due to digital television planning. As a result, analogue community television stations have only been permitted in areas where there is an incumbent service or where spectrum is available to be allocated on an ad hoc basis. For instance, Mt. Gambier in South Australia has been permitted to undertake a community television trial. But for regional areas in general, community television will not be realized until legislative changes are made to accommodate community television services in all television markets.

Programming on community television reflects a wide range of communities, including language groups, social justice groups, and gay and lesbian groups, as well as local information and magazine-style entertainment. Market research from 2005 revealed that up to 3.6 million Australians tune in to community television every week (over one-fifth of the population). Each station instituted a different organizational model at its commencement and, as a result, the programming, community access arrangements, and revenue-raising activities of the stations vary considerably. Funding sources include broadcast fees from program providers, facility rental fees, production fees for some programming, membership fees, donations, and grants. The stations were required to be not-for-profit when they applied for their class licenses and were expected to be guided by community broadcasting license restrictions in order to progress beyond the trial phase.

It is fair to say that the community television trial lasted longer than anyone expected. Despite the fact that the stations did manage to broadcast, no decision on the licensing arrangement was forthcoming. As the stations became increasingly frustrated by the lack of momentum, the bureaucrats also complained throughout successive review processes that they were unable to provide any real guidance or directives that would see the stations meet the expectations they had of community licensees. Community broadcasters were to represent the interests of the community they were intended to serve, and allow for community participation in programming as well as the running of the organization. But as the stations were not licensed as community broadcasters, the regulator was unable to enforce these obligations during the trial phase (including limits on sponsorship and sale of airtime).

In 1996, the regulator was instructed to report on the best use of the sixth free-to-air channel. That report recommended that "the sixth channel, if put to any use at all, should be used for community access television, as most socio-economic benefits presently appear likely to flow from this use."[26] Community access television was preferred as it was seen to be inclusive of multiple programming needs, freely available, and likely to reflect local interests and concerns. The sixth-channel report also found that long-term security for community television was required, "instead of continuing the open narrowcasting class licensing arrangements and the uncertainty that they generate."[27] As the ABA's report was not tabled in Parliament the sector saw no direct outcomes from these recommendations. Ralph McLean, former chairperson of MCT31, commented that many of community television's limitations were "imposed by virtue of it being 'on trial,' both literally and figuratively, for seven long years. Very few criminal trials last this long, but community TV has been 'on notice' all that time."[28] As McLean's sentiments from 2002 clearly articulate, those involved in the running of community television stations throughout the trial felt poorly treated in government decision-making processes.

Australia's community television trial has finally come to an end. In 2004, the government began awarding community broadcasting licenses, providing the stations with some permanency. Unfortunately, although the trial is over, the verdict is not so straightforward. Community broadcasting licenses are granted for a full five-year term. But there is no legislative guarantee that community television will be allowed to occupy its current spectrum when analogue transmission ceases. Furthermore, the community television audience will diminish as consumers replace their analogue televisions with digital sets (see below). Despite the so-called permanent licensing of community television, at the time of this writing, the situation remains far from resolved.[29]

Marginal Culture

Mark Lyons, in his book *The Third Sector: The Contribution of Nonprofit and Cooperative Enterprises in Australia*, points out that the greatest threat to nonprofit organizations today is the lack of appreciation within government of the particular nature and importance of the third sector. Whereas governments once damaged the third sector through nationalizing sections of it, out of a belief that government could do better, today they no longer see themselves as service providers. "The threat they offer to the third sector is quite different," writes Lyons. "It is the threat of non-recognition."[30] The treatment of community television in Australia reflects the apathy that Lyons describes.

Community broadcasting was introduced in the 1970s, along with a sweep of policies that were based on the principle of diversity. Multiculturalism, in particular, signified a new approach to the way in which diversity was managed. These programs sought to recognize difference and to cater to minority languages and cultures, replacing previous notions of national identity based on a unified and homogenous citizenry. The establishment of the Special Broadcasting Service in 1977 was seen as a means to meet the needs of multicultural Australia in the broadcasting environment. Although the Ethnic Television Review Panel considered the provision of ethnic broadcasting through community television, they concluded that "[community] television's overriding commitment to alternative special purpose programs is too limited to serve the needs of multicultural television. To locate multicultural television under the aegis of . . . community television would be to put it in the realm of broadcasting designed principally to meet minority group needs. This would run counter to the overriding objective of promoting multiculturalism among the community."[31] As this demonstrates, community television has been depicted as marginal and "alternative" from the start, when seen in relation to larger policy concerns such as multiculturalism. Diversity was still essentially distributed to viewers, rather than met through the participation of civil society groups. While SBS has successfully managed to bring a sense of cultural diversity to public service broadcasting, it has nonetheless been criticized for presenting a cultural product that is cosmopolitan but does not sufficiently cater to Australia's various diasporic groups.[32]

The issues of quality, diversity, and public service broadcasting are discussed at greater length in relation to European broadcasting in chapter 3. Although attitudes prevail that cast community broadcasting as inferior to public service broadcasting, this is not the only front on which notions of marginality have been propagated. Media policy expert Stuart Cunningham has observed that many government initiatives in which cultural diversity was given as a policy objective have dismissed community broadcasting. The Creative Nation policy (1994), in particular, "simply reiterated the status quo for community broadcasting, while all around it special initiative funding was being delivered for a wide variety of related initiatives."[33] In an early instance of community broadcasting being considered outside of "worthy" cultural funding, a 1976 decision to shift responsibility for the video access centers from the Australia Council to the Australian Film Commission (AFC) caused serious setbacks for the community television campaign: "Following the transfer, there was a change of emphasis towards more 'professional' production and the AFC's commitment to the video access project was revised. The Commission's rationalisation of funding priorities resulted in substantial disruption to the work of the video access centres and the eventual closure of most programs and for a time there was a decline in the activities of the community television lobby."[34] It is plain to see that when community is described, it carries with it a set of values and characteristics. Culturally, "community" is associated with "amateurism," as well as notions such as "political," "authentic," "social concern," "welfare," "therapy," and "worthy"—terms identified by media expert Gay Hawkins in her study of the mobilization of community in Australia's cultural policy context. As Hawkins points out, although these terms may challenge the hegemony of the professional and the national, "they are also invoked as terms of derision and dismissal, as signs of aesthetic fiascos and cultural lack."[35] Community is something that is often strived for, that becomes part of the political discourse at times, but is never fully realized. In the Australian cultural policy context, community is represented as being an *alternative*, a sincere yet problematic ideal that is not important in the greater scheme of things.

The cultural status of community broadcasting within Australia's broadcasting environment could be represented as being below the market, whereas public service broadcasting and cultural policy have pursued notions of difference that are seen to stand above the market:

PSB and CULTURAL POLICY
↓
MARKET
↓
COMMUNITY BROADCASTING

The marginalization of community media is often attributed to its failure to live up to its (largely self-proclaimed) desire to change broader media patterns of ownership and control. The radical edge of community media has been lost: "Over the past twenty years, this progressivism—the sense of the alternative society that community radio might help bring about, has been gradually marginalised by the growth of the sector as a whole as well as by the soft commercialism. . . . Community radio is seen to have shifted away from the original radical vision; indeed the sector is drifting and may wither and die. Above all, there is a view that it has failed to realise its potential."[36] Although recent alternative media theory has begun to revise this notion of "radical vision" as something necessarily in opposition to the mainstream media, in terms of policy justifications, it is diversity rather than radicalism that has been the stronger motivation behind community broadcasting in Australia. If anything, the particular diversity of community broadcasting does not fit comfortably with government ideas of a dense and varied cultural citizenry. Early attempts by government to shut down radical community media seem distant from today's reality; community broadcasting now suffers from not being "cutting edge" enough. Indeed, a greater degree of radicalism in terms of provocative political content or avant garde/experimental content might have helped community broadcasting's status—content such as that screened on SBS (whose government funding continues to grow). On Melbourne's community television station, Channel 31, programs from local football associations and religious groups, taped performances from comedy clubs and weddings air alongside programs by ethnic broadcasters and alternative media. The more "ordinary" associations, groups, and cultural products that make up a large part of community broadcasting are generally only mentioned in discussions of the sector's failures. For instance, Moran calls this aspect of community broadcasting "weak multiculturalism": "The mechanism of community radio that equates the needs of Aboriginal Australians with those of country and western fans, the needs of gay people with those of gamblers on the turf, the needs of prisoners with those of community sporting groups, smacks of a 'weak' multiculturalism that welcomes difference in the name of pluralism and cosmopolitanism rather than see that some differences are more important than others as evidence of continued social inequalities and subjugation."[37] Such assumptions about what community media *should be* are in direct tension with notions of public access and participation. The marginality of community broadcasting is reinforced by the policy approach to broadcasting based upon carefully controlled and predetermined cultural objectives. These themes are explored at much greater length in the context of free speech in North America (chapter 2), as well as in the context of changing notions of access that have entered policy debates due to the rise of the Internet (chapter 6). A greater awareness of how such values saturate Australian broadcasting policy, however, is required in order to see the possible uses of community broadcasting and its relevance for the emerging digital broadcasting environment.

Noncommercialism/Funding

Funding is a difficult issue for the Australian community broadcasting sector. The need to raise revenue sits in constant tension with the noncommercial ethic of the sector, which is reinforced by the license restrictions and the Codes of Practice. But with decreasing government funding for radio, and none for television, finding ways to raise money has become a major concern. Core government funding (funding that is guaranteed on an annual basis) stood at around $AU1.27 million in 1985 and was provided to fifty-six stations (approximately $AU22,000 per station). This increased until 1995 (with stations receiving on average $AU25,000 each), but dropped significantly from that point onwards. In 2002/2003 core funding stood at around $AU15,300 per station, or $AU3.58 million shared between 234 licensees. The new "targeted" funding introduced in 1996 supplements the core funding, but is not guaranteed and must be justified by the sector every three years. Taking into account the distribution of targeted funding together with core funding, the average amount per station for 2002/2003 works out to be $AU22,550. In real terms this represents a significant drop in funding since the original 1985 amount. Competition for government money has increased between stations, with many now operating without any government funding at all.[38] The CBAA summed up the situation in their report to the Local Voices Senate inquiry into regional radio as follows: "Our biggest dilemma is that what you might casually assume to be an abundance of riches (in spectrum terms) becomes a major issue for sustaining viable services if government support remains frozen or declines while new commercial and narrowcasting services continue to devour the corporate sponsorship pie."[39] Community television has not been included in the Community Broadcasting Foundation's distribution of core government funding (nor is there an "abundance of riches" in spectrum terms). With no government commitment to providing extra funds for television on the horizon, the stations are likely to have to continue to rely on sponsorship and the sale of airtime, as well as the lesser revenue sources of membership/subscriber fees and donations.

The general manager of the CBAA, Barry Melville, sees the increase in targeted funding as part of a general political trend:

> We have had an increase in recent years in additional targeted funding from the Government (infrastructure money). There is money for the satellite, money for the digital delivery network, money for the CBOnline project but it doesn't play out at the station level—it's never enough. It's increasingly the penchant of conservative governments to want to tie their funding to particular outcomes. It's a political control issue, I guess. They'll fund something as long as they control the outcome. They don't strongly favour handing it over to the CBF which would then convert the money to their discretionary funding. It's also about controlling the stakeholders too.[40]

Melville observes that the government's 1996 preelection policy statement, "Better Broadcasting," "was about transforming community broadcasting according to the policy imperatives of the day—what was new, what was groovy, what was exciting to government—which was about developing an online economy." He acknowledges the benefits of the targeted funding which "has allowed progress in the sector in terms of electronic communications and networking," but would like to see money now directed back to the stations.[41] The impact upon the Australian broadcasting sector is that stations are increasingly turning to the market in order to survive.

Accessing market-based revenue sources is more difficult for some broadcasters than others. Sandy Dann from Puranyangu Rangka-Kerrem Media in Halls Creek described the situation at their radio station: "We're just working on [sponsorship] at the moment, we do that in kind . . . the bakery might donate a pizza, so we'll make mention that we've got a pizza to give away from the local bakery, and we like to put that into local youth programs, for the young ones . . . so that at least we know that a group of kids out there has had something to eat . . . Halls Creek is a lovely, vibrant community, but it's also very oppressed in certain respects."[42] In contrast, one Sydney-based youth-oriented temporary licensee estimated in 2000 that its sponsorship potential was around $AU5 to $AU4 million.[43] It is almost impossible to generalize about the financial potential of either radio or television community broadcasters when the stations exist in vastly different communities. Generalizations are nonetheless common. In possibly the most confusing take on the funding of community radio, a government report into regional radio in September 2001 concludes:

> There were some calls . . . for the limits on sponsorship content to be lifted from 5 minutes per hour. The Committee is not persuaded that such a move would assist many stations. In its discussions with individual stations in the course of this inquiry, many were unable to fill the current 5 minutes. Increasing the level of sponsorship allowed would also have implications for the commercial radio broadcasters. It is ironic that radio stations which have grown from the community are unable to gain sponsorship support for their activities. Lifting the sponsorship time per hour would advantage few stations unless they advance their activities in obtaining sponsorship. Without proof of support for community stations as demonstrated by sponsorship support, there is little pressure for Government to subsidise further the community broadcasting sector.[44]

This position ignores the fact that some stations may never be able to achieve financial independence from government sources. At the same time, it protects the interests of the commercial sector by denying those community broadcasters who have the ability to raise more sponsorship revenue from doing so. What is apparent from the committee's report is that the real issue in terms of financing the community sector is not so much the ability of stations to participate in the market, but confusion over the appropriateness of that activity. The committee's viewpoint is one where market participation acts as proof of the sector's worth, yet where that activity may have "implications for the commercial radio broadcasters." The sector is depicted as inadequate when it cannot compete, and overstepping its role when it does.

The influence of the commercial lobby in restricting the financial growth of community broadcasting is a very real issue. This was particularly apparent in the case of the aspirant youth-oriented dance music stations: "When HITZ-FM went on air in Melbourne for a ninety-day test broadcast, it didn't take long for the commercial rock music stations to notice the slump in their ratings. HITZ-FM sounded terrific and programmed for a community that was not well served, so it went on air as it planned to continue. It gave FOX-FM and other competitors a real shock, so much so, they took their complaints to [the regulator]."[45] HITZ-FM's success came from the fact that they catered to a community of dance music listeners, a highly lucrative demographic, which placed the station in competition with commercial radio stations for audiences. During its time on air, a ratings survey found that the "Other FM" category had jumped from 1.8 to 16.1 percent of audience share in the 13–17 age group, and from 3.3 to 12.8 percent in the 18–24 age group.[46] HITZ-FM later found that it had its own competitor, another temporary community licensee called KISS-FM, who eventually took their format to Sydney and started up a commercial narrowcasting station called Rhythm-FM. These stations clearly represented a departure from the generally held image of the impoverished community broadcaster. In the case of the HITZ-FM story, it was the commercial broadcasters, rather than the audience, who most vehemently opposed community broadcasters' participation in the market. Despite HITZ-FM's popularity as an aspirant station (they commenced test broadcasts in 1992), the ABA rejected their application for a community broadcasting license in 2001 and the station was shut down. The regulator expressed concern over commercial arrangements between the station and a record company, involving a branded CD and a sponsorship deal. KISS-FM met a similar fate, this time due to their relationship with Rhythm: the sponsorship and advertising departments of the two services were authorized to represent each other without distinguishing who they were representing at any one time.[47]

Anxiety over commercialism in the community broadcasting sector also comes from within. Despite the fact that licensees are required to be not-for-profit and are limited in the amount of sponsorship that they can broadcast, activities that are seen to be in direct conflict with the community broadcasting ethic are common. Moran gives some examples of this "creeping commercialism":

> In Cairns, 4CCR has charged an Aboriginal group a fee for access to its airwaves. Before its present involvement with the Australian Fine Music Network, 2NSB Chatswood limited community programming in favour of a commercial-music type format purchased from an American consultant. 2SSS Canberra is operated as a service for the racing and gambling industry in the ACT [Australian Capital Territory]. Three stations (4CRB Gold Coast, 2CHY Coffs Harbour and 2GCR Goulburn) have been questioned about their high levels of sponsorship/advertising: 2CHY was opposed in its license renewal not only by FARB [Federation of Australian Radio Broadcasters] but also by some "S" class stations.[48]

A more recent example is the retransmission of John Laws's notorious commercial radio program on community radio.[49] Possibly the most controversial activity in the community television sector has been the sale of large blocks of airtime to commercial companies. These particular issues are beginning to be resolved through regulation: under the new license conditions, the number of hours that can be sold to commercial programmers and nonprofit organizations has been restricted. In recognition of the need for diverse revenue sources, the amendments did not prohibit the sale of airtime altogether and sponsorship has been increased from five to seven minutes.

Melbourne's 3RRR-FM had an estimated turnover of $AU1.1 million in the financial year 2000–2001, derived equally from sponsorship and subscriber income. Kath Letch, station manager of 3RRR FM and former president of the CBAA, emphasizes the need to uphold a community identity in order to maintain audiences. She identifies two influential factors that determine appropriate sponsorship: available business partnership opportunities and community acceptance.

> Fundamentally, the sector puts itself forward as an independent, non-commercial broadcast service—whether that's TV or radio—and sponsorship poses an inherent tension in that dynamic. Because although it's called "sponsorship" in reality it is on-air promotion with a tag and that's advertising. There aren't boundaries in the Act on what you can and can't take provided it's tagged. So that means that the decisions about what you will take operates at a station level rather than at a regulatory level and I think the decisions that stations can make in that regard are affected by their location. So for example, many community radio stations in large regional centres would run promotions for McDonalds or Hungry Jacks. There are only a small number of local businesses and only a smaller number that have any advertising budget. If you have a large take-away food chain that does have an advertising budget you are probably going to take them, and they will quite possibly be accepted by your community. So the test is: is it accepted by your community and is it accepted by your listeners. And there are many stations that could run a whole range of things that couldn't be run on 3RRR, not because of the type of service that 3RRR delivers but because of its type of identity in its community and its audience.[50]

Behind this thinking is a clearly audience-driven approach to sponsorship, whereby the listeners' desire for a community "feel" or standard is prioritized in order to retain audiences. The community ethic is as much an image—signifying the station's uniqueness—as it is a style of governance. In 3RRR's case, that image has proved to be particularly lucrative.

A number of stations have relied upon the education sector for at least part of their revenue. However, this has been a difficult partnership. From 1987, the tertiary sector fell on hard times as a result of changes implemented by the minister for employment, education, and training, John Dawkins. Some stations were threatened with closure, managing only to stay on air by gathering community support and, when it came down to it, just plain refusing to leave their microphones. In 1999, Lismore's 2NCR was forced to go it alone after a twenty-two-year history of university support. In one of the more notorious cases, Brisbane's 4ZZZ was evicted by a conservative student union that decided it did not want the radical left-wing broadcasters in the building. Although the education sector has been important in the development of community media, it is fair to say that dissemination of ideas via the media has never been "core business" for universities. However old-fashioned it may be, universities remain committed to print-based transmission of ideas and face-to-face lecturing. Web-based delivery of university teaching and research has potential, yet so far mostly conforms to a "business-as-usual" model of education. Although community radio and television in Australia have caught the attention of a few imaginative academics and board members, the larger structures and traditions that govern universities have failed to see the educative possibilities of the media.

Ethnic broadcasters have their own set of issues regarding funding. In order to comply with funding guidelines, ethnic programming must be mainly in a language other than English; contain no more than 50 percent music content; have a spoken-word content of no more than 25 percent religious material or references; be locally produced under the auspices of a recognized local ethnic community language group; and broadcast between 6:00 a.m. and midnight. There have been concerns voiced within the sector over the guidelines placed on ethnic stations. The guidelines are a restriction on programming freedom, particularly for stations wishing to cater to second- or third-generation migrants who still identify with their parent's homeland culture but prefer to listen to programming in English.[51] For instance, the ethnic community radio station 3ZZZ (Melbourne) serves fifty-eight ethnic communities with specialist programming. It broadcasts twenty-four hours a day and has an estimated listenership of over four hundred thousand. In the year 2000/2001, 3ZZZ received a total of $AU463,892 in grants from the Community Broadcasting Foundation. This is a substantial figure compared to grants received by nonethnic stations. However, 3ZZZ faces competition from SBS and full-time commercial ethnic radio, including two Greek radio stations, and pay TV outlets. Commercial ethnic broadcasters concentrate on the younger generations as opposed to 3ZZZ's older audience, but unless 3ZZZ begins to cater more to the younger generation, the station will face an aging and declining audience. And for most of the younger generation, English is their only language. The station will have to look at other sources of revenue for this programming unless language guidelines change.[52]

For television, the funding issues are amplified as a result of the increased transmission and production costs and complete absence of government funding. The Communications Law Centre remarks, in its report on the test trials, that "without question, the failure to identify an appropriate funding base for public television has been the most significant impediment to its development."[53] Although, arguably, spectrum issues related to broader broadcasting economics are surpassing cost as an impediment to growth, it remains a prominent issue.

Community television stations have existed on the brink of poverty. Equipment maintenance, including transmission, has been difficult. On a positive note, it has now been accepted at the government level that only a diversity of funding sources can provide the television sector with sufficient revenue to meet running costs. It is no longer a question of whether market participation is acceptable, but how much. If Letch's view is correct, then station viability depends on whether a station can maintain a community identity without alienating itself from business.

Localism

Localism is an attribute of community broadcasting that attracts less attention than it deserves. On the surface, the statistics are impressive: Perth's community television station reported in 2001 that it was screening 185 hours a month of local first-run programming;[54] the Brisbane station stated in a submission to the Australian Broadcasting Authority that local content accounted for over 40 percent of its total broadcast hours. For radio, the figures are similarly high, with two-thirds of stations claiming that they produce over one hundred hours a week of local programming. These figures are striking compared to the commercial broadcasting sector, where local content is on the decline. In 2001, the commercial broadcaster Southern Cross Broadcasting closed four of its regional production centers. This was but one more blow in a steady loss of localism in Australian commercial broadcasting since the 1980s.[55] The House of Representatives committee report titled "Local Voices," a result of an inquiry into regional radio, reports from the ABA's evidence that the number of networked stations increased by more than 80 percent between 1993 and 2000 due to the liberalization of ownership rules. Increased competition (due to a greater number of licenses) within local markets is also given as a reason for the loss of localism, with stations resorting to greater levels of program sharing in an effort to cut costs.

The benefits of localism should not be assumed. The provision of local news services is generally deemed to be the most necessary function of local broadcasting.[56] However, in the community sector it is local entertainment, cultures, and activities that make up the greater proportion of broadcasting content. Where this is seen by some to be a deficiency of the sector, the perpetuation and promotion of local culture deserves closer attention. The role of local events promotion, discussion of local issues through talkback or panel programs, as well as local music (Australian music quotas are given in the Community Radio Codes of Practice) are considered outside of the news genre yet are potentially significant sources of local information. It is evident, in any case, that the provision of localism in community broadcasting comes relatively easily—it is a by-product of access and community group participation. The involvement of groups within the production of broadcasting indicates that localism is integral to the structure and function of community broadcasting stations in the majority of cases (91.3 percent of community radio stations cite providing local groups with access to the media as their most important role). Where the issue of localism becomes problematic is how the worth of local content can be measured and evaluated. Localism is treated here from a production angle rather than as a provision-based service. Although community broadcasting may in fact serve the needs of local communities, it is the desire for access that drives local content as much as need.

There are further questions that surround justifications for community media based on localism. Community broadcasting stations are established where the motivation to produce exists within the local community. For this reason it can never be a blanket solution to the diminution of local content in regional areas, at least not without efforts to stimulate interest in media production, including training. At the same time, the opportunities presented by community broadcasting for developing skills and creativity in localities are still poorly researched and overlooked in policy circles in Australia.

Indigenous Media

The BRACS system has been important for the growth of the Indigenous media sector, but its success cannot be generalized. There is a BRACS station in Maningrida, the hub town of Arnhem Land in the Northern Territory. When I visited the town in 2004, the BRACS station was housed in the local school, which meant that access had to be via the teachers at the school, most of who are non-Aboriginal contractors. One non-Indigenous teacher had taken a special interest in the station. He had a background in video production but admitted that his skills were outdated and he could not use digital equipment. Nonetheless, he was dedicated to getting something to air on a weekly basis. On my visit, the teacher broadcast a SVHS tape of students at the school playing in the yard, which was the most he could manage that week. At other times, lessons from the classroom and cultural activities were shown. Despite the obvious lack of skills in the area, the BRACS station was still valued and the local people did tune in to the teacher's videos—despite the fact that the programs were often repeats that they had seen numerous times. Less than a month later, that teacher had moved south to a different town. I was told that other communities in the homelands around Maningrida were making better use of their facilities for both television and radio. However, the experience demonstrated something of the reality of BRACS. Without training, administration, and ongoing maintenance of the equipment, BRACS will never entirely meet the Indigenous population's media needs.

As outlined earlier, there are over one hundred facilities for radio and television broadcasting in remote Aboriginal communities. Although it proved an important step in getting infrastructure to these areas, BRACS attracted criticism from the start. The report that led to its implementation, *Out of the Silent Land*, was written without consultation—an oversight that may explain the problems that BRACS was to face. Funding structures for the ongoing use of BRACS were not considered, nor was the need for administrative structures and staff. Most of all, the report failed to predict that BRACS would be received and used differently around the country, according to community priorities and needs. Indigenous media researchers Helen Molnar and Michael Meadows write that BRACS was "a technological answer that could be neatly packaged and *given* to remote Aboriginal and Islander communities. By doing this, the government misunderstood the diversity of Indigenous uses of community video and television, and attempted instead to impose uniformity on Indigenous community media. It is not surprising then that as BRACS developed, it soon became clear that the government had little idea about how Indigenous people would really use it."[57] Another problem with the BRACS solution was that the taskforce falsely assumed that Aboriginal people in the cities and rural areas had access to national and community stations and did not need separate licenses. They failed to acknowledge that people in rural and urban centers can feel equal loss of culture and identity. This situation is beginning to be rectified. In recent years, a number of urban and rural Indigenous community radio groups have been granted community broadcasting licenses.

The benefit of community radio and television for Indigenous broadcasters is that it has provided a nonconditional means to the creation and distribution of content. Both national broadcasters currently screen and commission Indigenous content, but they are not run on an access policy. The commissioned programs are chosen for whether they meet the broadcaster's particular programming style and audience (to the dissatisfaction of many Indigenous producers). The Indigenous media sector is not entirely happy with the community broadcasting arrangements either—and for good reason. Under the community broadcasting license, Indigenous radio and television broadcasters must compete for spectrum and licenses with other aspiring community broadcasters despite the fact that Indigenous radio and television are a "first level of service"—the primary information and entertainment source—for many Indigenous people. Sponsorship restrictions also sit uneasily against demands from Indigenous groups for new approaches to policy making that cease to see Indigenous people in terms of "welfare" and dependency, and instead encourage social and economic reciprocity.[58]

During the 2005 review into the establishment of an Indigenous television service, Indigenous groups argued that a dedicated channel would allow for the expression of a dynamic and evolving Indigenous culture. The Australian government's decision to establish an Indigenous program fund will provide greater support for Indigenous media makers. However, it does not solve the problem of distribution—leaving metropolitan Indigenous communities without an autonomous, branded Indigenous channel. There is an apparent unwillingness on the part of the Australian government to make a commitment to identifying "air rights" (or spectrum rights) as a natural right possessed by first peoples alongside land rights.

Strengthening Indigenous media is likely to genuinely boost Australia's total cultural output. Aboriginal art and contemporary dance are recognized in cultural centers around the world for their innovation and uniqueness. With an ailing film industry that fails to inspire even local audiences on any large scale, greater support for Indigenous creative industries could be the key to reigniting Australia's cultural production, not to mention the public's interest in homegrown content.

Theory, too, must question whether Indigenous media should be defined as community media. If anything, my inclusion of it here is to show where it departs from community media and why it deserves separate study. Indigenous media and community media are aligned in many countries, as both have had to struggle for recognition within the dominant system. Furthermore, the movement in support of the political and cultural rights of Indigenous peoples have been brought to the forefront as one of the most important social movements of the twentieth century (acknowledging a struggle that stretches back through history), explaining its inclusion within alternative media discussions as defined in chapter 2. This becomes problematic in places such as Australia, where Indigenous media are diverse and spread across commercial, community, and national sectors. A "whole of media" approach is necessary to fully understand the need for Indigenous media.

In 2003, I worked with John Hartley to explore the issue of ethics in the reporting of Indigenous issues.[59] During the course of our interviews, Todd

Condie, editor of the *Koori Mail* (a commercially run Aboriginal newspaper), identified a number of unacceptable yet common problems in the mainstream media's reporting of Indigenous issues. Firstly, Aboriginal people are not always personally identified in news stories. He gives the example of Aboriginal trackers being called in to search for missing English tourist Peter Falconio in 2002. They were not identified by name or language group, and their role in the search was not stated. Says Condie, "It was just assumed that these old men came in from the bush like fauna to help the investigation."[60] He also asks audiences to pay attention to whether more than one Indigenous representative or leader is interviewed in relation to a particular issue: "the tendency has been for the mainstream media to look for one recognized representative to speak for all Aboriginal peoples, which is acceptable when the spokesperson is talking about their local area, but can be inappropriate when the issue is a national one."[61] Furthermore, the mainstream media predominantly cover high-profile Indigenous athletes, artists, and politicians, but overlook the coverage of community events or those taking place in remote and rural communities: "A cartoon which highlights this point appeared in one of the metropolitan dailies around the time of the Sydney Olympics, showing a white Australian leaning out of his 4WD which had just driven into an obviously remote Aboriginal community, yelling out: 'Why can't you all be like [Olympian] Cathy Freeman?' And the answer is 'we can't.' Journalists have to reflect what is really happening in the lives of Aboriginal people, no matter how challenging it is to get the information, instead of applying non-Indigenous values to their subjects."[62]

These concerns have certainly underpinned the development of Indigenous community media in Australia, so they are important in the context of this book. But where the problem is often cited as racial prejudice and stereotyping, the issue is much deeper than simply poor behavior on the part of journalists and editors. As Hartley points out, journalism is based upon principles of modernity and dedicated to a textual system that is centered upon government and business. As long as it fails to recognize Indigenous Australia as a polity unto itself, Indigenous issues will continue to be treated as a "problem." Condie's observation about Indigenous representatives in the news is a case in point. The right representatives are not asked to comment on an issue because the news media persistently treats Indigenous Australia as a subset of mainstream Australia—a "problem" to be dealt with in that arrangement. Furthermore, Indigenous representatives are rarely asked to comment on issues that do not directly involve them, such as international affairs. The news media fail to see Indigenous Australia as an independent power or culture in the international context. Journalism "is dedicated to the nineteenth-century modernist concept of the nation-state, which cannot 'recognise' nations such as these, and is therefore blind to 'people without a polity.'"[63] Of course, Indigenous Australia does have a nation (it has many), which, if recognized, would bring a range of discourses, issues, and personalities into the media that are currently overlooked. The problem is deeply political, but the media can play an important role. It is vitally important—for reasons of economic independence, autonomy, sovereignty—that community media studies does not try to represent Indigenous media as its own.

The Future: The Introduction of Digital Television

Digital terrestrial television broadcasting began in Australia in 2001, implemented through a conservative and cautious transition regime.[64] There was no provision in the Digital Television and Datacasting amendments (2000) for community television services to migrate to digital television along with the other free-to-air stations, nor was there any guarantee that they would do so at any future point during or after the simulcast period. High-definition television (HDTV) is the main feature of the policy. The rationale behind HDTV is that consumers will be enticed to replace their analogue sets with digital sets, assuming that they prefer superior quality over more content. But HDTV conveniently protects the interests of the existing free-to-air commercial stations for the duration of the transition phase. High-definition television is spectrum hungry; it requires large portions of spectrum. The triplecast obligation of the digital television legislation, which requires free-to-air broadcasters to transmit their signal in HDTV, standard-definition digital, and analogue formats, was described by the Australian Consumer's Association as a "bandwidth intensive white elephant" designed to take up spectrum that could otherwise be given or sold to new entrants.[65] The only means for new entrants to participate in digital television is through a new license category known as "datacasting." It was intended that these new commercial services would cater to niche markets, providing informational content such as stock market reports and the weather. However, the datacasting license was severely limited—it prohibited entertaining content and self-contained video material of more than ten minutes in duration. The datacasting plans failed to excite the market, leaving the commercial incumbents in a comfortable position (despite the fact that they have been restricted from delivering extra channels). The public service broadcasters are permitted to multichannel, but no extra funds have been provided to produce content for these channels. Australia's policy for digital broadcasting transition has made television slower to adapt to the changes brought about by convergence than other media and service industries, with the exception of radio.

Australia's cultural objectives have nonetheless been put under pressure by the introduction of digital television. With the increased spectrum capacity, a range of new players have stepped forward to express their interest in participating in digital television broadcasting, mostly from the press and telecommunications sectors. Somewhat more accustomed to competition policy approaches, these players have pushed arguments of consumer choice and the development of innovative new services via market forces. In the words of the experts, "the presence of these players ensured intense debate, signalled the break up of any consensus about the agenda within which debates would be constructed and conducted in both film and broadcasting policy alike, and ensured that any decisions taken were likely to be at most provisional."[66] Even though ultimately the Australian government opted to maintain the status quo in the short term, debate continues as to whether this approach will stand up, particularly in light of the slow consumer uptake of digital television. A convergent media environment has meant new emphasis on issues such as privacy protection, copyright, standards, access to infrastructure, and commercial robustness. Previous regulatory concerns that focused on cultural maintenance and support can no longer claim such distinct, or primary, importance.

The cultural role of community broadcasting is also being revised in light of new market pressures. Although spectrum scarcity excuses for denying permanent allocation to community television are less convincing with the introduction of digital technology, commercial interest in spectrum has also increased. The broadcasting inquiry report issued by the Productivity Commission states that "the major cost to the general community of community broadcasting is the opportunity cost of the spectrum they use" and recommends that the regulator conduct regular research on the demand for community radio and television programming.[67] Digital technology may deliver more channels through increased spectrum capacity, but it has also brought with it new pressures to see spectrum in purely economic terms. In such an environment, community broadcasting is in danger of being seen as a waste of a profitable resource.

The regulator has been trying to figure out a way to accommodate community television in the digital environment. But proposals so far have presumed that content will remain similar to that of the current trial stations. These suggestions, which have mostly centered on the carriage of a single standard-definition community television channel by another broadcaster (either a public service broadcaster or a commercial broadcaster), do not allow for community innovation beyond the current achievements of the sector. If anything, suggestions for the digital transmission of community television presume the static nature of community broadcasting, restricting and containing it rather than seeking a means for its advancement in the new digital environment.

Conclusion

Community broadcasting in Australia has struggled to overcome its position of marginality in an environment where the interests of the incumbent broadcasters are prioritized on the pretext of market stability. Television in particular has been considered an arena of controlled quality in which the status quo is maintained (favoring the commercial incumbents) in return for public interest requirements. This quid pro quo rationale, the presence of two national broadcasters, and a fixed approach to spectrum planning have made for a broadcasting environment in which access can only ever be a minor concern. The "political, technical, industrial, economic and social compromises," as the Productivity Commission report states, "have created a policy framework that is inward looking, anti-competitive and restrictive."[68] In such a framework, tradeoffs between economic and cultural imperatives are favored over transparency or flexibility. Access, as a principle, is marginal within such a system, an anomaly that does not fit with notions of prescriptive regulation over content.

The history of Australian community television policy, in particular, reflects this uncomfortable relationship. It has coincided with the rise of notions of cultural diversity, in which national identity has been redefined to account for and support the existing identities of the various cultural groups. This has included policies directed at particular cultures, for example, the development of multicultural, Aboriginal, and Torres Strait Islander policy frameworks, and the establishment of a national broadcaster with an ethnic broadcasting mandate (SBS television). But where multiculturalism has a defined and easily identifiable purpose (ethnic/migrant cultures and multilingualism), community policies are more often defined by what they are not. Community has been named in the cultural process as something other than high culture, as an effort to account for the various groups that were seeking recognition, funding, and cultural rights. In this cultural reorganization, community has been constructed as something that belongs at the fringes of culture. The inherent untidiness of community when viewed as an object of policy (where does it end and who is in charge?), its transient nature, and its status as something different from established forms of cultural enterprise (experimentation, voluntarism) fits uncomfortably with a regulatory environment of managed difference. In the television context, it is clear that the preferred means of maintaining Australian cultural standards is through content requirements rather than through access. Access becomes a concession to what is left over rather than a positively defined means to diversity.

Australian communications policy requires a clearer conception of what community access means if an adequate arrangement for the digital transmission of community television is to be found. This means thinking beyond the activities of the existing community television and radio stations and towards community access in general. There is now an opportunity to provide community broadcasters with a space in the digital television environment that would allow for a greater degree of experimentation and technical flexibility than has been possible with analogue technology. The set-aside of a significant amount of digital spectrum for use by community broadcasters would be one step towards a more open communications platform.

Notes

1. Community broadcasting was referred to as "public broadcasting" until the 1992 Broadcasting Services Act renamed it. For the sake of consistency I use the term "community broadcasting," even though most of the early literature uses the term "public." This also avoids confusing community-based media with public service broadcasting media, often referred to in Australia as "national" broadcasting.

2. Max Keogh in Phoebe Thornley, "Early Voices: Divergent Philosophies/ Aspirations of the Original Participants" (paper presented at the annual conference of the Community Broadcasting Association of Australia, Hobart, November 2001), 4.

3. Michael Thompson, "Some Issues for Community Radio at the Turn of the Century," *Media International Australia*, no. 91 (1999).

4. John Tebbutt, "Constructing Broadcasting for the Public," in *Australian Communications and the Public Sphere*, ed. Helen Wilson (Melbourne: Macmillan, 1989), 135.

5. Tebbutt, "Constructing Broadcasting for the Public," 135.

6. Tebbutt, "Constructing Broadcasting for the Public."

7. Part 5 of Schedule 2 of the Broadcasting Services Act 1992.

8. Susan Forde, Michael Meadows, and Kerrie Foxwell, "Culture Commitment Community" (Sydney: Community Broadcasting Association of Australia, 2002), iii.

9. Albert Moran, "Multiplying Minorities: The Case for Community Radio," in *Public Voices, Private Interests*, ed. Jennifer Craik, Julie James Bailey, and Albert Moran (Sydney: Allen & Unwin, 1995), 147–48.

10. Craig Liddell, *Diversity on the Airwaves: Histories of Australian Community Radio*, Community Broadcasting Foundation, and 2SER, 2005, at www.cbonline.org.au (accessed February 1, 2005).

11. Ian Cole in Craig Liddell, *Diversity on the Airwaves*.

12. Jim Beatson, "Is Australia a Suitable Model for the Development of Community Radio in Advanced Democracies? Participation, Access and Equity versus Public Accountability," unpublished paper (July 2000), 5.

13. In Alan Knight, "Won't Get Fooled Again: A Paper Detailing 25 Years of Brisbane's 4ZZZ," *CBOnline* 1, no. 6 (2001).

14. Knight, "Won't Get Fooled Again," 9.

15. Kevin Hayes in Knight, "Won't Get Fooled Again," 11.

16. Freda Glynn in Liddell, *Diversity on the Airwaves*.

17. Department of Aboriginal Affairs, *Out of the Silent Land: Report of the Taskforce on Aboriginal and Islander Broadcasting and Communications* (Canberra: AGPS, 1984).

18. Helen Molnar and Michael Meadows, *Songlines to Satellites: Indigenous Communication in Australia, the South Pacific and Canada* (Sydney: Pluto Press, 2001), 34.

19. Communications Law Centre, "Public Television Report: An Evaluation" (Sydney: White House and University of New South Wales, 1989/90).

20. Communications Law Centre, "Public Television Report."

21. Phillip Batty, "Singing the Electric: Aboriginal Television in Australia," in *Channels of Resistance: Global Television and Local Empowerment*, ed. Tony Dowmunt (London: BFI Publishing, 1993); Eric Michaels, *For a Cultural Future: Francis Jupurrurla Makes TV at Yuendumu*, vol. 3, Art & Criticism Monograph Series (Melbourne: Artspace, 1987).

22. Productivity Commission, "Inquiry into Broadcasting" (Canberra: Ausinfo, 2000).

23. This experiment, which offered a possible alternative to stand-alone services, remains the most significant broadcasting arrangement to date between community television and the public service broadcasters.

24. Terry Flew and Christina Spurgeon, "Television after Broadcasting: Pay TV, Community TV, Web TV and Digital TV in Australia," in *The Australian Television Book*, ed. Stuart Cunningham and Graeme Turner (Sydney: Allen & Unwin, 2000).

25. So called because of Australia's existing three commercial and two government-funded free-to-air broadcasters.

26. Australian Broadcasting Authority, "Inquiry into the Future Use of the Sixth High Power Television Channel: Report to the Minister for Communications and the Arts" (Sydney: Australian Broadcasting Authority, 1997), xi.

27. Australian Broadcasting Authority, "Inquiry into the Future Use of the Sixth High Power Television Channel," ix.

28. Ralph McLean in John Davey, "Guaranteed Free Access: A Look at Australian Community Television and Its Place in the Changing Media Landscape," *Metro*, no. 133 (2002): 129.

29. Across all of licensed broadcasting (community, commercial, and subscription) there is, strictly speaking, no "permanent" category of license, although this term is used colloquially to refer to the community license within the sector.

30. Mark Lyons, *Third Sector: The Contribution of Nonprofit and Cooperative Enterprises in Australia* (Sydney: Allen & Unwin, 2001), 221.

31. Ethnic Television Review Panel in Communications Law Centre, "Public Television Report."

32. Gay Hawkins, "Public Service Broadcasting in Australia," in *Communication, Citizenship, and Social Policy: Rethinking the Limits of the Welfare State*, ed. Andrew Calabrese and Jean-Claude Burgelman (Lanham, Md.: Rowman & Littlefield, 1999).

33. Stuart Cunningham, "Community Broadcasting and Civil Society," *Metro*, no. 110 (1997): 22.

34. Communications Law Centre, "Public Television Report," 15.

35. Gay Hawkins, *From Nimbin to Mardi Gras: Constructing Community Arts* (Sydney: Allen & Unwin, 1993), xix.

36. Moran, "Multiplying Minorities," 159.

37. Moran, "Multiplying Minorities," 159–60.

38. Forde, Meadows, and Foxwell, "Culture Commitment Community."

39. Community Broadcasting Association of Australia, "Response to the Productivity Commission's Review of Broadcasting Legislation Draft Report," at www.cbaa.org.au/Productivity%20Commission%20Dec%2099.html (accessed December 16, 1999).

40. Barry Melville, interviewed by Ellie Rennie, Sydney, July 6, 2004.

41. Barry Melville, interviewed by Ellie Rennie, Sydney, July 6, 2004.

42. Aboriginal and Torres Strait Islander Commission, "ATSIC Submission to the Inquiry into Regional Radio" (Canberra: ATSIC, 2000), 7.

43. Vincent O'Donnell, "Community Broadcasting: In Its Twenties Now," *Overland*, no. 158 (2000).

44. House of Representatives Standing Committee on Communications, Transport and the Arts, "Local Voices: Inquiry into Regional Radio" (Canberra: The Parliament of the Commonwealth of Australia, 2001), 40–41.

45. O'Donnell, "Community Broadcasting," 96.

46. Mick Counihan, "Hitz a Knockout," *Communications Update*, no. 123 (1996): 14.

47. Peter Marcato, "Different Values for Changing Times? The Melbourne 2001 Community Broadcasting License Grants," *3CMedia*, no. 1 (2005): 50–57.

48. Moran, "Multiplying Minorities," 158.

49. The program was the focus of an ABA inquiry known as "Cash for Comments" involving the broadcasting of paid product endorsements disguised as editorial.

50. Kath Letch, interviewed by Ellie Rennie, Melbourne, May 3, 2002.

51. Forde, Meadows, and Foxwell, "Culture Commitment Community," 58.

52. Ellie Rennie and Saba El-Ghul, "Supporting the Democratic Voice" (paper presented at the annual meeting of the International Association of Media and Communications Research, Porto Alegre, July 2004).

53. Communications Law Centre, "Public Television Report," 14.

54. Andrew Brine, interviewed by Ellie Rennie, Perth, July 2, 2001.

55. Anne Davies, "Broadcasting under Labor: 1983 to 1994," in *Public Voices, Private Interests*, ed. Craik, Bailey, and Moran.

56. House of Representatives Standing Committee on Communications, "Local Voices: Inquiry into Regional Radio."

57. Molnar and Meadows, *Songlines to Satellites*, 12.

58. Aboriginal and Torres Strait Islander Commission, "ATSIC Submission to the Inquiry into Regional Radio." See also Noel Pearson, "From Campbelltown to Cape York—Rebuilding Community," The Brisbane Institute, 2000, at www.brisinst.org.au/papers/noel_pearson_rebuilding/print-index.html (accessed October 9, 2000).

59. John Hartley, "'Their Own Media in Their Own Language': Journalism Ethics for a People without a Polity," in *Remote Control: New Media, New Ethics*, ed. Catharine Lumby and Elspeth Probyn (Cambridge: Cambridge University Press, 2003). The chapter includes a transcript of interviews with a number of Aboriginal media workers.

60. Todd Condie in Hartley, "'Their Own Media in Their Own Language,'" 64.

61. Condie in Hartley, "'Their Own Media in Their Own Language,'" 64.

62. Hartley, "'Their Own Media in Their Own Language,'" 64.

63. Hartley, "'Their Own Media in Their Own Language,'" 48.

64. 2003 for regional broadcasters.

65. Australian Consumer's Association, "Submission by Australian Consumer's Association to the Senate Environment, Communications, Information Technology and the Arts Committee Inquiry into Broadcasting Services Amendment (Digital Television and Datacasting) Bill 2000" (Canberra: Senate Committee for the Environment, Communications, Information Technology and the Arts, 2000), 4.

66. Tom O'Regan and Ben Goldsmith, "Meeting Cultural Objectives in a Digital Environment" (paper presented at the Rethinking Public Media in a Transnational Era Conference, New York University, January 11–14, 2001), 14.

67. Productivity Commission, "Inquiry into Broadcasting," 275–76.

68. Productivity Commission, "Inquiry into Broadcasting," 5.

CHAPTER FIVE

Development

The Ballymun Media Centre (County Dublin, Ireland) was once located in a flat on the second floor of a grey building practically indistinguishable from others around it. All had walls marked with graffiti and dark, unwelcoming stairwells. Now the community media group is housed within a new and impressive community building; a curving, glass-fronted space contains offices, sound studios, a theater, a dance hall, a darkroom, and a bar. When I last visited, the community center was getting the final touches done to its flash new interior. It stood in stark contrast to the towers of the older "project" that still awaited demolition.

Many miles away is the city of Bamako in Mali. In 1993, community media expert Alfonso Gumucio Dagron visited Bamako to research a media group funded by the Food and Agricultural Organisation (FAO) and the United Nations Development Program (UNDP). He writes, "In a country often so dry and austere, the garden in the middle of the CESPA [Centre de services de production audiovisuelle] building in Bamako looks like an oasis. Somehow it symbolises the very perspective of the project, which aims to create many oases of participatory communication in the remote, rural communities of Mali."[1]

Ballymun and Bamako are both examples of community media within programs intended to improve the lives of local residents. These two "oases" are attempts to rebuild and improve localities through community media. Bamako belongs to a long and controversial history of communications development. Ballymun signifies a new deployment of "community" by local governments as part of their neighborhood development strategies.

This chapter seeks to understand the use of community media for development purposes, in particular the assumption that the establishment of community media will lead to positive social change. It also considers how existing community media fits within this design (for instance, the Ballymun media group has been around longer than the city's current neighborhood regeneration program). It looks at the promotion of community as a legitimate partner for government and development agencies, and of media and technology as empowering tools for local communities. Community media initiatives that are involved in these programs are part of a wider shift in the way culture is viewed. George Yúdice, a professor of American and Latin American studies, writes that "culture is increasingly wielded as a resource for both sociopolitical and economic amelioration, that is, for increasing participation in this era of waning political involvement, conflicts over citizenship . . . and the rise of what Jeremy Rifkin has called 'cultural capitalism.'"[2] It is a shift towards seeing culture as a means to solve political and economic problems.

The communications policies that are designed for social improvement in the First and Third Worlds (sometimes referred to as the North and South[3]) are related, although rarely discussed within the same study. Participatory communication (Third World) projects are defined by their high level of community involvement and organization and are considered successful when they have been "appropriated" by the community.[4] Although the term "participatory communication" refers to a field wider than community media (health communication, education projects, etc.), there is a body of community media theory that situates itself within this discipline. The World Association of Community Radio Broadcasters (AMARC) also deploys participatory development notions in its descriptions of community broadcasting. Participatory communication projects are often small-scale, seeing specific bottom-up solutions as being more effective than general macro policies. Furthermore, they are seen to provide a means for networking within the community and between communities, rather than simply a means to relay information from communicator to receiver. Their uniqueness in this respect means that participatory media projects often rely upon and generate innovative relationships between the community and relevant nongovernmental organizations (NGOs), development organizations, and other institutions. Participatory communications theorist Jan Servaes emphasizes the level of responsiveness within such projects: "With this shift in focus, one is no longer attempting to create a need for the information disseminated, but instead, information is disseminated from which there is a need. Experts and development workers respond rather than dictate, they choose what is relevant to the context in which they are working. The emphasis is on information exchange rather than persuasion, as was the case in the diffusion model."[5] Spending more time in the field, maintaining contact, and keeping promises are also characteristics of neighborhood development approaches in some First World countries that seek to "connect" with communities. Both are examples of interventions by government or other institutions to alleviate issues of scarcity and/or social unrest. Neighborhood development media (Ballymun) and community-based development media programs in the Third World (Bamako) both work to put into practice reflexive, or generative, policies. Of course, the political circumstances that these groups work in are vastly different, as are the obstacles they face. Third World community media often work under legal systems or regimes that are unsympathetic, sometimes hostile, to their cause. However, it is still worth comparing First and Third World community media to understand the wide application of social change objectives.

Justifications for community media based upon social change are not new, but their current prevalence indicates a favorable policy climate. This turn, that sees culture as a driver for change, has emerged in response to the disparities produced by the globalization of capital and the Information Age. Theoretically, the justifications for community media that look to postmodernity, networks, and new social movements are also closely associated with this policy shift. Out of it comes a new set of questions for community media. Firstly, are the approaches and achievements of Third World participatory communications applicable to First World countries? The rhetoric of both Third World development and third way politics promotes "connecting" or "partnering" with community, raising questions of how the local is implicated within global agendas. Are such policy approaches constructive for the communities they claim to reach?

Community media in the Third World is a vast and complicated area to map. However, some of the best intellectual work on community media concentrates on this area. I have selected a few examples in order to examine the implications of the social change rationale for community media in both Third World and First World contexts.

Community Media as Third World Development

Gumucio has gathered anecdotal stories and facts to portray some of the achievements of grassroots participatory communications projects. The impermanency of the projects—their tendency to be based upon temporal and cultural moments and their changing motives and outcomes due to financial and organizational constraints—stand out in his report. It is apparent that diversity of experience and flux are part of the nature of participatory media.

The community project CESPA in Mali was inspired by similar FAO projects that had been successfully run in Peru and Mexico. The goal of the CESPA was to train, mobilize, and organize the local population in the use of video in order to "facilitate the development of new techniques for agriculture, and for improving community management capability and increased participation."[6] Eighty percent of Mali's population lives in rural areas, which extends over the Sahara and the Sahel. The country's reliance on seasonal rains, and constant battles with natural disasters, make it one of the most difficult places to live. The CESPA attempted to alleviate problems of food production through the creation of "pedagogic packages" that combined local knowledge and perception with information from specialists to create videos about agricultural concerns. In its first decade, the CESPA had completed 22 such packages (designed for different ethnic groups within Mali), as well as 116 motivational videos, 23 cultural programs, 20 institutional videos, as well as theater sketches and "newsmagazines" for television. In 1993, CESPA became an independent company, generating its own income. The CESPA has been viewed as the most successful participatory communication project in West Africa and the financial independence of the project is generally considered one indication of its success. However, since its incorporation, the video training aspects of the project have been removed—the "process became less important than the product."[7] For Gumucio, community participation in development communications projects outweighs economic gain. The measures of success are local and culturally specific, yet based upon an idea of social change.

Development community media projects generally fill some important need, from Mampita in Madagascar, which broadcasts messages on lost or stolen animals to help their owners recover them, to Radio Kwizera, which sends messages from refugees—who have lost contact with others due to war and genocide—along the Tanzanian border to their families in Burundi and Rwanda.[8] Three important observations arise out of Gumucio's survey:

- Talk of the "impact" of community media can be misleading; often "impact" is narrowly defined according to the immediate goal pursued by the investors (funding agencies), rather than a true description of the long-term benefit for communities. "Impact often patronizes over communities rewarding instant 'behavioural change,' and turns its back on those that didn't behave well, didn't drop their traditional unhealthy practices."[9]

- Participatory media projects in rural areas are not isolated or marginal for those involved: "for several hundred thousand refugees along the border between Tanzania, Rwanda and Burundi, Radio Kwizera is far from being an 'isolated' communication tool." Community media, in particular radio, can be the most direct and influential media that people come into contact with, not only because they may live in an area without other media, but because it speaks of issues that have a direct impact on their lives. Levels of access and involvement can far outweigh our experience of media in the cities. "Isolation exists in terms of access to other benefits: credit, roads, or services, however in terms of communicating, a community that has its own media channels is far better than a community that doesn't have any."
- Gumucio also asserts that "all community based participatory experiences show that a local radio station, video project, or any other communication experience has helped in the struggle to bring to the community what was long needed." For instance, locals said of a community speaker system in their local town (in the Philippines) that they would not have obtained electricity, roads, and clean water as quickly if they were not able to voice their needs.

Participatory communication does have transformative potential. But the expectations and assessments that come with that can be problematic. The vast majority of community media projects in the Third World rely upon donor funding for equipment and other expenses. Institutions such as the World Bank, the Inter-American Development Bank, the European Union, and UNESCO are just some of the major organizations that have funded cultural programs. When Canadian anthropologist Alan O'Connor visited a radio station in Ecuador he became aware of how problematic this can be:

> There have been problems in recent years with aid. The federation is very suspicious of whom [sic] it accepts help [from]. At present there are technical services, training and technical advice from ALER [the Latin American Association for Educational Radio]. After several years of building this relationship, the radio is affiliated with this organization. Oxfam America is also involved through a local organization. This raises problems because all of these local organizations are informally affiliated with a political party and are not disinterested. They're attempting to gain support for their party. They provided a trainer *chosen by them* to the disappointment of a local person and the organization's hopes. Also tape recorders, cassettes, salaries for popular reporters. There was an attempted imposition of a western hierarchical structure with a director paid more than the others, but the Federation successfully resisted

this. Oxfam Britain is providing help with bilingual school materials. . . . The influx of large amounts of money (and in rumors it gets inflated) creates the possibility of tension and suspicion within the organization. This is a serious problem because their strength has always been in their unity.[10]

Apart from the internal problems that donor involvement can cause, the guidelines for administering funding mean that some projects will be deemed worthy while others will not be. Cultural projects often end up piggybacking on other projects for education or urban renewal as culture is less easy to quantify. There are substantial methodological problems in developing indicators for culture. Although some do work on indicators based upon social justice, cultural institutions and funders are increasingly turning to other, more measurable factors, in order to justify their investment.[11] The criteria by which projects are assessed can therefore shape what community media gets made and by whom. Only by measuring the complex, long-term outcomes of community media projects can we understand their use—but this is a difficult task.

Community media studies has understandably been preoccupied with methodology in recent years. How do you measure community outcomes? One way is to spend time with communities to observe the way they use and produce community media. Ethnographic approaches, whereby researchers visit the community and draw conclusions based on their observations, interviews, and so on, can be problematic. I sympathize with one cultural theorist's admission that she felt shocked by the idea of observing people and then writing about them as it "seemed to be a betrayal of the people observed, and a potential reporting of them to the authorities."[12] Such approaches are also in danger of misrepresentation, bringing the researcher's own cultural assumptions to bear upon others' lives, circumstances, and traditions. O'Connor, during the course of his own ethnographic research, further discovered that communities do not always see researchers as allies: "Later Eusebio told me that people often come to visit the radio. He said they wouldn't have talked to me without the letter of introduction. He told me about an American academic who had visited recently and grudgingly said that I seemed different. Still, he said, all these people come to visit and we never see any result. It's not worth the time."[13] Nonetheless, community media engages at the level of the everyday and research methods do need to connect with specific communities in order to measure outcomes. The local nature of community media is significant for information sharing in communities as communication occurs on the communities' own terms. Research methods—and project design—do need to take this into account. A good example from a UNESCO-commissioned report is a project called Nebanna (a Bengali word meaning "first rice"), which used the social networks of women to diffuse information via information communication technologies (ICTs). Individual women, known as "information agents," receive computer training and establish groups in their immediate locality. One task of the participants is to write diaries, which help project workers to understand local information needs and knowledge and encourage self-expression. The women then experiment with a range of communication approaches and produce a newsletter that includes information gathered from the Internet that they consider relevant to the community. The information from the newsletter then gets circulated throughout the community, and the content is shared with those who cannot read through talk. The project is successful in its goal of information provision and has been a useful test of new research practices. The research utilizes existing networks to incorporate local knowledge and practice.[14]

This is an ethnographic approach to community media evaluation, but it's designed to take into account the local context and to provide ongoing findings through a continual cycle of research and project development. The methodology combines ethnography (involving in-depth interviews, participant observation, diaries, and surveys) with action research. Rather than trying to evaluate sites on their own, the researchers train locals in the area to come up with data, which is gathered over long periods. The local researchers, who are intimately involved in the "communicative ecology," contribute their observations and findings to a website. The participants get to contribute to the ongoing development of the project via this process. The ethnographers who designed the project, Don Slater and Jo Tacchi, write that they have found that the "strongest links between social and technical networks have grown over time through gradual, local, and organic developments and in response to a community of users."[15] Their work demonstrates that research can help resolve the complex issues that face community media; for one thing, it can create better communication channels between communities and those that determine their access to communication.

The Development Tradition and Its Problems

New approaches to participatory communication in the Third World, such as the Nebanna project, seek to break away from top-down governance. This shows that development theory is now deep in the process of coming to terms with its own past. Having undergone the scrutiny of the postmodernist gaze (an almost therapy-like experience), it is now painfully aware of its past failures and influences. Theorist Arturo Escobar writes of "the inability of development to bring lasting improvement in the social condition of much of Asia, Africa, and Latin America, on the one hand, and on the other, the epistemological crisis that seems to affect the field."[16] The development project has failed in its objective of overcoming scarcity at large (generally it has advanced the debt crisis, poverty, and ecological destruction) and lost the intellectual and political arguments it once relied upon to justify its existence. However, the development industry continues to operate, and even its harshest critics do not wish to stop the resources that it manages to lever. Finding new methods and approaches to social change, in the hope of redirecting resources towards more fruitful projects, has become the goal of much writing in the field today.

A story by development worker Bella Mody demonstrates the problematic area of communications development. In the early 1970s, Mody worked for an organization with the unnerving name of the NASA-India Satellite Instructional TV Experiment (SITE). Recounting the story of her experience with SITE's Kheda Communication Project, Mody tells of how the group assumed that "knowledge served as power under all conditions," an assumption with devastating consequences.[17] The agency had decided to confront the legal and human rights violations being committed by landowners with the complicity of local government. With a considerable tone of irony, Mody writes, "All that was needed to dismantle caste, class and gender abuse was the harsh glare of investigative documentaries and drama on local TV." The documentary crew first created and broadcast programs exposing the lack of infrastructure in the area in order to motivate local government towards greater efficiency. They then moved on to "more serious problems of exploitation, such as family agribusinesses not paying their labor the legal minimum wage," incorporating interview material gathered in local villages. "As the daily coverage continued, daily laborers could not believe the government agency was standing up for them against the local economic power structure, but neither could the economic powers. The federal government agency, full of physicists, TV producers, social scientists, was dabbling in rural development."[18] The consequence of this "dabbling" was that huts owned by interviewees were burnt down by paramilitary gangs commissioned by the farmers. The police, having also been paid off by the farmers, never arrived. Not only did the Kheda Communication Project show that "communication through technology alone was impossible," it also revealed the disastrous implications of "context-free research" and "ungrounded theory."[19]

Since Mody's personal collision with the failings of communication development, academics and institutions have begun to look towards participation as a means to fulfill a new (agenda-less) development agenda.

The Epistemological Crisis of Development Communications

Early development communications was founded upon the sender-receiver communication model that suggested the media could "effect" or guide people's thinking directly. In the late 1950s when communications development began to be practiced, this theoretical paradigm was already being discredited. Research such as that of Katz and Lazarsfeld asserted that "intervening variables" (a person's predisposition, for example) could modify the effectiveness or meaning of a message.[20] Despite this, research commissioned by agencies such as UNESCO continued to employ the media effects model, possibly out of a belief that people living within traditional societies were more easily influenced than those in industrial societies. One book famously suggested that the media could act as a hypodermic needle, injecting sensibilities into traditional peoples that would encourage modernization.[21] In later studies, the effects model was replaced by a more technology-centered model that endorsed the setting up of communications infrastructure in nonindustrialized countries as a means towards the diffusion of innovations.[22]

The notion of modernization was central to both the effects and innovation approaches. Modernization promoted an idea of "progress" that was firmly grounded in the Enlightenment concepts of science, reason, and individualism. The Enlightenment project assumed that there was only one possible answer to any problem[23]—a universalism that guided the drive towards a particular type of political order. In development, this was manifested in the promotion of technology and infrastructure, as well as political pressure upon Third World governments to implement macro policies that would lead them either towards capitalist economic systems, or, in some instances, the modernism of Soviet-style statism. Industrialization and urbanization were seen as the goals of development, best implemented through Western methods of production and labor and centrally controlled by bankers and economists. The so-called problems of the Third World were viewed as internal, rather than the product of international economic arrangements and power.[24]

Here is an example of the thought that prevailed, taken from a United Nations Department of Social Affairs publication written in 1951: "There is a sense in which rapid economic progress is impossible without painful adjustments. Ancient philosophies have to be scrapped; old social institutions have to disintegrate; bonds of cast, creed and race have to burst; and large numbers of persons who cannot keep up with progress have to have their expectations of a comfortable life frustrated. Very few communities are willing to pay the full price of economic progress."[25] Discourses such as these became dominant in international institutions but also within the social imaginary—the daily discourse that continued to classify and characterize places now named "Third World." Notions of poverty, deprivation, illiteracy, and helplessness were problematized within this category, perpetuating the powerlessness of these geographic and cultural spaces. As a result, subordination was provoked through discourse that proclaimed to alleviate it. Some scholars, in particular the South American dependency theorists (*dependistas*) of the late 1960s and 1970s, began to confront development by pointing out that the problems at stake were in fact caused by global capital flows and power. Dependency theory addressed the problematic nature of Western power structures that were being deployed through development programs. However, in terms of communication, it reinforced the linear model of communication: "source-transmitter-channel-receiver-destination."[26] Although an important shift in understanding development, dependency theory still, essentially, saw communications as something that was imposed upon the receiver, framing it as an issue of imperialism.

The participatory communication approach arose out of the dialogical pedagogy of Paulo Friere, as well as the UNESCO debates of the 1970s, which culminated in the MacBride Report (see chapter 1). These approaches supply the principles upon which participation has been implemented. The more detailed and specific concerns with grassroots media and local specificity is mostly discussed in terms of the postmodernist revision of development, or "postdevelopment" as it has been called.[27] This approach sees conceptions of power and discourse as being the necessary theoretical framework from which new approaches to development must emerge: "reconceptualizing the field in terms of power demands that we consider development communication as an intervention created and justified through institutional discourse operating in a global system."[28] For Escobar, development is a colonizing discourse. The problematization of poverty "brought into existence new discourses and practices that shaped the reality to which they referred. That the essential trait of the Third World was its poverty and that the solution was economic growth and development became self-evident, necessary and universal truths."[29] When the discourse around women, peasants, and the environment in development contexts is analyzed, it becomes apparent that development as a whole is a highly problematic construct. Intimately tied to our political structures and idea of the "social," development has been a successful apparatus for "producing knowledge about, and the exercise of power over, the Third World."[30]

Postdevelopment is an attempt to make visible the colonizing discourses and actions of development. It maintains the idea that intervention is possible, and that something must be done, but replaces the concept of development with the less problematic "social change." Some discourses of participatory communication maintain that it is the process rather than the product that is important. However, it is difficult to see any difference between participatory communications development that establishes community media stations and the broader field of community media without the idea of some kind of "project," or social goal, within its definition. Escobar contends that "We may understand postdevelopment as opening the possibility of reducing the role of development as a central organizing principle of social life in Asia, Africa, and Latin America, as a heuristic device for seeing local realities in Asia, Africa, and Latin America differently, and finally as a way to strive for other potential principles for thinking about and reconstituting the world. If we imagine postdevelopment in these ways, then we have to admit that postdevelopment already exists in what we have called here (place-based) practices of difference."[31] Perhaps it is the case that the true goal of postdevelopment media is community media itself (a "place-based practice of difference"), entirely run by the community according to its own system and imperatives. Where participatory communication departs from community media—and perhaps also from postdevelopment—is when the claim to bringing about social change is not generated from within the group but by outside planners. I will return to the implications of "planning" in the second part of this chapter.

Considering participatory media as a means for communities and individuals to alter power relationships through grassroots activity is one way to deal with the fact that the project of development is saturated with cultural and historical biases.[32] Relinquishing the idea of "development" (but not necessarily the resources that development institutions provide) avoids endorsing imperialistic, paternalistic, modernizing projects while retaining the idea that something can be done. By framing it as a means of empowerment instead of development, the emphasis on participation directs the debate towards the "on the ground" usefulness of community-based media as a means to social change.

The possible contradiction of postdevelopment theory lies here. A reading of grassroots media as the only means to embrace and elevate local culture without implicating it within modernist development agendas reaches a dead end when it attempts to see such media as drivers of large-scale social change. One critique of postmodernity is that by acknowledging the authenticity of many voices, postmodernism ghettoizes those voices, seeing them only in terms of their own logic and specificity. It therefore cannot successfully engage in the realities of the political economy.[33] Postdevelopment *does* attempt to seek social change nonetheless, and in this way it steps back from its own postmodern stance. At a theoretical level, postdevelopment is confusing due to its reliance upon local specificity—an apparent resistance to accepting any kind of macro view—while still maintaining an idea of social change. The result is that community media is caught between local, community-specific use—which does as it likes—and the aspiration (often from outside) to change the world. If nothing else, that is a big responsibility for communities to bear. Are they a "failure" when change does not eventuate?

Civil Society in the Third World

One possible reason why social change is being led by NGOs and social movements is that governments are increasingly driven to respond to global economic pressures at the expense of domestic welfare. Neo-liberalism, which is sweeping through much of the globe, involves trade liberalization, privatization, and the reduction of state-supported social services. As a result, the left has shifted its focus from "the takeover of power" to issues of "civil and human rights and quality of life." Writes Yúdice:

> Conventional and even progressive political parties have succeeded in doing very little to counter [neo-liberal] policies, both because the institutionalized political process is largely dysfunctional in responding to social needs and because enormous pressures from international financial interests not only have discouraged reform but have actually worsened conditions, such as the ever increasing gap in income distribution. Consequently, the most innovative actors in setting agendas for political and social policies are grassroots movements and the national and international NGOS that support them.[34]

It is these conditions that have fostered the turn towards seeing culture in general, and community media in particular, as a means to social change. Nongovernmental organizations, which also work within nondemocratic states, have therefore been significant in framing civil society as the answer to political and economic problems. But asserting that civil society is capable of democratizing economic and political life must lead us to ask: what will foster civil society?[35]

If civil society and its associations are not pre-political (in the way that community is), but rather the product of a particular stage in capitalist democracy, it follows that a state's political structure will determine the presence or absence of civil society. Some have questioned the notion that civil society is an appropriate prescription for Third World development. Discussions of civil society and its newfound popularity suggest a universality of human experience.[36] In reality it is a structure that requires a stable system of individual rights, including freedom of association.[37] To ignore this is to overlook the difficulties faced by the Third World in attempting the long-term stabilization of civil society.

For community media this raises two issues: firstly, whether community media requires an existing and mature civil society, and secondly, whether the prescription of community media as a solution ignores fundamental political issues. Do the difficulties encountered by community media in the industrialized world (such as funding and management issues) become insurmountable in places where there is no support-bed or framework for civil society? Or is it the case that community media in the Third World can only be understood outside of theoretical conceptions of civil society and the liberal democratic state? South Africa (technically a "Second World" country) is an interesting case in point. Since the end of apartheid, South Africa has been attempting to repair the enormous inequities brought about by the country's history of enforced discrimination. Civil society played a crucial role within that transition, both in popular resistance to apartheid and in the transition to democracy.[38] Community media has come into existence as a part of the democratization process. However, economic and cultural legacies of the apartheid era remain, displaying the difficulties that community media projects face in their attempt to expand civil society within a transitional democracy.

South Africa developed a framework for community radio within its 1993 Independent Broadcasting Authority (IBA) Act. Under the act, community radio stations are required to be nonprofit entities, must serve a particular community, must encourage community participation, and may be funded by sponsorship or advertising. It was intended from the start that four-year licenses would be made available to community radio stations. However, delays caused by problems in the IBA's own internal structure meant that the stations had to exist on twelve-month interim licenses until hearings could be held. Apart from the predictable problems that licensing delays have caused (time-consuming annual renewal processes and an inability to develop long-term plans), many stations suffer from a serious lack of resources and volunteers.[39]

Mabalane Mfundisi of South Africa's National Community Radio Forum states that community radio is sometimes seen as "exploitation of the poor, by the poor,"[40] highlighting the lack of a voluntarist culture in communities with high unemployment and a history of political and economic subjugation. For Pheladi Gwangwa, former head of the licensing unit of the Independent Communications Authority of South Africa, community apathy towards the running of the stations has to do with the fact that "people still need to be schooled into the working of democracy."[41] Researcher Jo Tacchi comments that "simply understanding what community radio is and can be for communities, and how they can be managed transparently, is recognised as an issue by people on all sides of the community radio debate in South Africa."[42] What is apparent in the South African example is that the absence of a robust civil society complicates the establishment of community radio. On the one hand the lack of volunteerism—a cultural phenomenon taken for granted in many First World countries—inhibits the internal running of the stations. Furthermore, as the external environment—the local economy and infrastructure—remain characterized by scarcity, the structures that could provide ongoing funding and assistance cannot be relied upon.

Others write of the seemingly insurmountable rift between the need for state building in Third World politics and the transition to democracy that requires a level of individual liberty.[43] State legitimacy is required to foster stability and manage economic inequalities, ethnicity, religious conflict, and external influences. However, a strong, interventionist state can run counter to the expansion of civil society and participation. Furthermore, strategies for economic growth can conflict with public-good policies. In Latin America, in particular, government efforts to raise their countries above Third World status have involved the commercialization of broadcasting, auctioning spectrum that was previously used by community groups. These factors put into question the ability of community media organizations to become part of the permanent political setting.

Despite this, community media initiated by development agencies can be immensely important for those involved. It gives individuals and communities the ability to express themselves, which in turn can have direct consequences in the political arena. But the claim to stimulating broader social change and overcoming scarcity through community mobilization requires complex examination, taking into account the micro and the macro. Although the development project should ultimately aim to make itself unnecessary, community media as a driver for social change may not have the ability to foster social change in the absence of the "project." Development communications (and all of its problems) will replace community media in the absence of broader political change.

Radio Sagarmatha

Community radio emerged in Nepal following the democratization of the political system in 1990. I visited Kathmandu in 2003, when Radio Sagarmatha was hosting the eighth annual conference of the World Association of Community Radio Broadcasters (AMARC). Radio Sagarmatha was one of the first independent community broadcasting stations in South Asia. Its setup is impressive, with well-equipped studios and a five-hundred–watt transmitter, which is pitched on the rooftop of their four-story building. At the time, the station was producing a wide variety of programs, ranging from classical (South Asian) music to health programming, news, and entertainment. Highest priority was given to their news and current affairs programming, which was seen as important for the democratic process. A number of stations in Nepal were also making significant headway into women's rights, allocating time slots to women's discussions on sensitive topics such as patriarchal practices and rape.

On February 1, 2005, King Gyanendra sacked the government and closed the international airport. All communications, including e-mail, were initially cut. Although services were restored within a matter of weeks, radio stations were restricted from broadcasting news programs; only "entertaining" content was permitted. As a result, the only news program that the people of Nepal have been able to listen to (on standard radio receivers) comes from the state-run Radio Nepal.

Radio Sagarmatha is a peace-building media, encouraging discussion and openness without favoring any political faction. However, it faces some significant challenges. In places without sufficient democratic process, subtle and adequate analysis of the issues is not available within the public sphere at large. It is unrealistic to expect that community radio can provide full in-depth analysis under these circumstances. Finding independent views and sustaining debate on complex issues such as policy intervention can often be beyond the scope of volunteer-run station programming, even in the best of circumstances. With restrictions on news and current affairs, it is almost impossible. However, the community radio stations of Nepal are making do, despite decreasing audiences and empty newsrooms. Some have begun to produce "entertaining" drama programs that discuss social issues and political themes. Lengthy discussions of elections at local scout groups are intended to surreptitiously remind people of the democratic process they are missing out on. One group even sacrificed a radio transmitter at their local temple to remind those in the vicinity of their democratic needs.

Development in the First World: Ireland and the United Kingdom

Influential third way thinker Anthony Giddens calls for "an alternative development."[44] Such a revision of development would involve a move beyond welfare approaches that act as modernity's insurance against external risk, to strategies that see risk and uncertainty as manufactured and as things that can be confronted through an organized, yet reflexive, strategy. It is an attempt to move away from dependency and stagnation, and towards self-development for the prevention of poverty and social exclusion.

Giddens suggests that an alternative development is not simply a transfer of resources from the First to the Third World (convincing rich countries to give to the poor and then restructuring Third World political systems to align with those of the First World). An alternative development must be "a challenge to modernity rather than an attempt to generalise it successfully everywhere."[45] This might involve, for both the First World and the Third World, attention to the initiatives of most economically deprived groups: Indigenous social movements or local "self-help" organizations, for example. Development should not be seen as imposition upon the Third World, a "solution" imposed from above, but as a worldwide concern: "An alternative development: isn't that just what we see emerging—or struggling to emerge—within the more developed societies also? And isn't such an alternative development at the same time the only way in which it would be remotely possible for the reconstruction of welfare in the North to be compatible with increasing prosperity in the South? What is at issue here is the coming into being of a post-scarcity society—a process still perhaps led by those in the wealthier countries, but worldwide in its implications."[46] Partly thanks to Giddens, who has had significant influence on contemporary social policy in leftist governments, modernization is being revised in the First World as well as the Third World. The high-rise council housing of the old Ballymun, which has become a symbol of a failed top-down approach to social problems, is a part of this. Although governments constructed high-rise housing in order to resolve real problems faced by economically disenfranchised communities (such as sanitation and the provision of hot water and heating) it is now apparent that these public housing projects created as many difficulties as they attempted to resolve. They became isolated areas of poverty, attracting crime and drug use.

Technology, media, and culture are also implicated in First World development strategies. In 1987, the residents of Ballymun first campaigned to have their housing issues addressed. In response, the Dublin Council spent 57 million Irish pounds in the mid-1990s, refurbishing 150 of the flats. The project did not address the needs of the five thousand homes situated over Ballymun's two square miles, nor did it resolve the structural deterioration of the buildings themselves.[47] The current redevelopment has emerged out of Dublin City's Strategic Plan, a twelve-year framework for change that targets Ballymun for development due to its low employment and education rates. In July 2002, the first of the blocks was demolished, and residents began relocating into the new low-rise dwellings. But this second approach to urban renewal is more than simply an "edifice complex."[48] Ballymun signifies a new approach to urban development, where social and technological spaces are seen to be as important as the physical structure in which they stand. The regenerated Ballymun is an e-town, with computing and Internet connection available to all residents. Furthermore, consultation with communities is also seen as vital to the fulfillment of the strategic plan.[49]

Community radio has existed in Ireland since 1995; community television, however, has been slower to develop. A community forum was established in Dublin to discuss community concerns and filter ideas from civil society through to government. A subsection of this forum is the Community Media Forum. The campaign to establish a community television channel in the Dublin area has worked through this forum, although the national campaign for community television is much older and has involved many more individuals and groups around the country. In March 2001, Ireland established its first legislative commitment to community television by allowing for community channels for cable or MMDS (wireless) distribution. These services are to be self-funded and represent local interests. Community channels are created through "community content contracts" awarded by the Broadcasting Commission of Ireland (BCI). Applicants must be representative of the community and programs must address the interests of the community. Although there is no nonprofit stipulation, the channel must ensure that no monetary reward beyond covering costs is involved.

The policy is somewhat problematic.[50] Communities are only defined by geographic localism, which excludes communities of interest. There is no ongoing funding arrangement for these services. Most crucially, there are no requirements for access or participation, meaning that the community's involvement could be minimal, depending on the contractor. Groups such as the Ballymun Media Centre currently have no broadcast outlet.

According to Margaret Gillan, speaking as the manager of Community Media Network (CMN), the community television channel has gained momentum in policy circles over recent years as it is seen to fulfill the government's mandate of "partnership": "Setting up a website can be used as an excuse to avoid real participation, and the National Development Plan

Beaumont Street Studios

The neighborhood development approach to community broadcasting can also be seen in Huddersfield, a small town in West Yorkshire. Beaumont Street Studios, established in 1985, was initially a response to social problems within the local black community. In its early days, the center offered only sound recording studios and training, but it has now diversified into multimedia, as well as radio and video training and production. Beaumont Street Studios runs short-term radio broadcasts—called Creative FM—under the Restricted Service License scheme. The studio is also involved in the New Deal for Musicians and the New Deal for Creative Industries, both New Labour strategies to bring unemployed people back into the labor market. For this the studio provides a training and mentoring program, designed towards supportive, work-focused learning. After one year of operating, the New Deal for Musicians project had managed to train numbers in the hundreds. As training manager Jeni Vine explains:

"A lot of our work at the moment is grant-funded work at an access level. So it's working with people who are long term unemployed or kids that didn't go to school. The sort of projects where people's basic levels of literacy and numeracy tend to be very low and their motivation tends to be very low. And it's using the media that we have to interest people in understanding their situation better and developing self-confidence and developing skills that will take them forward. So it's not so much about training people up for jobs in the industry so much as training people up for a job."[a]

Beaumont Street Studios have no core funding and their annual income varies from year to year depending on what funding is available. According to Vine, in the year 1999/2000, the annual income was around half a million pounds. "That's running a whole range of programs, some of those are commissions, some of them are working on European funded projects, some of them are training, some of them are commercial."[b] The commercial operations include sound studio rental and short-courses for businesses. But the majority of funding comes from grant-based projects, including the New Deal for Musicians.

---

[a] Jeni Vine, interviewed by Ellie Rennie, Sheffield, March 1, 2001.

is supposed to be big on participation. You set up an 'interactive' website but who can access it? The whole process is an offshoot of partnership and partnership is the government's format for progress ever since the 1990s."[51] This new interest in community media is not exclusive to Ireland. The United Kingdom introduced full-time community radio in 2004. The policy rationale behind the new license category (known as "access radio," with nonprofit local television still under review) is not unlike Dublin's. It seems that participation in the form of community media is now experiencing a much more favorable policy climate in the United Kingdom and Ireland than ever before.

Beaumont Street Studios' training manager, Jeni Vine, has taken her community media experience into research. Her study, which compares three different community media training projects in England, deliberately implicates itself within current U.K. policy objectives. For Vine, community media fits within social policy that looks beyond short-term solutions to social and economic exclusion. In her opinion "that is what community media has always sought to do and can now find a platform for." Vine sees the need for "a rationale for community media that includes not only the potential individual gains for trainees but also the gains for the local community."[52] Central to her thesis is the argument that learning through creative production is a more profound, empowering, and ultimately productive way to learn than experience gained through traditional education.

The U.K. government's influential Creative Industry Task Force report explicitly states that the dissemination of media production skills can lead to economic development: "Engaging learners in doing creative work, such as design, music and media production, and writing rather than transcribing, provides not only a more fulfilling, accessible and intuitive experience of the basic ICT technical skills, it also encourages and requires the development of creative thinking, one of the most important drivers of the knowledge-based economy."[53] The Community Media Association (CMA) in the United Kingdom has been making the most of the Blair government's community rhetoric. The organization's former general manager, Steve Buckley, has commented, "The government has majored on social inclusion, reform of life-long learning, community access to communication information technologies, local democracy, e-government etc. All these things tie in with new agendas within the community media sector. And we've been able to argue fairly successfully that community media reaches lots of themes and topics that the government wants to reach and that have been reflected in statements of ministerial support for community media at a high level."[54] In March 1999, the chancellor of the exchequer allocated 252 million pounds to support community-based learning centers. This was matched with 250 million pounds from the New Opportunities Fund (money levied from lottery profits). Combined, the funds were intended to support the development of seven hundred learning centers, only some of which are community media centers (CMCs)—providing facilities equipped with radio, television, and web content production technology. At the time, the CMA described this development as "possibly the most important opportunity ever for getting financial resources into Community Media development."[55] Steve Buckley estimated that since then, 10–20 million pounds in capital funds have come into the community media sector as a result of the forty to fifty funding proposals which have been made to the ICT Learning Centre by community media groups. The CMA also made a successful bid for a mobile radio training unit for the London area.[56]

Knowledge and motivation were also identified as key benefits of community broadcasting in Peter Lewis's 1978 study of Britain's early community cable television experiments. The cable experiments did not succeed, marred as they were by "changes of governments and lack of policy" that left community media groups without a platform for broadcast.[57] As a result, they have persisted as audio and video training centers, with production outcomes but no ongoing means of distribution (see chapter 3). Their funding has been predominantly from grants, either from government or philanthropic organizations. Reliance upon grant funding places pressure upon community organizations to justify their projects in terms of measurable social outcomes and to focus their efforts upon target groups. Contemporary discourses that connect community media to neighborhood development and social regeneration therefore often arise in the absence of adequate policy and funding arrangements.

Although community media has always been justified on the grounds of its ability to provide training, these new discourses display aspirations of knowledge-economy growth and a concern for globalization. Whereas previous approaches to community media focused upon their capacity to affirm local identity, new approaches seek to build *localities*, seeing the local in the context of global flows of capital. This approach accepts the contention that globalization has made economic and cultural forces less inhibited by nation-state borders. One ramification of this is that cities and regions become more significant, as they are capable of attracting industry and tourism through lifestyle appeal as well as economic incentives. In recognition of this, city councils and local and regional governments are increasingly looking to enhance their sense of place. With a dual agenda of social/neighborhood regeneration and competitiveness within the global economy, these policy approaches have a specific focus on local culture rather than the nation as a whole. The mobilization and coordination of funding bodies, arts, heritage and tourism agencies, as well as private and third sector groups, is central to this trend. In disenfranchised areas, the goal is to encourage a more active and reflexive citizenry capable of taking advantage of the opportunities of the new economy.

The United Kingdom's New Labour government, with its third way approach (see chapter 1), sees social capital as a means to prosperity. Communications technology, with its capacity to extend knowledge-economy growth, is also of central importance. Succinctly summarized by Giddens, "In the new information economy, human (and social) capital becomes central to economic success. The cultivation of these forms of capital demands extensive social investment—in education, communications and infrastructure."[58] The inclusion of communications into local development policies becomes an issue of local agency. There are three identifiable aims driving the push towards information technology within local policy:

- The "global positioning" approach, where ICTs and media are used to attract inward investment into cities
- The "endogenous" development approach to ICTs and media which seeks to reconnect the economic, social, and cultural fragments within localities; and
- The delivery of public services via media and ICTs and the establishment of new channels of communications between citizens and authorities/ government.[59]

With its focus upon social capital, as well as content production and training, community media is a logical fit within the second of these objectives. It "may help underpin the development of a 'virtuous circle' where improved social cohesion is linked with a renaissance of urbanism, local economic development and civic culture."[60]

Some correlations between new approaches to Third World development and the politics of the third way can thus be seen. In both participatory development in the Third World and neighborhood development, the assumption is that "connecting" with communities will bring forth new approaches to improving local conditions. Both see this as crucial in order to get beyond the failed modernization solutions of the past. Globalization is accepted as a phenomenon that requires correction—it will lead to greater disempowerment of those outside of the economic networks unless strategies are put in place to counteract such forces. These strategies are implemented at a local level—social change is seen as having to come from within communities rather than from without. Finally, both rely upon a relationship between an agency and the community, and are therefore working at the intersection of civil society and the state and/or economy.

Implicit within this is the idea that it is necessary to foster civil society (although in coordination with the state). Civil society theorist John Keane writes that:

> The language of civil society can also be used for the purposes of calculating political strategies of achieving a predefined or assumed political good. In contrast

to empirical-analytic-interpretive approaches, which are concerned with such intellectual tasks as naming, categorising, observing, theorising, comparing and understanding a complex reality of institutionally structured action, strategic usages of the distinction between civil society and the state have an eye for defining what must or must not be done so as to reach a given political goal. The term "civil society" is bound up with efforts to calculate the tactical means of achieving or preserving certain ends.[61]

As has been outlined in this chapter, both neighborhood development and Third World development rely upon the idea that civil society is a means to achieve a positive political end.

Localization

Communications development and neighborhood development both base policy within a sense of place. Within these programs the local is valorized as the site from which legitimate change must occur. In order to separate itself from the modernist past, these projects maintain that direct connection with the community concerned is necessary. Power is redistributed to the local level.

Globalization can create favorable conditions for community renewal in that it can have a "push-down" effect, allowing power at the local level to find expression.[62] As with the participatory development approach to community media, neighborhood development acknowledges the inequalities that globalization produces. However, it seeks relevance within this system rather than recognition of cultural relevance for its own sake and seeks inclusion within the knowledge economy through education and skills transfer.

In participatory development, the emphasis upon local place and culture is intended to help avoid generalizing perceived community needs. Programs based upon uniformity, in some critiques, are seen as imperializing (although this is problematic, too, as it casts the local community as powerless against any influence). In other treatments, uniform approaches ultimately fail due to a kind of self-blinkered misdirection (as in Mody's example). Participatory communications is wary of globalization due to the history of development.

Huesca and Escobar look to new social movement theory as a means to resolve issues of place and globalization in development theory.[63] New social movements have arisen out of the context of globalization and signify a challenge to the power structures enforced by the rise of global capital. This "globalization from below" utilizes technology and networks to coordinate resistance and to stimulate social change. "New social movements are generally understood to be small, decentralised, and democratic in their structure; cyclical and diffuse in their temporal arrangement; and action driven toward identity construction in their orientation. In the most general sense, new social movements have been defined as heterogenous groups forming outside formal institutions and operating in discontinuous cycles to forge collective meanings and identities that direct action."[64]

Escobar asks whether it is possible to launch a defence of place as the starting point for social action within a world increasingly characterized by globalization. The two contradictory phenomena of global communication networks and the assertion of place within the global context can, combined, allow the concerns of the powerless to be expressed. By asserting the importance of place in terms of development—a continuing focus on local projects—development will work to build coalitions between places through communities' use of communications technology. Seeing community media and development projects in terms of globalization is important in order to see beyond the immediate groups and to account for networks and transnational communities. It takes community media out of its immediate broadcast reach and, in this way, acknowledges the role it plays in influencing and maintaining social movements across the globe—elevating "local knowledges into different constellations of knowledge and power through enabling networks."[65] It is what some have called "grounding" the conflation of unanchored knowledge and power in globalization theory.[66] Whereas popular conceptions of the ramifications of information communication technologies emphasize "flows" over "places,"[67] this theory holds that only through understanding of the lived reality of local experience can the nature and potential for participation in the information economy be seen.

But to view globalization as the primary justification for community media or development media projects risks ignoring the local for its own sake, outside of the global context. It should be remembered that community media predates current concerns of globalization. Local uses that do not intend to elevate people into the knowledge economy (as the third way rhetoric suggests) or that do not connect affiliated resistance groups (as postdevelopment suggests) should not be disregarded. If skills and networks are the criteria for funding of community media projects, then other uses—identity, entertainment—may miss out. Furthermore, if training programs focused upon specific groups take priority, then other financial needs, such as infrastructure and station management, may not be met.

Beyond Development Communications and Towards Community Media

Participation is not appropriate to all situations, nor can it be mapped out according to a stringent policy design. It should not be something that experts deliver to the masses but a process that responds to each situation. Prescribing how it should occur goes against the nature of true participation.[68] Participatory communications has had to come to terms with the limitations of community-based change. There are no fast results and no outcomes that can be predefined. These observations go back to the problem of attempting to define communities as knowable and measurable entities. Concepts such as "community" can "disguise radical differences in meaning because the processes of community production themselves diverge remarkably according to group capacities and interest. Yet the treatment of communities as if they are comparable (by, say, a planning agency) has material implications to which the social practises of people who live in them have to respond."[69] In the policy context, a rhetoric that sees community as a project to be constructed may work to entrench false notions of community and may fail to see actual needs. The theoretical progression that participative development communications has undergone is instructive in this instance. What is at stake is the way in which communities are packaged and treated within policy approaches that seek to overcome scarcity.

Gumucio warns that "myths emerge when the knowledge of reality is limited." The influences of dependency theory and the day-to-day struggles against dictatorships through much of Latin America idealized the notion of community-based social regeneration: "Anything from the community level had an aura of purity and rightfulness. This was not really a bad thing, considering the hard times that the progressive movement was living in Latin America." However, Gumucio adds that "times have changed, and communities have revealed themselves as less compact entities."[70] The challenge for research and development is to recognize the difficult nature of community-based change. Furthermore, policy needs to take into account what is already happening at the local level rather than attempt to "do community better." Gillan, of the CMN in Ireland, has expressed dissatisfaction with Dublin City's community forum. Referring to their website, she points out the claim that without the forum "the community does not have a platform from which to air their views": "There are lots of platforms! . . . The community workers co-op is one of them, for example. People created platforms but little notice is taken of them, that is the problem. This is the one the Government likes, and this is the one they've decided we're going to have."[71] The community forum, for Gillan, is fraught with problems, mostly to do with the way the forum has been structured by the city. By comparison, the Community Media Forum, while a member body of the city community forum, had an independent existence. Gillan attributes its achievements, particularly its part in the campaign for community television, to this fact. Where government strategies seek to shape civil society, or require them through "partnerships" to comply with government settings, they risk ostracizing the community. In a true partnership, Gillan points out, one partner does not have the upper hand. Furthermore, she sees the campaign for community television as a complex struggle, involving many groups over a long period of time—a history that is easily overlooked when the city's efforts are seen as the only interface.

Participatory communications cannot be "a strategy to make target audiences 'feel' more involved and, therefore, more acquiescent to manipulative agendas. It is not a means to an end but legitimate in its own right."[72] This insight applies to all practices that seek to create social change through the mobilization of community. Despite the fact that the complexity of civil society groups makes "partnership" a difficult idea, this is often what civil society groups seek and desire. Civil society relies upon both government and other agencies and networks for its survival, and it is only in relation to such structures that it finds its role. Therefore, there are no answers to be found by abandoning attempts to connect groups and institutions.

But we do need to acknowledge the dynamics that such partnerships create. Policies that seek to "empower" communities can deflect the state's own responsibilities. Civil society becomes negatively implicated in the political climate: it gets told to function better, be more active, involve more citizens. When civil society takes on the responsibility of solving problems such as poverty, unemployment, or crime it may be setting itself up for failure. Community media projects based upon social change imperatives are taking on a similar risk.

In summary, civil society cannot be promoted or rolled-out. The history of communications development demonstrates the sensitivity involved in using community-based projects to achieve social change outcomes. Activism risks "NGOization," communities can be made to conform to ways of operating that may not suit their needs, and the type of social change achieved may not match up with expectations. Policies and development programs should not prevent communities from defining and expressing themselves. When we discuss community media only in terms of social outcomes, we are in danger of overlooking what is really going on in the community sphere. This is perhaps something more ordinary, less ambitious than we might like to believe. But that does not mean that it is not worth exploring or resourcing. Furthermore, unless it is seen for what it is, with all its difficulties, problems, perceived inadequacies and surprises, then community media may fail to meet expectations. This will have a direct result on the way in which it is legislated and the resources it is granted. The idea that community media can be something other than development motivated is a much more promising notion. The final two chapters look at that possibility.

Notes

1. Alfonso Gumucio Dagron, *Making Waves: Stories of Participatory Communication for Social Change* (New York: Rockefeller Foundation, 2001), 115.

2. George Yúdice, *The Expediency of Culture* (Durham: Duke University Press, 2003), 9.

3. Although the terms "First World" and "Third World" are problematic, the terms "North" and "South" reinforce geographic notions of exclusion. The latter terms also seem absurd to me, living in Australia with a reasonable standard of living and freedom. Instead, I prefer to use First World and Third World, only to suggest the struggle for empowerment. I agree with Melkote and Steeves, that "a Third World exists within the so-called First World and vice versa." See Srinivas R. Melkote and H. Leslie Steeves, *Communication for Development in the Third World: Theory and Practice for Empowerment*, 2nd ed. (London: Sage, 2001). In fact, this supports my attempt to find correlations between development and neighborhood development policies. Furthermore, as Gumucio points out, the term "developing countries" denies the fact that many Third World countries have been going backwards in terms of economic and social development.

4. Gumucio, *Making Waves*.

5. Jan Servaes, "Introduction: Participatory Communication and Research in Development Settings," in *Participatory Communication for Social Change*, ed. Jan Servaes, Thomas L. Jacobson, and Shirley A. White (Thousand Oaks: Sage, 1996), 16.

6. Gumucio, *Making Waves*, 116.

7. Gumucio, *Making Waves*, 119.

8. Alfonso Gumucio Dagron, "Art of Aerialists: Sustainability of Community Media" (paper presented at the OURMedia III Conference, Barranquilla, May 2003), 16–17.

9. Alfonso Gumucio Dagron, "Call Me Impure: Myths and Paradigms of Participatory Communication" (paper presented at the OURMedia I Conference, Washington, D.C., May 2001), 5.

10. Alan O'Connor, "Mouth of the Wolf: Anthropology and Radio" (paper presented at the OURMedia I Conference, Washington, D.C., May 2001), 5.

11. Yúdice, *The Expediency of Culture*, 15.

12. Charlotte Brunsdon, *The Feminist, the Housewife, and the Soap Opera* (Oxford: Clarendon Press, 2000), 5.

13. O'Connor, "Mouth of the Wolf," 7.

14. Don Slater and Jo Tacchi, *ICT Innovations for Poverty Reduction* (New Dehli: UNESCO, 2004), 4–5.

15. Slater and Tacchi, *ICT Innovations for Poverty Reduction*. The network OUR-Media is an important forum for discussing research methodologies for community media studies. Papers on this topic can be found on their website at www.ourmedianet .org.

16. Arturo Escobar, "Place, Power and Networks in Globalisation and Postdevelopment," in *Redeveloping Communication for Social Change*, ed. Karin Gwinn Wilkins (Lanham, Md.: Rowman & Littlefield, 2000), 165.

17. Bella Mody, "The Contexts of Power and the Power of the Media," in *Redeveloping Communication for Social Change*, ed. Wilkins, 190.

18. Mody, "The Contexts of Power and the Power of the Media," 190.

19. Mody, "The Contexts of Power and the Power of the Media," 191, 194.

20. Elihu Katz and Paul F. Lazarsfeld, *Personal Influence: The Part Played by People in the Flow of Mass Communications* (Glencoe, Ill.: The Free Press, 1955).

21. David Lerner, *The Passing of Traditional Society* (Glencoe, Ill.: The Free Press, 1958).

22. Everett Rogers, *Diffusion of Innovations* (New York: The Free Press, 1962).

23. David Harvey, *The Condition of Postmodernity* (Oxford: Blackwell, 1990), 27.

24. Melkote and Steeves, *Communication for Development in the Third World*.

25. United Nations Department of Social Affairs in Arturo Escobar, *Encountering Development: The Making and Unmaking of the Third World* (Princeton: Princeton University Press, 1995), 4.

26. Jan Servaes, *Communication for Development: One World, Multiple Cultures* (Cresskill, N.J.: Hampton Press, 1999), 46.

27. Karin Gwinn Wilkins, "Accounting for Power in Development Communication," in *Redeveloping Communication for Social Change: Theory, Practice and Power*, ed. Karin Gwinn Wilkins (Lanham, Md.: Rowman & Littlefield, 2000).

28. Wilkins, "Accounting for Power in Development Communication," 207.

29. Escobar, *Encountering Development*, 24.

30. Escobar, *Encountering Development*, 9.

31. Escobar, "Place, Power and Networks in Globalisation and Postdevelopment," 168.

32. Srinivas R. Melkote, "Reinventing Development Support Communication to Account for Power and Control in Development," in *Redeveloping Communication for Social Change*, ed. Wilkins, 39.

33. Harvey, *The Condition of Postmodernity*, 118.

34. Yúdice, *The Expediency of Culture*, 5–6.

35. Yúdice, *The Expediency of Culture*, 95.

36. David L. Blaney and Mustapha Kamal Pasha, "Civil Society and Democracy in the Third World: Ambiguities and Historical Possibilities," *Studies in Comparative International Development* 28, no. 1 (1993): 3.

37. Blaney and Pasha, "Civil Society and Democracy in the Third World," 4–5.

38. Robert B. Horwitz, "Negotiated Liberalisation: Stakeholder Politics and Communication Sector Reform in South Africa" (paper presented at the Rethinking Public Media in a Transnational Era Conference, New York University, January 2001); Heinz Klug, "Extending Democracy in South Africa," in *Associations and Democracy*, ed. Erik Olin Wright, *The Real Utopias Project* (London: Verso, 1995).

39. Gumucio, *Making Waves*, 251.

40. Mabalane Mfundisi in Jo Tacchi, "Transforming the Mediascape in South Africa: The Continuing Struggle to Develop Community Radio," *Media International Australia*, no. 103 (2002): 72.

41. Pheladi Gwangwa in Tacchi, "Transforming the Mediascape in South Africa," 72.

42. Tacchi, "Transforming the Mediascape in South Africa," 72.

43. Mahmood Monshipouri, "State Prerogatives, Civil Society, and Liberalisation: The Paradoxes of the Late Twentieth Century in the Third World," *Ethics and International Affairs* 11 (1997).

44. Anthony Giddens, *Beyond Left and Right* (Cambridge: Polity Press, 1994), 152.

45. Giddens, *Beyond Left and Right*, 158.

46. Giddens, *Beyond Left and Right*, 163.

47. Ollie McGlinchey (Manager of the Ballymun Community Media Co-operative), interviewed by Ellie Rennie, Dublin, August 2, 2002.

48. Shearer cited in Stephen Graham, "Towards Urban Cyberspace Planning: Grounding the Global through Urban Telematic Policy and Planning," in *Technocities*, ed. John Downey and Jim McGuigan (London: Sage, 1999), 17.

49. At www.dublin.ie/background.asp.

50. Community Media Network, "Proposed Amendments to the Broadcasting Bill" (Dublin: Community Media Network, 2000).

51. Margaret Gillan, interviewed by Ellie Rennie, Dublin, August 1, 2002.

52. Jeni Vine, "Community Media Training: A Tool in Combating Social Exclusion" (MA diss., Hallam University, U.K., 2001), 3.

53. Department of Culture, Media and Sport, "Creative Industries Task Force Inquiry into the Internet," 2000, at www.dcms.gov.uk (accessed March 25, 2001).

54. Steve Buckley, interviewed by Ellie Rennie, Sheffield, March 1, 2001.

55. Community Media Association, "Community Media Centres: New Funding for the Digital Generation," 2000, at www.commedia.org.uk (accessed March 7, 2000).

56. Steve Buckley, correspondence, 2002.

57. Peter M. Lewis, *Community Television and Cable in Britain* (London: British Film Institute, 1978), 71.

58. Anthony Giddens, *The Third Way and Its Critics* (Cambridge: Polity Press, 2000), 52.

59. Graham, "Towards Urban Cyberspace Planning," 17.

60. Graham, "Towards Urban Cyberspace Planning," 19.

61. John Keane, *The Media and Democracy* (Cambridge: Polity Press, 1991), 41.

62. Giddens, *The Third Way and Its Critics*, 62.

63. Escobar, "Place, Power and Networks in Globalisation and Postdevelopment"; Robert Huesca, "Conceptual Contributions of New Social Movements to Development Communication Research," *Communication Theory* 11, no. 4 (2001).

64. Huesca, "Conceptual Contributions of New Social Movements to Development Communication Research," 421.

65. Escobar, "Place, Power and Networks in Globalisation and Postdevelopment," 171.

66. Stephen Graham and Simon Marvin, *Splintering Urbanism: Networked Infrastructures, Technological Mobilities and the Urban Condition* (London: Routledge, 2001); Roger S. Slack and Robin A. Williams, "The Dialectics of Place," *New Media & Society* 2, no. 3 (2000).

67. Manuel Castells, *The Rise of the Network Society*, vol. 1 (Malden, Mass.: Blackwell, 1996).

68. Servaes, "Introduction: Participatory Communication and Research in Development Settings," 23.

69. Harvey, *The Condition of Postmodernity*, 204.

70. Gumucio, "Call Me Impure," 11–12.

71. Interview with Gillan.

72. Servaes, "Introduction: Participatory Communication and Research in Development Settings," 23.

CHAPTER SIX

Access Reconfigured

So far, this book has been structured around geographical regions. Now it is time to travelinto the virtual territory of the Internet. The networks of the Internet, it is often asserted, are the pathways to a more lively and powerful civil society: "the characteristics of the Internet to shrink costs, maximize speed, broaden reach, and eradicate distance provide transnational advocacy networks with an effective tool for mobilisation, organisation and expression that can potentially maximise their leverage in the global arena."[1] Even more important, the Internet has demonstrated that there is an alternative way to structure communication; a structure in which access, cooperation, and collaboration are the core organizing principles.

Within its short history (and shorter theorization), the Internet has been a topic of both hope and fear. Many promoted an optimistic communications future. Not only had advances in communications technology made the world smaller, readers were told, they had also made it more accessible and democratic. But now Internet theorists are less sure. Although it is still the case that "the Internet represents a radical departure in terms of the ownership and control of electronic media," there is also a fear that existing interests will "protect themselves from the competitive threat the Internet represents. The old, in other words, is bending the Net to protect itself against the new."[2] The concern now is that if "the future" is here, then it is beginning to look a lot like the recent past. This chapter will discuss the survival of the

---

A version of chapter 6 appeared in *Javnost: The Public* 10 (2003): 1, 49–62.

Internet "commons"—its accessible and open architecture and what this means in terms of how we see community media. The conceptual framework of the commons will be extended to explore the issues involved with community media's transition to a convergent media environment in the final part of this chapter.

Community Media and the Internet

What exactly is community within the vast, decentered, and global terrain of Internet content? Does the Internet's potential for participation at the edges (with no central control) mean that it is the perfect domain for community expression? Its facilitation of communication in real time, the formal and informal congregation of users according to their interests, the end-to-end technical design—all of this makes it the technological platform with a seemingly natural affinity for the spaces, groups, and networks of civil society. Early impressions of the Internet led to expressions of this sentiment. For instance, one user wrote this of his discovery of the virtual community: "Millions of people on every continent also participate in the computer-mediated social groups known as virtual communities, and this population is growing fast. Finding WELL [Whole Earth 'Lectronic Link] was like discovering a cosy little world that had been flourishing without me, hidden within the walls of my house; an entire cast of characters welcomed me to the troupe with great merriment as soon as I found the secret door."[3] However, discussions of community formations on the Net complicate, rather than clarify, attempts to locate community media activity. These early descriptions of the Internet saw it as a realm immune from control, as if the Internet were the perfect public sphere where people could organize into communities without the restrictions of time and space that have encumbered traditional communities.[4] This depiction of the Internet, as well as its swift growth and apparent ability to defy regulation or control, inspired a wave of *cyberdemocracy*—a belief that the technology would increase society's democratic potential. The accessible and participatory nature of the Internet was seen to make it an ideal democratic space wherein people could communicate freely and participate in forums built for collective decision making. One of the first to theorize about the Internet, Nicholas Negroponte, wrote in 1995 that "the access, the mobility, and the ability to effect change are what will make the future so different to the present," and that digital information would be an "empowering" force beyond people's expectations.[5]

The excitement expressed by early Internet participants at the possibilities for a new democratic space is understandable. If they are to be criticized, it is for how easily they made grand sweeping statements out of their experiences of what was essentially a closed community of techno-literate libertarians. The particular voluntarist and utopianist history that has been instilled into discourses of the Internet is just one history. In fact, the Internet as it is known today is the result of collaborations between public and private research institutions, corporations, and publicly minded individuals, as well as organized and informal groups. To look only at the radical elements of the Internet is to deny the complicated and contradictory relationship between commercial and noncommercial relationships involved.[6] The Internet was not the product of uncorrupted "hippy artisanship"[7] but of a combined effort from private industry, government and civil society groups, and individual pioneers. Those that warn of "certain economic, political, and legislative trends that threaten to convert the Internet into yet another commercial medium, stripped of its unique potential for facilitating progressive political debate and transformation"[8] often ignore this history. Much cyberdemocratic discourse also ignores the vast body of literature that warned against technological determinism. Writes Nicholas Garnham: "In spite of the assaults of critical theorists, romantics, and postmodernists and growing popular suspicion, science and technology, and the technologically determined view of progress linked to it, retains high prestige and currency, perhaps particularly in relation to information and communication technology, at both popular and elite level[s]."[9] The task of positioning the Internet within existing political theory is still far from completion.

It is no longer possible to rely upon these cyberdemocratic discourses in attempting to define the role that the Internet will play in the advancement of civil society. Cyberdemocracy has finally become outdated with the recognition that the participatory appearance of the Internet was just one possible path of development. The ability for the Internet to be shaped through market forces or the state's design was, and is, entirely feasible. Discussions of commercialization on the one hand and surveillance and privacy—such as the FBI's Carnivore software—reflected a new sweep of concerns. Law professor Lawrence Lessig's mantra that "Code is Law," which centered on how the Net's architecture could be altered to accommodate regulation, became the new, less optimistic, depiction of the Internet. Conveniently summarizing an entire book in one paragraph, Lessig writes, "Nature doesn't determine cyberspace. Code does. Code is not constant. It changes. It is changing now in a way that will make cyberspace more regulable. It could change in a way that makes cyberspace less regulable. How it changes depends on the code writers. How code writers change it could depend on us."[10] "Code" sent a warning through academic and policy circles that a different, commercialized

Internet might be just around the corner. But even though the early beliefs about the Internet were to be dampened by the likes of Lessig (who has since become a major advocate of the creative commons, discussed below), it can be said that the ethos of free information exchange within early cyberdemocracy claims must have attracted media activists and communities in need of an accessible platform. Although it was falsely deterministic, this promise was in some ways a self-fulfilling prophesy, fueling interest in the Net and expanding its user base. Such interest in the democratic uses of the Net led to some astoundingly effective innovations by groups that were otherwise considered to be without media power. Most famous of these was the experience of the Zapatista movement in Mexico. In 1994, this Indigenous army utilized global information networks to express their demands directly, without having to use state-controlled media channels. The Zapatistas managed to create a wide network of radical media communication that allowed them to communicate and mobilize civil society groups around the world.[11] What the Zapatistas described as a five hundred–year struggle received global attention for the first time, due to the Internet.

In her book on the Internet and civil society, Pippa Norris writes reservedly that it is unreasonable to expect total political transformation from the Internet. However, the "restructured opportunities for information and communication available via digital politics will potentially have positive consequences for civic society, altering the balance of relevant resources and slightly levelling the playing field."[12] Using a sample from the *Yearbook of International Organizations*, she finds that about a quarter of all civil society associations have an online presence (approximately 12,400 groups worldwide). And this is excluding social movement networks or other unregistered types of community groups. The number and diversity of groups on the Net, from the International Potato Center to the Nordic Youth Committee, is a testament to its use as a civil society forum. The Internet is a commons, "a virtual Hyde Park Corner where a plurality of multiple actors can and do find opportunities to network, organise and express their viewpoints."[13] This simple survey of the status of civil society's use of the Internet and of the content level is useful, but it does not tell us much about the implications for civil society, or what it means for community-based media activities.

So what is community media on the Internet? Without the mechanisms of governance—licensing, regulation, incorporation—that clearly define community broadcasting as belonging within the third sector, it is difficult to identify exactly what on the Internet can be considered community media. Communities that utilize the Internet negotiate their own terms and boundaries more often than not. Resources and enthusiasm determine their presence on the Net but their activity is not enshrined by application to a bureaucratic authority. The Internet involves a different idea of access than that discussed thus far.

Access and the Internet Commons

As discussed in chapter 2, access television in many parts of the world, including the United States, is subservient in a system organized around the principles of contemporary liberalism in that it appeals for access to something owned by someone else.[14] Access has been requested in many places at numerous times (in the women's movement, in overcoming racially designated borders), but it is not a unifying political goal in itself. Seeking access is not so much the attempt to institute a fundamentally different regime, but a process of reform that occurs on multiple fronts within a complex system. It is the process of identifying the spaces where power is used to block freedom and seeking to shift it. Access cannot help but sound like a challenge or a demand—it is the opposite of exclusion and alienation, and yet it is also a recognition that these dynamics exist.

But community broadcasting also suggests an alternative regime through the act of demanding a space and using it differently than the general governance of the airwaves. The difficulty of community broadcasting comes not from its ambitions to change wider patterns of ownership and control, but that it is made to exist within overall policy arrangements that are antithetical to its design. The policy question of how to accommodate community broadcasting—how to provide access—has generally presupposed its subservience, or accommodation, within that system. An alternative policy regime is difficult to imagine.

And yet, in a wider sense, a new conception of access is being imagined, if not pursued. What in the past has been a politically ambiguous word (more of a political process and a tool than a system of governance), "access" has come to describe a new type of politics: "Access has become the ticket to advancement and personal fulfilment and as powerful as the democratic vision was to earlier generations. It is a highly charged word, full of political significance."[15] Lessig writes that in the digital age, "the central question becomes not whether governments or the market should control a resource, but whether a resource should be controlled at all,"[16] suggesting that we need to relearn the benefits of protecting resources from private and public control. Some have called it "a new public interest," one that is based on an alternative regime where access is no longer about gaining access to a controlled territory, but where that territory is freely accessible to begin with. Inspired by the rise of the Internet, this policy approach argues that open and accessible communications platforms are the most guaranteed pathway to the development of new ideas—and for the reinvigoration of political life. Although the Internet itself has changed since the debate began, the very fact of its rapid ascendancy as a communications platform has brought a new significance to notions of access and what it makes possible. How does this relate to the old idea of community broadcasting and the public interest it has fought for?

The rise of the Internet has had broad political consequences for all sectors of the media.[17] What this means for community media is nicely summed up by community website developer Gabrielle Kuiper. If there is a future for community media, Kuiper believes, then it will need to be constructed out of DIY materials. In true communitarian style, the technologies used will be the equivalent of mud bricks: "anyone can learn how to make mud bricks, build their own houses and teach other people how to build them."[18] So the technologies of the Internet that will be of most benefit to communities are the ones that are free, accessible, easily available, and hopefully not too complicated to use. Kuiper works with the group Catalyst, which is located in an old ice-cream factory in a suburb of Sydney. Catalyst (a low-cost Internet service provider) assists community groups in achieving an online presence, also providing training and free software based on open source code (which can be distributed free of charge). By pioneering free software, Catalyst constructs technology that can be built upon, adapted, and repurposed by other groups. For community access, this technology is the handmade brick of Kuiper's metaphor. Access here is something that is free to all, where information can be copied without permission and where the community can create its own spaces and technologies.

The technical initiatives of open source and end-to-end design can be credited with having made the Internet the unusually accessible and participatory communications platform that it is. End-to-end design is the result of a system of protocols that allow computers to share data by "packet-switching"— shifting recognizable packets of data by labeling them and routing them to their destination.[19] As a result, there is no reason why a computer should send a packet through the same route twice, avoiding the need for a central machine: "End-to-end says to keep intelligence in a network at the ends, or in the applications, leaving the network itself to be relatively simple."[20] This system means that permission is not required in order to participate in the Internet.[21] And as the source code that implements the protocols is visible, anyone can participate in the construction of new layers of protocols, and so develop new applications or produce new versions of existing ones. In the case of free software (meaning software distributed under the GNU Public License that prevents it from being copyrighted[22]), this is accompanied by a philosophical idea, or ethic, about access to technology and how it can be engineered to encourage participation. As the software cannot become proprietary, it is kept in the public domain as a free, common resource. Furthermore, the technology is collaborative, with a capacity-building potential, and educative in that the code is visible to be analyzed and learned.[23] Richard Stallman, founder of the free software movement, explains that free software has nothing to do with price; "it is about freedom":

- You have the freedom to run the program, for any purpose.
- You have the freedom to modify the program to suit your needs. To make this freedom effective in practice, you must have access to the source code, since making changes in a program without having the source code is exceedingly difficult.
- You have the freedom to redistribute copies, either gratis or for a fee.
- You have the freedom to distribute modified versions of the program, so that the community can benefit from your improvements.[24]

This is a direct challenge and alternative to the way technical and artistic works are usually managed. Proprietary (privately owned/copyrighted) software is not free—in other words, the public is not allowed to use it as they wish. In U.S. law, when you create a work you are automatically assigned the rights to that work. There is a trend around the world to make copyright bigger in scope and duration. This effectively creates monopolies over ideas/technologies that restrict use by others. So in order to make a program free, Stallman had to come up with a legal means of keeping it that way, which he called *copyleft*. Free software comes with the stipulation that even if you make modifications to a piece of software that carries the copyleft license, it must remain open (free) for others to copy. This is an alternative to the dominant way of organizing property:

> Open source is a way of organising production, of making things jointly. The baseline problem is that it is not easy for human beings to work together and certainly not to produce complex integrated systems. One solution is the familiar economy that depends on a blend of exclusive property rights, divisions of labour, reduction of transaction costs, and the management of principle-agent problems. The success of open source demonstrates the importance of a fundamentally different solution, built on top of an unconventional understanding of property rights configured around distribution.[25]

Perhaps the most well-known example of code innovation by civil society entrepreneurs is Linux. Prior to the 1984 telecommunications legislation in the United States, the monopoly telephone company AT&T had been restricted from participating in the computing industry. When researchers Ken Thompson and Dennis Richie at the company's laboratories created an operating system that could be run as a common platform for programs to run on, AT&T found that they were not permitted to sell the innovation. Instead, Thompson and Richie convinced the company to give it away.[26] However, when AT&T was split up in 1984 and permitted to participate in the computing industry, it decided to make Unix proprietary. By this time, "a generation had devoted its professional career to learning and building upon the Unix system."[27] Understandably, they felt betrayed. Stallman responded by developing a free version of Unix, which was later linked to a concurrent project developed by Finnish computer science student Linus Torvalds, creating GNU/Linux (popularly known as just Linux). The intention behind GNU and Linux was to create, or maintain, a software-sharing community. Linux is now the fastest growing operating system in the world, and in May 2002 the four major distributors of Linux decided to join together to create a standardized Linux distribution system. What is most significant about the Linux story is that it is estimated to be the result of the efforts of over one hundred thousand independent and voluntary enthusiasts. By comparison, Windows 2000 had a staff of five hundred working on its development over a period of two to three years. Due to its transparency as open source code, Linux is generally considered to be a far more robust system than Windows.[28] Although it is uncertain whether Linux will ever be able to outdo the Windows market, there is at least one other example where an open system has reached a majority of users: the Apache web server code, developed by volunteers outside of any company structure (in a manner similar to Linux), is currently used by two-thirds of the servers on the World Wide Web.

For Lessig, the Internet is a commons in which no one has "the exclusive right to choose whether the resource is made available to others."[29] It is akin to a public park or beach that anyone can access or a language that anyone can learn without having to seek permission. The commons is a resource that is held "in common," and the Internet, due to its technical architecture, is seen as the ultimate example of this. In another version of the commons philosophy, alternative media researcher Graham Meikle makes a clear distinction between types of interactivity that allow for a degree of choice in content (such as video game interactivity) and those that enable people to "influence and contribute to the content of the exchange."[30] In making tiered distinctions between types of interactivity, Meikle demonstrates how the issue is more complex than simply that of the conventional binary of participation and broadcasting. For Meikle, conversational forms of interactivity are "unfinished." The unfinished nature of this interactivity means that it allows others to add to existing works and so continue the creative process. As a result, it is a type of interactivity that leads to the new, bringing about "possibilities of a future that, in this case, we don't back into; one that may not look like what's gone before."[31] Such "intercreative" designs are therefore a catalyst for innovation. As with Lessig, Meikle sees the possibility of a future rich with new ideas and democratic potential as residing in the existence of open (rather than closed) systems, in the particular end-to-end technology, and in open source software.

Although the commons debate has become popular through discussions of the Internet, the revival of the commons as a political concept is much broader: "The American commons include[s] tangible assets such as public forests and minerals, intangible wealth such as copyrights and patents, critical infrastructure such as the Internet and government research, and cultural resources such as the broadcast airwaves and public spaces."[32] Within all of these spaces there is a fear that too much private control leading to the restriction of access will be against the public interest. The historical example most often referred to is the "enclosure movement" that occurred in England around the mid-eighteenth century. At that time, the British aristocracy pressured Parliament into letting them take possession of large areas of forests and meadows which had previously been available for common use. Enclosure of common land was the culmination of a series of changes that had been taking place since the fifteenth century which resulted in modern capitalism, including methods of production, price movements, and property relations. The peasantry that used the land to begin with were the ultimate losers; they were forced to hand over resources they had shared and relied upon to wealthy landowners.[33]

As this book has shown, notions of collective creativity and organization have persisted throughout the capitalist era through community organization. These notions have also proved vulnerable to government regulations that have turned public resources over to corporate interests, or to corporate interests that have challenged the legal grounds of shared property. In the past, in the area of community media, the public interest has been upheld through measures such as content quotas for locally produced television, subsidies and tax incentives for film and television production, and the reservation of spectrum for public and community broadcasters. All of these policies were intended to retain a "space" for activities considered to stand over and above private, individual gain. But, as discussed in chapter 4, straightforward public interest language and policies of cultural protection have not adequately served the myriad communities that have sought participation in the media via community radio and television. Now, with the advent of new technologies, the complexity that participation brings to the cultural landscape has become difficult to ignore. The revival of the idea of the commons stems from a desire to reframe the importance of shared ideas and resources in relation to changes within economics and communications. It speaks to the dilemma of the public interest by taking into account the emergent cultural forms and characteristics of new media.

The early, pre-broadband Internet, with its open, commons-style architecture, represents a moment in which participation and media access were taken to a new level. It flipped the media access debate from one where private property (ownership and control) is presupposed, to one where openness and collective interest are the starting point. As one commentator points out, this is more than a matter of software: "Even if open source were just a story about software, it would still be an interesting problem for social scientists thinking about large-scale cooperation. And it would still have significant implications for economic growth and development."[34] The issue has profound consequences for how we build, manage, and distribute ideas, and it challenges the political economy of postindustrial capitalism. What does this have to do with community media? Everything. Community media has persistently challenged the way communication is managed in just this way.

The New Public Interest

The argument for the commons is about protecting the spaces where openness exists and creating new spaces for that to occur. Permission is not required for involvement in a commons because the ruling structure allows for participation. The impact of this upon the ideas world of policy has been substantial. The threat of losing that narrowband moment has sparked a new policy push, away from a concern about how to regulate the Internet to concerns for how to make sure that it remains free and accessible.

This has been described as the "new public interest."[35] The public interest is generally used to refer to something highly valued, a collective good that is seen as more important than other legitimate demands and interests.[36] The prevailing understanding of the public interest—the "old," familiar, public interest—has thus negated selfishness and personal gain in favor of a common good that may require compromise from individuals. It is a "matter which might affect the public life of society"—the general welfare—stemming from first principles, or "basic social and political values."[37] Because it is the thinking behind public service broadcasting (and content requirements) in broadcasting policy, the public interest has, through its insistence on what is "best for all," come to represent the collective.

The new public interest is something altogether different. It involves embracing a range of possible publics that may conflict with or contradict each other. There is no claim to what the "good" is, only a striving for it; more players and more ideas means a greater chance that some kind of progress will emerge, either in the form of economic advancement or the advancement of democracy. When partnered with a commons-style notion of access, the communitarian ideal is transformed into a more dispersed, random, and inconclusive idea of the good life. The difference between this idea of media democracy and the more cautious, regulated idea of the (old) public interest in broadcasting policy is clear: policy approaches that seek to uphold the new public interest are important for community broadcasting as they admit the existence of multiple publics—something that has always been a feature of the community media rationale.

Enclosure

"Open" technologies such as the Internet can change—and usually do—in ways that favor corporate interests. The public's ability to participate and innovate may be restricted in the process. The "enclosure" of the Internet is similar to the eighteenth-century enclosure of the English commons. The America Online (AOL) story has become a notorious case in the recent history of enclosure, not least because the company argued both for the Internet commons and against it, changing its tune when it suited its interests. It also demonstrates how regulation can have an impact upon the Internet and the communities that make use of it.

America Online began as an extremely well-marketed online computer network that people joined in order to communicate with others. America Online was not an end-to-end system. Although users could participate in discussions and services on AOL, they did not have the capacity to change the application, or to add to the technology in any way. America Online was a preselected environment, and users would stay within its constructed boundaries. When households began connecting to the Internet, AOL faced fierce competition from this vast territory of accessible, multiple communities. It had no choice but to become an Internet service provider, to offer its customers access to the Internet, but to also provide that access easily through AOL content and guidance from its portal. It was a solution that worked well for AOL, at least for a time.

When broadband cable technology emerged, AOL faced another serious threat to its market dominance. Cable-delivered broadband offered much faster access to the Internet than AOL's narrowband telephone-line access. According to FCC figures, at the end of 2000, 7.1 million American households and businesses subscribed to broadband, with 96 percent of the population living in areas where broadband was available. The majority of U.S. broadband subscribers were using cable networks rather than other competing technologies such as DSL (telephone wire–delivered broadband).[38] As the cable companies were delivering broadband without allowing use of their "pipes" to ISPs other than their selected affiliates, AOL could not participate in this growing market. America Online joined the growing number of lobbyists—commercial interests and public interest advocates—who were campaigning for open access to the cable companies' broadband technology.

America Online's lobbying efforts suddenly changed, however, with the opportunity for a merger with Time Warner, a company owning a large percentage of cable infrastructure in the United States. America Online now argued that the public interest would best be served by the merger as it would enable AOL to achieve more efficient cable broadband services for consumers. After intense lobbying efforts from both sides, the Federal Trade Commission (FTC) and the FCC eventually ruled that the merger could go ahead, but on the condition that access to cable infrastructure for other ISPs was increased over a period of five years. The primary concern of those opposed to the AOL-TW merger was that those who controlled the physical layer—the cables—could restrict the potential for innovation by implementing closed networks. Furthermore, at the code and content layers the company could limit people's ability to leave its confines through the implementation of walled-garden business strategies. Such strategies include the privileging of one provider over another; controlling the first screen a user encounters; controlling the frame around an image; monitoring and controlling the speed, amount, and kind of data a user sends; and providing content that discourages users from traveling outside its confines, or even keeps them from knowing about other options. All of these strategies indicate that new media can be built to behave in a way that prohibits participation and self-expression. We can identify community media on the Internet as it retains the principle of access and participation, actively constructing "mud brick" technologies and building free spaces.

The Limits of the Commons

Perhaps not surprisingly, commons advocates have met with some serious resistance from powerful private industry bastions (such as the recording industry in the United States). The commons agenda has been depicted as communist, anarchist, and anti-American as it challenges the ability of free market players to dominate. But this is far from the truth. Those who support the commons do not believe that commercial enterprise should be banned from the Internet. If anything, they endorse competition over anticompetitive practices that seek to limit how ideas and technologies are used. By keeping ideas out of the public domain, copyright stifles the extent to which information can be repurposed and shared. But commons supporters argue that some degree of reward for enterprise is needed to encourage innovation and development. Some believe that copyright is necessary as it allows creators to reap rewards, but that copyright should be curtailed so that its life span and application are more reasonable.[39] In this way, the commons is a much bigger issue than community media, which is based on altruistic values and nonprofit enterprise. Community activity is but one part of a wider innovation system, but it is a necessary part. Amateur activity, as well as the activity of groups such as Catalyst (based upon stimulating greater social good), provide spaces from which new ideas can emerge.[40] Economic outcomes may flow from some of this activity. The commons argument requires that we look more closely at the relationship of community to the market and to recognize that they are interconnected.

There is another, more fundamental, way in which the commons is far from radical. In essence, the commons is a well-established construct within property law. Property, in legal terms, does not refer to an object (for instance, a piece of land), but to a system of governance that determines who can claim what as their entitlement (I own that land because there is a system in place that permits me to make a claim to it under certain circumstances). When the commons is understood as a system of governance it loses its radical overtones. In a commons arrangement, rights do exist, both generally and between people using the land. Often, that entitlement to use the land is expressed through customs of use, rather than explicitly, but the fact remains that a commons is a system—a regime of rights. The complete absence of property rights is usually described in law as "open access"—meaning that anyone can use a resource, even it will infringe on the rights of others to use it or destroy the resource all together. In a commons, the resource is shared according to established use and customs. Therefore, the commons need not be seen as a radically new concept or one that is free from rule. In fact, describing the Internet as a commons cancels out the earlier cyberdemocracy arguments that idealized its lack of governance. The commons argument places the Internet firmly within a framework of rights and social guarantees, long established in Western democracies, using property arrangements to achieve that.

The threat to the corporate world is not that the Internet commons seeks to eliminate property and ownership, but that it provides a basis for a revision of how the system of property is managed. It asserts that society has changed and therefore the fundamentals of economic exchange and law must follow suit. The commons is a useful construct for understanding and implementing community media. It is a means to achieve access to a resource with a system of management that benefits the community rather than carves up the resource into allotments for private gain. And it allows for experimentation, sharing, and collaboration without the hindrance of restrictive, profit-motivated rules and technologies. Conceptually, it asks us to see community media as a legitimate system that can be used to stimulate innovation. It defines community media positively, for what it can achieve, rather than negatively, by what it opposes.

Will the commons play a part in future communications policy? There is still a long way to go in figuring out how to design policy and laws that create a communications commons. And there are other unresolved issues. As I have outlined elsewhere, the innovation commons is essentially a utilitarian concept, meaning that it is intended to provide the best possible outcome for the most number of people.[41] Utilitarianism does not make claim to a right and wrong way of doing things, but says that circumstances should determine decision making to some degree. The argument for an innovation commons is utilitarian because it asserts that the greatest good will come out of that particular arrangement, and that law must adapt to suit technological change. This is fundamentally opposed to the Anglo-American tradition that sees property rights as "natural" and therefore guaranteed against meddling by the state on the basis of social convention. This tradition claims that property rights are derived from our natural right to derive sustenance and to reap the reward of our labor. It is considered to be a "more substantial foundation for intellectual property rights,"[42] which guarantee that the inventions of our personality and the products of our labor are not taken away from us.

In this way, utilitarian arguments such as the innovation commons have proved to be vulnerable to a prevailing notion of property that relies upon unassailable natural rights and the guarantee that the owner, at least, will benefit from his or her labor regardless of changing social structures. Critic Richard Spinello, for instance, argues that although the innovation commons is good for society, the common good is still best protected by the right to property as we cannot know the end result of technological innovation. Natural rights (private property rather than the commons) provide a surer and more stable path to a well-functioning society.[43] The commons fails on the same charge as community: it is an imprecise entity with unknowable outcomes. For the commons to become a reality, rigorous research into creative/ cultural innovation systems needs to be undertaken—either that, or a significant leap of faith will be required.

However, market-driven arguments can also be used against commons policies. Where utilitarian arguments are used to promote the commons, nations with fragile markets may deem that they are better off protecting monopoly or oligopoly corporate interests.[44] Even if the commons arrangement may suit grassroots movements and small enterprise, governments are likely to favor retaining old structures for the sake of the national economy. The commons has proved to be a powerful concept in the rethinking of communications policy, but unless its outcomes can be measured and viable pathways implemented, it may never have a substantial impact on the way that the media is regulated.

Community-based media still fits better with commons theory than notions of the public interest being met only through monopoly or oligopoly public service broadcasters. It presents us with a new way of thinking about community media that resolves many of the issues addressed in previous chapters, such as freedom of speech, access, the value of amateur participation, and innovation at the margins.

From Old to New Media

There is a common assumption that broadcast media is, and has always been, a "closed" network. Meikle writes, "Early Net technologies—email, bulletin boards, newsgroups—produced so much optimism and excitement at least partly because they were seen to enable participation on a scale, and to a degree, not possible with established media. Any of us could, in theory, take part. An interactive technology was one in which we could get to them as easily as they could get to us."[45] But hasn't community broadcasting always been a media platform in which anyone can take part? In the commons of community broadcasting, participation and broadcasting go together. It is an open system that everyone can participate in as long as their use of that resource complies with the established norms. Although not end-to-end— apparently the best platform for the stimulation of innovation—community broadcasting's access mandate brings it close to this principle, despite being a broadcast media. Participation, framed in contrast to the mass media, has always been used as a justification for community media, but this has been overlooked in the commons argument. Community media proves that innovation arising out of open networks is not restricted to the Internet, but possible on any platform where a commons can be established.

Catalyst

In the late 1990s, Gabrielle Kuiper and community television pioneer Matthew Arnison began working on an automated calendar website where groups could post their events onto the Internet without people in a central location having to key in the entry. The site—known as Active (www.active.org.au)—was extended to include a space for community news and opinions, which could also be easily posted. Active became a forum for community news and debate, listing not only events but descriptions, explanations, and journalistic information focused upon Sydney's activist community.

Active had a global impact through its role in the development of the Indymedia phenomenon. Prior to the anticorporate/globalization rally held during the World Trade Organization meeting in 1999, Indymedia's main function was to provide a physical space for community-based media in the United States. Active had been launched in Sydney in January of that year. When Active webmasters heard about the upcoming protests, they decided to attempt a web broadcast of the event. A site was developed at Catalyst that enabled the uploading of images and video onto the site. Arnison, in the United States at the time, met with the Seattle Indymedia Center and suggested that the Active source code be used by the Seattle center for its coverage of the event. Returning to Sydney, Arnison worked throughout the night during the protests to keep the site going "while tear gas was floating in to the Indymedia office in Seattle."[a] The infamous Seattle protests attracted the world's attention, and on the weekend of June 18 the site reached one million hits. Indymedia became possibly the most notorious activist site on the web, retaining its structure as an open forum for news, opinion, and events through the automated posting system. Within six months of the Seattle protests, over thirty Indymedia sites were established in cities throughout the United States and around the world. There are now over seventy in existence, spawned from the original code and adapted to fit local languages and aesthetics.

Sydney Indymedia has, in the past, had a presence on 2SER community radio, where it has imitated its own web format by encouraging listeners to send in their own short audio documentaries. The entire program was then digitized and uploaded back onto Sydney Indymedia. According to Kuiper, the radio program "was a recognition that you get your message across more effectively if you put it out across different media," attracting wider audiences according to their media usage.[b] Activities of video groups such as Actively Radical prompted Catalyst to invest in video capturing equipment in order to incorporate video documentaries onto the site. Community media is becoming a multi-platform phenomenon.

---

[a] Gabrielle Kuiper, interviewed by Ellie Rennie, Sydney, May 17, 2002.
[b] Interview with Kuiper.

Community media has a tendency to occupy available space where it can be found. Microradio in the United States, pirate stations in Europe, and the first Indigenous community television stations in Australia have all preceded rather than followed policy. In Italy, low-power stations have sprung up utilizing free spectrum to broadcast television content as an alternative to stations owned by Berlusconi. In the United Kingdom, a test was conducted at the June 2002 Community Media Summer Festival that saw community television distributed to the local neighborhood by wireless broadband, using spectrum that is freely available for use within a one hundred–meter radius. These are just some examples of a history of community media initiatives that have "routed around" legislative hurdles in order to be seen or heard. More famously, in 1999, when the independent radio station B92 in Belgrade was suspended under the Milosevic regime, the station persisted by video streaming its programming on the Net. In the process it gained the attention and support of the international community and was eventually distributed for rebroadcast in Serbia via satellite.[46] The group Catalyst, discussed above, was formed by community television campaigners who were dissatisfied with the activities of the community television station in Sydney at the time. Indymedia was developed as a means to coordinate large groups of activists during the Seattle demonstrations and to allow independent reporting of events by the activist community. In all examples, new media territory was crossed as a tactic to survive or make do—in order to persist. Community media is a multi-platform phenomenon that often finds innovative ways to reach its audience.

In many cases, the groups that utilize the Internet emerge from or seek partnerships with broadcasters. Kuiper, comparing the content of Sydney Indymedia with the Indymedia sites of other cities, said that it would have been a "much more effective and useful site if it had made contact with existing community media when it started off."[47] By restricting discussions of innovation to the Internet, the processes of information sharing, collaboration, and flexibility to move between media platforms are not taken into account.

Therefore, although community media has been forced into radio and television structures designed to meet other interests, it has also been a challenge to that system—an innovation commons that has gone largely unrecognized. It has been seen as amateur in comparison to the public interest represented by public service broadcasting and it has been seen as a waste of resources by those who would prefer to use the spectrum (or cable capacity) for commercial gain. These new arguments for participation in the media and innovation at the margins do have a history, and it is a history in which community media has played a significant part.

Community and the Network Society

Depending on how you look at it, community media is becoming either more relevant or less relevant as culture and technology change. On the one hand, community access and participation have a higher status. As new media theorist Jeremy Rifkin writes:

> Inclusion and access, rather than autonomy and ownership, become the more important tests of one's personal freedom. Freedom is a measure of one's opportunities to enter into relationships, forge alliances, and engage in networks of shared interest. Being connected makes one free. Autonomy, once regarded as tautological with personal freedom, becomes its opposite. To be autonomous in a network world is to be isolated and disconnected. The right not to be excluded, the right of access, on the other hand becomes the baseline for measuring personal freedom. Government's role in the new scheme of things is to secure every individual's right of access to the many networks—both in geographic space and cyberspace—through which human beings communicate, interact, conduct business, and constitute change.[48]

Although the way in which we view community media may change as technologies become more participative, the notion of community itself becomes more relevant. In fact, the new economy has coopted community within its project of network relations. Community is both a means to the development of fruitful relationships that may extend and enhance networks and information flows, and that which contributes value to this new social configuration. Manuel Castells, one of the first to consider the Internet's social impact, writes that this is a politics where "a structural logic dominated by largely uncontrollable flows within and between networks creates the conditions for the unpredictability of the consequences of human action through the reflection of such action in an unseen, unchartered space of flows."[49] Community furnishes this otherwise bleak social vision with some kind of meaning, albeit a meaning that is made up of a myriad of different concerns, efforts, and tastes. Reaction against the destructuration of society takes the form of "affirming basic cultural, historical, or biological identities (real or reconstructed) as fundamental principles of existence. The society of flows is a society of primary ascription communities, in which affirmation of the being (ethnic identity, territorial identity, national identity) becomes the organizing principle for a system that in itself becomes a system for itself."[50] In other words, the forces of globalization need not be seen as random and alienating—not if we take into account the way in which communities continue to operate through "uncharted spaces."

Where Castells's work is descriptive, the role of community within the "society of flows" is, for others, something that must be prescribed and promoted. Rifkin speaks of two types of access—community and commercial. He wants us to ask what type of access it is that we seek to institute, asserting that it is the networks of community that are more valuable, and more lasting—they are "the wellspring of social trust" and a means to self-fulfillment. Community plays a vital role in the maintenance of networks and social relations within the network society, but, more importantly, it makes it worthwhile. However, as people's participation in the media increases, community media *as a concept* may change or fade. Matthew Arnison discusses the blurred lines between activism and creative freedom: "I like to think the free software movement is a very strong activist movement, but somewhat hidden. This is because the people involved don't really think they are activists, and other activists don't realise what is going on. . . . For once they can write software to do what they want, rather than what they can get paid to write, and they get to join a huge family of other people sharing the process of writing software."[51] Arnison defines participation as activism, even though the people involved are not aware of it as such. In the free software movement, media production is not identified as media activism by many who create it, as the idea of resistance is less obvious when the technology is open to begin with. The words "community media" could be substituted for that of "activism" and the point would still be the same—that participation may become so commonplace that people will not be aware that they are changing the traditional structures of the media. How will community media be defined when participation is as much a characteristic of the mainstream media? The line between community media and other media may cease to exist.

But perhaps that is too optimistic a vision. So far I have discussed access as having changed from "access to" towards "access as openness." The free software movement only emerged when enclosure became an issue (which is why Meikle and Lessig seek to make people aware that free software is an important democratic movement). In some respects, defining community media on the Internet has been a matter of self-definition—an identity group in itself rather than an institutionally designated sector—as the boundaries between types of participation are not enshrined or delineated by the governmental categorizing that occurs in the field of broadcast regulation. As the Internet is increasingly threatened by the enclosure strategies of private companies seeking to control the technology, the nature of community involvement and activism may become more clearly defined, particularly if commons-style spaces are created in order to ensure that access remains. In the realm of television and radio, community media requires adequate definitions in order to make it distinct from commercial and government broadcasters and to uphold its status as a legitimate sphere of media activity. As long as the media is not an open resource, community media is an important category by which to ensure that participation exists.

The central argument of public interest advocates in the commons debate, including the AOL merger, was that the government should be regulating to restrict anticompetitive practices likely to stifle innovation through the provision of access; not simply the carriage of commercial enterprises who can compete at auction for access, but free access for anyone—a true commons. The new public interest is not far removed from that which has been called upon in the past to support the establishment of community media. Community media has relied upon diversity, difference, access, and participation as the primary justifications for its existence. Such values have never fully conformed to a public interest that has sought top-down solutions in defence of the majority good. As John Keane writes, a "theory of civil society and public life that clings dogmatically to the vision of a unified public sphere in which 'public opinion' and 'the public interest' are defined is a chimera." For the sake of democracy, "it ought to be jettisoned."[52] Philosophically, the new public interest is not incompatible with community broadcasting. It is hardly new at all.

Notes

1. Pippa Norris, *Digital Divide: Civic Engagement, Information Poverty and the Internet Worldwide* (Cambridge: Cambridge University Press, 2001), 172.

2. Trevor Barr, *newmedia.com.au* (Sydney: Allen & Unwin, 2000), 123; Lawrence Lessig, *The Future of Ideas: The Fate of the Commons in a Connected World* (New York: Random House, 2001), 16.

3. Howard Rheingold, *The Virtual Community: Homesteading on the Electronic Frontier* (New York: HarperPerrenial, 1994), 1–2.

4. Mark Poster, "Cyberdemocracy: Internet and the Public Sphere," in *Internet Culture*, ed. David Porter (New York: Routledge, 1997).

5. Nicholas Negroponte, *Being Digital* (Rydalmere: Hodder & Staughton, 1995), 231.

6. Gerard Goggin, "Pay Per Browse? The Web's Commercial Futures," in *web.studies*, ed. David Gauntlett (London: Arnold, 2000).

7. Richard Barbrook and Andy Cameron, "The Californian Ideology," *Muse*, no. 3, 1995.

8. Tamara Villareal Ford and Geneve Gil, "Radical Internet Use," in *Radical Media: Rebellious Communication and Social Movements*, ed. John Downing (Thousand Oaks: Sage, 2001), 201.

9. Nicholas Garnham, *Emancipation, the Media, and Modernity: Arguments about the Media and Social Theory* (Oxford: Oxford University Press, 2000), 66.

10. Lawrence Lessig, *Code and Other Laws of Cyberspace* (New York: Basic, 1999), 109.

11. Ford and Gil, "Radical Internet Use," 219. See also Manuel Castells, *The Rise of the Network Society*, vol. 1 (Malden, Mass.: Blackwell, 1996).

12. Norris, *Digital Divide*, 23.

13. Norris, *Digital Divide*, 190.

14. Thomas Streeter, *Selling the Air: A Critique of the Policy of Commercial Broadcasting in the United States* (Chicago: University of Chicago Press, 1996).

15. Jeremy Rifkin, *The Age of Access* (London: Penguin, 2000), 15.

16. Lessig, *The Future of Ideas*, 14.

17. Terry Flew, *New Media: An Introduction* (Melbourne: Oxford University Press, 2002).

18. Gabrielle Kuiper, interviewed by Ellie Rennie, Sydney, May 17, 2002.

19. Michael Froomkin, "The Internet as a Source of Regulatory Arbitrage," in *Borders in Cyberspace: Information Policy and the Global Information Infrastructure*, ed. Brian Kahin and Charles Nesson (Cambridge, Mass.: MIT Press, 1997).

20. Lessig, *The Future of Ideas*, 34.

21. Barry M. Leiner et al., "A Brief History of the Internet, ISOC," 2000, www.isoc.org/internet/history/brief.shtml (accessed October 2, 2001).

22. GNU is a recursive acronym for "GNU's Not Unix." It is pronounced "guh-NEW."

23. Interview with Kuiper.

24. Richard Stallman, "The GNU Project," in *Free Software Free Society: Selected Essays of Richard M. Stallman*, ed. Joshua Gay (Boston: Free Software Foundation, 2002), 18.

25. Steven Weber, *The Success of Open Source* (Cambridge: Cambridge University Press, 2004), 225.

26. Lessig, *The Future of Ideas*.

27. Lessig, *The Future of Ideas*, 53.

28. James Gifford, interviewed by Ellie Rennie, Sydney, May 17, 2002.

29. Lessig, *The Future of Ideas*, 20.

30. Graham Meikle, *Future Active: Media Activism and the Internet* (Sydney: Pluto Press, 2002), 31.

31. Meikle, *Future Active*, 33.

32. David Bollier, *Public Assets, Private Profits: Reclaiming the American Commons in an Age of Market Enclosure* (Washington, D.C.: New America Foundation, 2001), 2.

33. J. M. Neeson, *Commoners: Common Right, Enclosure and Social Change in England, 1700–1820* (Cambridge: Cambridge University Press, 1993).

34. Weber, *The Success of Open Source*, 17.

35. Patricia Aufderheide, "Competition and Commons: The Public Interest, in and after the AOLTW Merger," 2002, at arxiv.org/html/cs.CY/0109048 (accessed April 22, 2002).

36. Anthony Smith, "The Public Interest," *Intermedia* 17, no. 2 (1989): 11.

37. Denis McQuail, "Mass Media and the Public Interest," in *Mass Media and Society*, ed. James Curran and Michael Gurevitch (London: Arnold, 1996), 69.

38. Aufderheide, "Competition and Commons."

39. See Lessig's Creative Commons license at www.creativecommons.org.

40. Ellie Rennie, "Creative World," in *Creative Industries*, ed. John Hartley (Malden, Mass.: Blackwell, 2005).

41. Ellie Rennie and Sherman Young, "Park Life: The Commons and Communications Policy," in *Virtual Nation: The Internet in Australia*, ed. Gerard Goggin (Sydney: UNSW Press, 2004).

42. Richard A. Spinello, "The Future of Intellectual Property," *Ethics and Information Technology* 5 (2003).

43. Spinello, "The Future of Intellectual Property."

44. Rennie and Young, "Park Life."

45. Meikle, *Future Active*, 29.

46. Meikle, *Future Active*.

47. Interview with Kuiper.

48. Rifkin, *The Age of Access*, 240.

49. Manuel Castells, "Flows, Networks, and Identities: A Critical Theory of the Informational Society," in *Critical Education in the New Information Age*, ed. Manuel Castells (Lanham, Md.: Rowman & Littlefield, 1999), 59.

50. Manuel Castells, "Materials for an Exploratory Theory of the Network Society," in *American Cultural Studies: A Reader*, ed. John Hartley and R. E. Pearson (Oxford: Oxford University Press, 2000), 243.

51. Matthew Arnison in Meikle, *Future Active*, 107.

52. John Keane, *Civil Society: Old Images, New Visions* (Cambridge: Polity Press, 1998), 189.

CHAPTER SEVEN

Self-Representation

In his alternative history of radio in America, Jesse Walker introduces us to two former microradio broadcasters, Joe and Zeal. Neither of them wanted to be democratic in the way they ran their station. They are only half kidding when they say they were dictators (not even benign dictators), and stipulate that the king should be the poorest man in the town. Nonetheless, Kind Radio in San Marcos, Texas, was committed to local politics, "not the local patriotism of mindless boosterism and downtown cliques, but the kind that believes in digging up dirt, relieving human misery, and celebrating the lives that the locals really had."[1] At one point, before the FCC closed it down for operating without a license, some programmers at the station decided that some form of organization might be a good idea. "So Joe and Zeal started calling programmers' meetings, just like the dissidents wanted, and then they turned them into parties. Pretty soon, most of the rebels were having too much fun to worry about fighting among themselves or establishing a formal sort of government."[2]

This book has endeavored to show that, even at its least organized, community media is democratic media. Community media has tested the principles of access and free speech through everyday endeavor. It also allows us to represent ourselves to others, on our own terms. Although that may sound fairly straightforward, it does have profound consequences for democracy. These final few pages are intended to bring together the themes of this book—the place of community in contemporary politics, the role of civil society organizations, social change, and access to communication resources—to see why self-representation is so important.

As a movement, community media has fought for the public's right to controlled communication resources (spectrum, cable, code) and continues to do so. It is this aspect of community media that many concentrate on when considering its democratic potential—it allows for participation in the distribution of media information, ensuring greater diversity of viewpoints and encouraging free speech. The struggle for access has meant that advocacy tends to dominate discourse and, as a result, descriptions of community media often fail to take into account its complexity and contradictions. We know that community media is democratic in that it promotes free speech, but often its outcomes are small-scale and transient. Our theories of community media need to begin from its reality; a reality that involves ordinary folk producing all kinds of stuff, some of which may be hard to even recognize as democratic. Community media shows us just how complex and unpredictable media democracy can be. It is a democracy where self-appointed kings such as Joe and Zeal can still reign.

Chapter 1 described the theoretical history of community media studies, arriving at a contemporary understanding that avoids positing community-based media in opposition to the mainstream media. The media as a whole is a more complex field than some early arguments for community media allowed. The Indymedia slogan "don't hate the media, make the media" better describes the attitude of many who produce. They want to be part of the media and they understand intimately the power of communication, both for the self and for the group. It is not about having a gripe with the establishment necessarily, but it is about asserting difference—either from other aspects of the media or just in general. Community media is not just do-it-yourself (DIY), it is also do-it-your-own-way (DIYOW?). I suspect that even if the mainstream media behaved as the perfect model of ethical reporting and artistic endeavor, community media would still exist.

In places where the media is controlled by repressive nondemocratic governments, it is understandable that community media has become, or seeks to become, a counterforce. It demonstrates that speaking out is a right and when the right is taken away, people will go to great lengths to get it back. When so much information and culture is administered via communication technologies, denying access to them seems a hostile move. In some situations it is. Community media's role in peace building and overcoming negative assumptions to do with gender and race has been well documented. But is there a common factor between these projects and those that are more random and less social-change focused? Does there need to be?

Community media belongs within the sphere of civil society in that it is constructed by groups that share an interest or something to say. Its creators range from hobbyists to activists and include everything in between. Some of it is highly organized while other parts eschew any kind of formal structure. When people make community media it is often for the love of it. The only generalization that can be made is that it gives voice to those who might otherwise be denied a chance to participate. But out of that opportunity some immensely useful, far-reaching, and innovative things emerge. Women's radio programming in Nepal, for example, has helped to change patriarchal practices by giving women a public forum to express themselves. Zoom Black Magic Radio, which (while it operated) was the only black-oriented station in Fresno, California, broadcast grassroots music, rights talk, and promotions for black businesses.[3]

What these examples show us is that community media deals in representation. Not necessarily representation of political issues or political leaders (as has traditionally been the domain of the mainstream media)—but representation of the individual and community. Every instance of community media—whether alternative, social-change focused, or minimalist in its approach to free speech—involves self-expression. Representing oneself, ideas, creativity, or politics is an act of participation. It shows us what is occurring in civil society, through personal stories, local concerns, or just through straightforward, unhindered commentary. And that has consequences for democracy.

Self-expression

Community radio and television may not be very different than what they were two decades ago, but the context in which they work has altered drastically. New technologies have enabled widespread participation in the media. With it has come a greater acceptance of the fact that people can, and do, produce media outside of professional contexts. For instance, 44 percent of U.S. Internet users created content in 2003, even though the majority only had dial-up access rather than broadband.[4] Although this is not necessarily "community media" activity—much of the activity may be for commercial purposes or social interaction—it shows that people are learning to participate in the media to a point where it has become normalized. Fansites and blogs demonstrate that some of these uses blur the boundaries between private and public communication, taking journalistic forms, personalizing them, and asking others to participate. This has been described as the era of "read-write" media, where people don't just consume media, they also create it. It appears that the early community media advocates were right about some things at least: that media creation does not have to be for the talented few and that participation in media production increases as equipment gets cheaper and easier to use. It means that people are expressing their fears, desires, thoughts, and opinions to each other and forming media networks to pursue interests that they share. Representing oneself to the world via media technologies has become common practice.

Self-representation is only beginning to be theorized in community media studies. Zines, for instance, are being studied as a highly personalized media form that is introducing new production practices into the mediasphere, thereby acting as an alternative to the dominant structures of commerce and governance.[5] In chapter 4, self-expression was discussed in relation to the politics of development; a domain where broader social causes have come to define community media but where attention is now being directed at the act of media creation itself. For Rodriguez, "citizens' media" can bring about transformation in the way the individual and community understand their power: "[A]lternative media spin transformative processes that alter people's sense of self, their subjective positionings, and therefore their access to power."[6]

Rodriguez's theory of citizens' media is the most in-depth attempt to understand self-representation. It is an attempt to get beyond the outdated theoretical frameworks that brought community media to the attention of media studies academics in the 1970s and 1980s and to bring community media into contemporary thinking about power, citizenship, and media use. Contemporary theories of citizenship attempt to transcend the division between liberalism and communitarianism (discussed in chapter 1) by focusing on the ties and commitments of citizens themselves. Kymlicka writes: "Citizenship is intimately linked to liberal ideas of individual and rights and entitlements on the one hand, and to communitarian ideas of membership in and attachment to a particular community on the other. Thus it provides a concept that can mediate the debate between liberals and communitarians."[7] Citizenship theory tries to account for our allegiances and differences in order that politics may be fairer on the individual. Just as community media studies emerged in a climate of increasingly powerful transnational media, so the current revision of its role and use—not just by Rodriguez but others discussed in chapter 1— is inextricably tied to the anxieties and hopes of our time.

Radical democracy and citizens' media are "quotidian politics"—a politics of the everyday, a recognition that occurrences in daily life shape citizens and are implicated in power relations. Cultural codes that circulate through the media, arts, fashions, and social interaction demonstrate the myriad ways that we can choose to express ourselves and the multiple identities that make up contemporary life. Citizens choose to interact with the world through informal networks. They decide which issues they want to engage in and use improvised and surprising tactics to make their point.[8] Nikolas Rose writes that we are now experiencing a proliferation of "forms of politics and types of contestation which cannot be calibrated in terms of the dichotomies of traditional political thought."[9] The activities of civil society have expanded, or shifted, to become the foreground upon which many of our issues, conflicts, and cultural activities are played out.

There is a relationship between our social, political, and cultural landscapes and our ability to engage with media at different levels and through multiple means. Whether there has been a recent proliferation of cultural and political groups, tastes, identities, and issues is debatable. It does appear to be the case, however, that we are witnessing or recognizing this activity more acutely and with greater interest than in the past. It is now a recurrent theme of political thought that issues of national sovereignty and identity are being challenged by "the globalisation of flows of money, communications, products, persons, ideas and cultures, and the localisation of local economic regions, world cities, regional identities, lifestyle sectors and so forth."[10] This recognition, if not the activity itself, is tied directly to our information systems, our access to media, and our increasing ability to participate in and distribute ideas.

Community media theory is now coming into line with this intellectual awareness. It has moved beyond binary notions of power (the people vs. corporations, or the people vs. government media), demonstrating that community media works in small ways and on multiple fronts to alter the individual's and the community's relationship with the world. This empowerment is achieved by "strengthening the symbolic dimension of everyday life: that is, opening social spaces for dialogue and participation, breaking individual's isolation, encouraging creativity and imagination, redefining shared social languages and symbols, and demystifying mass media."[11] It alters historical power configurations in the process.

This is a useful way of thinking about community media, but how do these outcomes flow through to change at the institutional level? It describes a constant renegotiation of democratic forces and an ephemeral "swelling of the democratic,"[12] but what pathways does this present us with? Radical democracy and citizens' media theory ask us to view democracy through the lens of the citizen's identity, responsibility, demands, and roles, and to recognize the complex power relationships that this entails. But in the end, theories of citizenship are still concerned with the same old questions of democracy and justice.[13] This book has attempted to bring the contribution of citizens' media to bear upon communication policies and political trends in order to sum up where community media sits in the current media environment and where it might go next. In the end (and we are at the end of the book), the question of media and democracy must come back to the straightforward problem of whether democracy is actually working in terms of adequate governance and how power can be managed for the people. Can community media make democratic societies work better? Can it make undemocratic ones more democratic?

Without self-representation, a part of our political reality is going unrecognized. There is a gap, a political failure: people are unable to put their ideas into the mix of concerns that democratic nation-states were invented to resolve. Community media, in the emerging communications landscape, has an important role to play.

Democracy, Governance, and the Media

Democracy itself is not a "thing" that we can ever reach or even directly point to. It is a concept, a goal, an ideal. We construct political institutions so that they will come to resemble something like democracy and, in doing so, assist us to achieve democracy's central principle: that power will be exercised in the interests of the people. But we have not been able to realize that goal and we have not figured out how to build institutions that get us particularly close to it. Representative democracy, whereby elected representatives make decisions on behalf of the citizenry, is as much as we have been able to manage. It involves voting, elections, universal suffrage, the right to stand for office or to form political associations, freedom of religion, and, consequently, pluralism.

Within this arrangement, the media has had to take a central role. Whether that scenario is adequate has been highly disputed. Some believe democracy would not exist at all without the contemporary media as it promotes freedom, civic virtue, and individual rights. For others, the media itself is undemocratic—controlled by a small number of elites who determine what information is available and how it is disseminated. Regardless of which side you take, you cannot deny that the media is the primary means through which people understand the nation and the related configurations that tie us together (culture, business, community); an understanding that informs our democratic choices. The question of democracy has therefore become a question of how we stay informed and whether we see ourselves as participants, as active citizens.

When representation is discussed in relation to the media, it usually involves the question of whether we are adequately represented by our leaders.

This investigation has been driven by a growing phenomenon of political apathy across all Western democracies. Although democracy seems to be an unstoppable force, with an astounding number of countries transferring from communism or authoritarianism since the 1990s, this rise has coincided with an ailing interest in democratic processes within countries where it is long established. Politicians are held somewhat responsible for this; their combative style in Parliament, old-fashioned institutions, and aloof personalities fail to muster much confidence from the public. The media are also seen as a central culprit; they are increasingly hostile in their reporting on politicians and their actions, promoting negativity towards political processes which then discourages citizens from voting or campaigning. People's level of participation has changed across the board. Importantly, feelings of political efficacy are at an all-time low ("efficacy" meaning our sense of whether we have any say in what happens politically in the world). We know this because political scientists have been asking people whether they feel they can make a difference for a number of decades. In the mid-1960s, around 30 percent of people in North America and Europe agreed with the statement "Whatever I say, whatever I do, I can't influence the government." Over the last ten years, between 70 and 80 percent of people responded that they agree.[14] We feel as though we have little say in the way the world is run.

Efficacy has been one of the central themes of the civil society debate. The pro–civil society commentators argue that participation in civil society can increase people's sense of efficacy and thereby lead to democratic renewal. There are three problems with this argument. Firstly, as discussed earlier, that argument has been difficult to prove. What is to say that participation in a civil society activity such as microradio—let's take Joe and Zeal as an example—will lead these two citizens to have greater faith in American political candidates or the systems of governance that determine local, national, or global outcomes? The connection is hard to accept. Joe and Zeal still "hate big government" despite the fact that they ran a radio station that takes credit for the defeat of one local candidate.[15]

Secondly, seeing civil society as the solution to political apathy puts the responsibility back on the citizen and the community. This has been one of the major critiques of third way politics. Empowerment and social inclusion may sound like admirable ideals, but they turn attention away from the responsibility that government has to its citizens. If democracy rests on the ability of civil society to reactivate itself and make people behave as better citizens, then when democracy isn't working it becomes the fault of civil society. This argument casts community as a thing in demise that is taking democracy down with it. This may appeal to those civil society theorists who are nostalgic for a past without the media (it discourages face-to-face communication) or women's rights (women in the workplace means families and volunteer groups are suffering). But it is unconvincing for those of us who recognize that new media technologies have stimulated networks and given people new avenues for participation at the global level, and for those of us who know that the gender and identity rights gained via social movements are a good thing. Civil society is not to blame; it is the institutions of government that are out of touch with the people, not the other way around.

Thirdly, there is nothing to guarantee that civil society groups will behave in a democratic way. Civil society groups, including those that utilize community media, can also be undemocratic and it is this tendency that makes some critics skeptical of any attempt to support or shape it. Civil society includes groups that wish to restrict the freedom of individuals. For instance, some ethnic groups demote others by clinging to a sense of their cultural superiority. If anything, community media makes this visible. When access defines how community media is organized, then a program that one person finds progressive will most likely be accompanied by something that they find offensive or irrelevant. Giving control to civil society is not the answer to political apathy and a realistic investigation of community media demonstrates this. But it can assist in the way that representative democracy works.

Stephen Coleman, professor of e-democracy at Oxford University, believes that new media technologies offer an opportunity to correct some of the problems of representative democracy. He calls his model "direct representation." This is not straight-out direct democracy but a hybrid model. Direct democracy—what Coleman doesn't advocate—would entail creating technologies that could allow us all to participate in decision making. We would determine policies by voting on each and every one of them, bypassing elected officials (or directing them) so that rule would be by the people directly. But this option has not eventuated and there are many who are glad it has not. For one thing, it is unlikely that people would want to vote on everything or take the time to. Even if they did, some argue that they would make ill-informed choices and that their decisions would not necessarily be the best ones in the long run. However, as Coleman asserts, the problem with the alternative—representative democracy—is that we are left feeling detached and distant from the political process.

For Coleman, the issue of representation is not that we all want to be able to talk to our politicians directly, but that we do want our politicians to know what it feels like to be us. We want them to empathize with our situation and, in doing so, be less remote from our daily lives. This is not about face-to-face contact with politicians—the last thing most of us want is to have to talk to a politician or for a politician to expect us to sit down and formulate policies with them. But if communication was not just one-way from politicians to the people, but from the people to the politicians, then the dynamics of politics would change in such a way where politics would (hopefully) become more responsive. Coleman talks of how we might be able to synthesize the best of representative democracy with the best of direct democracy. In his words, "As digital ICTs open up the possibility of developing relationships in which governments can be more collaborative and conversational, the possibility of direct representation . . . emerges. Direct representation would not bind representatives to the precise will of the people, but would connect them to a knowledge and understanding of public will, in ways that would be far more sophisticated than reliance upon opinion polling or media mood setting."[16] Anthony Giddens promotes what he calls "dialogic democracy," which also involves better communication between governments and their citizens. This does not entail direct talk with politicians and involvement in the policy process (generally called "deliberative democracy"), rather dialogic democracy is about furthering cultural cosmopolitanism. Giddens asserts that it is being open to deliberation, rather than where it occurs, that is important. "This is why I speak of democratisation as the (actual and potential) extension of dialogic democracy—a situation where there is developed autonomy of communication, and where such communication forms a dialogue by means of which policies and activities are shaped."[17] Dialogic democracy takes into account that the forces of culture, communication, and technology have repercussions for democratic processes: "Many of the most important changes which affect people's lives today do not originate in the formal political sphere and can only in some part be coped with by it. . . . Such changes form the social revolutions of our time . . . they press for, and themselves in some part represent, processes of democratisation, but these democratising influences and pressures cut across the political arena and destabilise the liberal democratic system as much as they reinforce it."[18] Giddens understands that people now understand their nation and role as citizens through the media and cultural sphere. Factors outside of politics promote contemporary democracy but they also free us from having to participate in the formal political sphere. Media democracy is therefore important on two levels: it promotes democracy and it also provides a means for autonomous dialogue.

The problem of political apathy is intrinsic to contemporary democracies as the conditions of democracy encourage us to participate in spheres outside of formal politics. As community media demonstrates, we are not apathetic when politics is on our own terms and carried out through our own networks and processes. The disconnection lies between the dry, old-fashioned sphere occupied by politicians and the public service, and the spaces where we actually engage with what is going on in the world—the media, entertainment, culture, groups, and families. As it stands, representative democracy appears not to be representing the reality of its citizens. For that to be achieved, we need to find ways for citizens to represent themselves to the nation and for politics to be responsive to that. As Coleman points out, this does not have to mean that politicians are locked in to the "precise will of the people," but it does mean that they behave in a more responsive manner and demonstrate an understanding of our reality.[19]

Civil society cannot directly influence the way people participate in political life. In fact, it encourages them to participate in spheres outside of formal politics and to "make their own politics" in a way. We also know that politics is inflexible and unlikely to change its institutions and ways of doing things—representative democracy is here to stay. But the media is changing drastically. People are communicating more, and therein lies the opportunity to make connections between civil society and the state that can bring the citizenry and the processes that determine their lives into some kind of responsive relationship.

Community media also shows us that not everyone thinks the same way we do. It brings to the surface opinions and activities that we may not agree with. We might not want to know the people who think differently from us, but if we are able to see their thoughts and opinions on a more regular—and personal—basis, we might be less surprised by the world. And the democratic process would at least appear to be working, even when it didn't go our way.

Can community media democratize democracy? In many respects, it is already doing its part and showing us what is going on at the level of the individual and community. What it does not have is the support that it deserves or recognition of its important place within the communications landscape.

Keep Talking

I am hesitant to conclude that community media could perform a greater role in society if it just corrected some of its faults, such as issues of quality and the problems of access discussed in this book. One of the important aspects of community media is that anything can happen. To try to make it more organized and efficient may prevent some of its innovations from emerging. Joe and Zeal had the right idea: throwing a party is probably going to produce better results than forming a committee in the world of community media.

But we can begin to revise the way we value community media and the roles we prescribe to it. For one thing, we need to recognize that it is part of a contemporary media landscape, where communication technologies have brought new aspects of society into the purview of politics. Identity, difference, and community relationships figure in the way we see the world because they are making themselves known on a larger scale than ever before. Traditional news does not have sole claim on politics; entertainment, creative participation, and protest are just as important. Disinterest in politics means that interest has shifted to other domains—to the private world, to community affiliations and networks, to the activist domains where citizens feel as though they do have power. Within this landscape, community media is not "marginal" or even "oppositional." It is something very relevant: a movement for access to the spaces we know we are capable of occupying.

To review the themes of this book:

- The problem of aesthetics should now be one of education. The media is increasingly read-write and participative. Community media will no doubt change as more people become fluent in media making.
- The problems of free speech and access are taking on new significance as a result of the commons movement. Emerging configurations of labor, capital, and property need to be considered in the construction of technological spaces and speech rights.
- The problem of development becomes one of self-representation. Community media has demonstrated that, as far as communication and culture are concerned, the Third World is rich with ideas.
- The problem of marginality is an out-of-date perception. It exists because our institutions are out of touch with changes taking place at the everyday level through lifestyle, culture, and social movements. Our political institutions are antiquated, not community media.

Community, as one theorist describes it, is "precisely the conversation where nobody knows what he or she will say before he or she has said it."[20] Community media allows that conversation to occur.

Now it's your turn.

Notes

1. Jesse Walker, *Rebels on the Air: An Alternative History of Radio in America* (New York: New York University Press, 2001), 1.

2. Walker, *Rebels on the Air: An Alternative History of Radio in America*, 6.

3. Walker, *Rebels on the Air: An Alternative History of Radio in America*, 208.

4. Pew research figures, 2004.

5. Chris Atton, *Alternative Media* (Thousand Oaks: Sage, 2002).

6. Clemencia Rodriguez, *Fissures in the Mediascape* (Cresskill, N.J.: Hampton Press, 2001), 18.

7. Will Kymlicka, *Contemporary Political Philosophy: An Introduction*, 2nd ed. (Oxford: Oxford University Press, 2002), 284.

8. Nick Couldry, *The Place of Media Power: Pilgrims and Witnesses of the Media Age* (London: Routledge, 2000).

9. Nikolas Rose, *Powers of Freedom: Reframing Political Thought* (Cambridge: Cambridge University Press, 1999), 2.

10. Rose, *Powers of Freedom*, 2.

11. Rodriguez, *Fissures in the Mediascape*, 63.

12. Rodriguez, *Fissures in the Mediascape*, 22.

13. Kymlicka, *Contemporary Political Philosophy*.

14. Stephen Coleman, "Direct Representation: A New Agenda for E-Democracy" (paper presented at the Australian Electronic Governance Conference, Melbourne, April 2004), 6; Robert Putnam, *Bowling Alone: The Collapse and Revival of American Community* (New York: Simon & Schuster, 2000), 47.

15. Walker, *Rebels on the Air*, 2.

16. Coleman, "Direct Representation," 15.

17. Anthony Giddens, *Beyond Left and Right* (Cambridge: Polity Press, 1994), 115.

18. Giddens, *Beyond Left and Right*, 111.

19. Coleman, "Direct Representation," 15. See also Stephen Coleman, "A Tale of Two Houses: The House of Commons, the Big Brother House and the People at Home" (London: Hansard Society, 2003).

20. Wilhelm S. Wurzer, "The Political Imaginary," in *On Jean-Luc Nancy: The Sense of Philosophy*, ed. Darren Sheppard, Simon Sparks, and Colin Thomas (London: Routledge, 1997), 97.

Useful Websites

Alliance for Community Media (access television, United States)
www.alliancecm.org

CBOnline (Australia)
www.cbonline.org.au

The Communication Initiative, "Making Waves" (participatory media, Third World)
www.comminit.com/making-waves.html

Community Media Association (United Kingdom)
www.commedia.org.uk

Community Radio Forum (Ireland)
www.craol.ie

Global Village CAT (access television worldwide)
www.openchannel.se

Indymedia
www.indymedia.org

OURMedia (international research network)
www.ourmedianet.org

Prometheus Radio Project (low-power radio, United States)
www.prometheusradio.org

World Association of Community Radio Broadcasters (AMARC)
www.amarc.org

Bibliography

Aboriginal and Torres Strait Islander Commission. "ATSIC Submission to the Inquiry into Regional Radio." Canberra: ATSIC, 2000.

Ang, Ien. *Living Room Wars: Rethinking Media Audiences for a Postmodern World.* London: Routledge, 1996.

Atton, Chris. *Alternative Media.* Thousand Oaks: Sage, 2002.

Aufderheide, Patricia. "Competition and Commons: The Public Interest, in and after the AOLTW Merger." 2002, at arxiv.org/html/cs.CY/0109048 (accessed April 22, 2002).

———. *The Daily Planet: A Critique on the Capitalist Culture Beat.* Minneapolis: University of Minnesota Press, 2000.

Australian Broadcasting Authority. "Inquiry into the Future Use of the Sixth High Power Television Channel: Report to the Minister for Communications and the Arts." Sydney: Australian Broadcasting Authority, 1997.

Australian Consumer's Association. "Submission by Australian Consumer's Association to the Senate Environment, Communications, Information Technology and the Arts Committee Inquiry into Broadcasting Services Amendment (Digital Television and Datacasting) Bill 2000." Canberra: Senate Committee for the Environment, Communications, Information Technology and the Arts, 2000.

Barbrook, Richard, and Andy Cameron. "The Californian Ideology." *Muse,* no. 3, 1995.

Barr, Trevor. *newmedia.com.au.* Sydney: Allen & Unwin, 2000.

Batty, Phillip. "Singing the Electric: Aboriginal Television in Australia." In *Channels of Resistance: Global Television and Local Empowerment,* edited by Tony Dowmunt, 106–25. London: BFI Publishing, 1993.

Bibby, Andrew, Cathy Denford, and Jerry Cross. *Local Television: Piped Dreams?* Milton Keynes: Redwing Press, 1979.

Blaney, David L., and Mustapha Kamal Pasha. "Civil Society and Democracy in the Third World: Ambiguities and Historical Possibilities." *Studies in Comparative International Development* 28, no. 1 (1993): 3–24.

Blumler, Jay G. "Public Service Broadcasting before the Commercial Deluge." In *Television and the Public Interest: Vulnerable Values in West European Broadcasting*, edited by Jay G. Blumler, 7–21. London: Sage, 1992.

———, ed. *Television and the Public Interest: Vulnerable Values in West European Broadcasting*. London: Sage, 1992.

Bollier, David. *Public Assets, Private Profits: Reclaiming the American Commons in an Age of Market Enclosure*. Washington, D.C.: New America Foundation, 2001.

Brunsdon, Charlotte. *The Feminist, the Housewife, and the Soap Opera*. Oxford: Clarendon Press, 2000.

Buckley, Steve. "If I Had a Little Money..." Community Media Association, 2000, at www.commedia.org.uk (accessed March 1, 2001).

Calabrese, Andrew, and Janet Wasko. "All Wired Up and No Place to Go: The Search for Public Space in U.S. Cable Development." *Gazette* 49 (1992): 121–51.

Castells, Manuel. "Flows, Networks, and Identities: A Critical Theory of the Informational Society." In *Critical Education in the New Information Age*, edited by Manuel Castells, 37–38, 44–64. Lanham, Md.: Rowman & Littlefield, 1999.

———. "Materials for an Exploratory Theory of the Network Society." In *American Cultural Studies: A Reader*, edited by John Hartley and R. E. Pearson, 414–26. Oxford: Oxford University Press, 2000.

———. *The Rise of the Network Society*. Vol. 1. Malden, Mass.: Blackwell, 1996.

Chapman, Robert. *Selling the Sixties: The Pirates and Pop Music Radio*. London: Routledge, 1992.

Cohen, Jean L. "American Civil Society Talk." In *Civil Society, Democracy and Civic Renewal*, edited by Robert K. Fullinwider, 55–88. Lanham, Md.: Rowman & Littlefield, 1999.

Cohen, Jean L., and Andrew Arato. *Civil Society and Political Theory*. Cambridge, Mass.: MIT Press, 1992.

Coleman, Stephen. "Direct Representation: A New Agenda for E-Democracy." Paper presented at the Australian Electronic Governance Conference, Melbourne, April 2004.

———. "A Tale of Two Houses: The House of Commons, the Big Brother House and the People at Home." London: Hansard Society, 2003.

Communications Law Centre. "Public Television Report: An Evaluation." Sydney: White House and University of New South Wales, 1989/90.

Community Broadcasting Association of Australia. "Response to the Productivity Commission's Review of Broadcasting Legislation Draft Report." CBAA, 1999, at www.cbaa.org.au/Productivity%20Commission%20Dec%2099.html (accessed December 16, 1999).

Community Media Association. "Community Media Centres: New Funding for the Digital Generation." 2000, at www. commedia.org.uk (accessed March 7, 2000).

Community Media Network. "Proposed Amendments to the Broadcasting Bill." Dublin: Community Media Network, 2000.

Couldry, Nick. "Mediation and Alternative Media, or Relocating the Centre of Media and Communication Studies." *Media International Australia*, no. 103 (2002): 25–31.

———. *The Place of Media Power: Pilgrims and Witnesses of the Media Age*. London: Routledge, 2000.

Counihan, Mick. "Hitz a Knockout." *Communications Update*, no. 123 (1996): 14–16.

Cunningham, Stuart. "Community Broadcasting and Civil Society." *Metro*, no. 110 (1997): 21–25.

———. "The Cultural Policy Debate Revisited." *Meanjin* 51, no. 3 (1992): 533–43.

Cunningham, Stuart, and Terry Flew. "Policy." In *Television Studies*, edited by Toby Miller, 50–52. London: British Film Institute, 2002.

Davey, John. "Guaranteed Free Access: A Look at Australian Community Television and Its Place in the Changing Media Landscape." *Metro*, no. 133 (2002): 126–33.

Davies, Anne. "Broadcasting under Labor: 1983 to 1994." In *Public Voices, Private Interests*, edited by Jennifer Craik, Julie James Bailey, and Albert Moran, 3–14. St. Leonards NSW: Allen & Unwin, 1995.

de Certeau, Michel. *The Practice of Everyday Life*. Berkeley: University of California Press, 1984.

Department of Aboriginal Affairs. *Out of the Silent Land: Report of the Taskforce on Aboriginal and Islander Broadcasting and Communications* (Canberra: AGPS, 1984).

Department of Culture, Media and Sport. "Creative Industries Task Force Inquiry into the Internet." 2000, at www.dcms.gov.uk (accessed March 25, 2001).

Dionne, E. J., Jr. "Introduction: Why Civil Society? Why Now?" In *Community Works: The Revival of Civil Society in America*, edited by E. J. Dionne Jr., 1–14. Washington, D.C.: Brookings, 1998.

Dowmunt, Tony. "Swindon Viewpoint, Aberdeen Cable, Cable Authority and the Grapevine Channel." In *Local Television Revisited: Essays on Local Television 1982–1993*, edited by Dave Rushton, 22–26. Edinburgh: Institute for Local Television, 1990/1994.

Downing, John. "Community Access Television: Past, Present and Future." *Community Television Review* (August 1991): 6–8.

———. *Radical Media: Rebellious Communication and Social Movements*. Thousand Oaks: Sage, 2001.

Edwards, Catherine. "Response to Public Notice CRTC 2000-127." Unpublished paper. Calgary, 2001.

Eijk, Nico van. "Legal and Policy Aspects of Community Broadcasting." In *The People's Voice: Local Radio and Television in Europe*, edited by Nick Jankowski, Ole Prehn, and James Stappers, 235–46. London: John Libbey, 1992.

Engelman, Ralph. *The Origins of Public Access Cable Television.* Columbia, S.C.: Journalism Monographs, no. 123 (1990).

———. *Public Radio and Television in America: A Political History.* Thousand Oaks: Sage, 1996.

Escobar, Arturo. *Encountering Development: The Making and Unmaking of the Third World.* Princeton: Princeton University Press, 1995.

———. "Place, Power and Networks in Globalisation and Postdevelopment." In *Redeveloping Communication for Social Change*, edited by Karin Gwinn Wilkins, 163–74. Lanham, Md.: Rowman & Littlefield, 2000.

Etzioni, Amitai. "Old Chestnuts and New Spurs." In *New Communitarian Thinking*, edited by Amitai Etzioni, 16–36. Charlottesville: University Press of Virginia, 1995.

Flew, Terry. *New Media: An Introduction.* Melbourne: Oxford University Press, 2002.

Flew, Terry, and Christina Spurgeon. "Television after Broadcasting: Pay TV, Community TV, Web TV and Digital TV in Australia." In *The Australian Television Book*, edited by Stuart Cunningham and Graeme Turner, 69–88. Sydney: Allen & Unwin, 2000.

Ford, Tamara Villareal, and Geneve Gil. "Radical Internet Use." In *Radical Media: Rebellious Communication and Social Movements*, edited by John Downing, 201–34. Thousand Oaks: Sage, 2001.

Forde, Susan, Michael Meadows, and Kerrie Foxwell. "Culture Commitment Community." Sydney: Community Broadcasting Association of Australia, 2002.

Froomkin, A. Michael. "The Internet as a Source of Regulatory Arbitrage." In *Borders in Cyberspace: Information Policy and the Global Information Infrastructure*, edited by Brian Kahin and Charles Nesson, 129–63. Cambridge, Mass.: MIT Press, 1997.

Fuller, Linda K. *Community Television in the United States: A Sourcebook on Public, Educational, and Governmental Access.* Westport, Conn.: Greenwood, 1994.

Galston, William A., and Peter Levine. "America's Civic Condition: A Glance at the Evidence." In *Community Works: The Revival of Civil Society in America*, edited by E. J. Dionne Jr., 30–36. Washington, D.C.: Brookings, 1998.

Garnham, Nicholas. *Emancipation, the Media, and Modernity: Arguments about the Media and Social Theory.* Oxford: Oxford University Press, 2000.

———. "The Media and the Public Sphere." In *Communicating Politics*, edited by P. Golding, G. Murdock, and P. Schlesinger, 45–53. Leicester: Leicester University Press, 1986.

———. "The Myths of Video." In *Capitalism and Communication: Global Culture and the Economics of Information*, edited by Nicholas Garnham, 64–69. London: Sage, 1990.

Giddens, Anthony. *Beyond Left and Right.* Cambridge: Polity Press, 1994.

———, ed. *The Global Third Way Debate.* Malden, Mass.: Polity Press, 2001.

———. *The Third Way and Its Critics.* Cambridge: Polity Press, 2000.

Goggin, Gerard. "Pay Per Browse? The Web's Commercial Futures." In *web.studies*, edited by David Gauntlett, 103–12. London: Arnold, 2000.

Graham, Stephen. "Towards Urban Cyberspace Planning: Grounding the Global through Urban Telematic Policy and Planning." In *Technocities*, edited by John Downey and Jim McGuigan, 9–33. London: Sage, 1999.

Graham, Stephen, and Simon Marvin. *Splintering Urbanism: Networked Infrastructures, Technological Mobilities and the Urban Condition*. London: Routledge, 2001.

Gumucio Dagron, Alfonso. "Art of Aerialists: Sustainability of Community Media." Paper presented at the OURMedia III Conference, Barranquilla, Colombia, May 2003.

——. "Call Me Impure: Myths and Paradigms of Participatory Communication." Paper presented at the OURMedia I Conference, Washington, D.C., May 2001.

——. *Making Waves: Stories of Participatory Communication for Social Change*. New York: Rockefeller Foundation, 2001.

Habermas, Jurgen. *Between Facts and Norms: Contributions to a Discourse Theory of Law and Democracy*. Translated by William Rehg. Cambridge, Mass.: MIT Press, 1996.

Halleck, DeeDee. "Paper Tiger & Deep Dish: A Brief History." *Community Media Review* 24, no. 2 (2001): 28.

Harrison, J., and L. M. Woods. "Defining European Public Service Broadcasting." *European Journal of Communication* 16, no. 4 (2001): 477–504.

Hartley, John. *A Short History of Cultural Studies*. London: Sage, 2003.

——. "'Their Own Media in Their Own Language': Journalism Ethics for a People without a Polity." In *Remote Control: New Media, New Ethics*, edited by Catharine Lumby and Elspeth Probyn, 42–66. Cambridge: Cambridge University Press, 2003.

——. *Uses of Television*. London: Routledge, 1999.

Harvey, David. *The Condition of Postmodernity*. Oxford: Blackwell, 1990.

Hawkins, Gay. *From Nimbin to Mardi Gras: Constructing Community Arts*. Sydney: Allen & Unwin, 1993.

——. "Public Service Broadcasting in Australia." In *Communication, Citizenship, and Social Policy: Rethinking the Limits of the Welfare State*, edited by Andrew Calabrese and Jean-Claude Burgelman, 173–90. Lanham, Md.: Rowman & Littlefield, 1999.

Hedman, Lowe. "Sweden: Neighbourhood Radio." In *The People's Voice: Local Radio and Television in Europe*, edited by Nick Jankowski, Ole Prehn, and James Stappers, 62–77. London: John Libbey, 1992.

Hewson, Chris. *Local and Community Television in the United Kingdom: A New Beginning?* Sheffield: Community Media Association, 2005.

Higgins, John. "Community Television and the Vision of Media Literacy, Social Action, and Empowerment." *Journal of Broadcasting & Electronic Media* 43, no. 4 (1999): 624–44.

——. "Which First Amendment Are You Talking About?" *Community Media Review* 25, no. 2 (2002): 11–15.

Hirst, Paul Q. *Associative Democracy: New Forms of Economic and Social Governance*. Cambridge: Polity Press, 1994.

———. "Can Associationalism Come Back?" In *Associative Democracy: The Real Third Way*, edited by Paul Hirst and Veit Bader. London: Frank Cass, 2001.

———. "Democracy and Civil Society." In *Reinventing Democracy*, edited by Paul Q. Hirst and S. Kibilnan, 81–95. Oxford: Blackwell, 1996.

Hoffman-Reim, Wolfgang. "Trends in the Development of Broadcasting Law in Western Europe." *European Journal of Communication* 7 (1992): 147–71.

Hollander, Ed. "The Emergence of Small Scale Media." In *The People's Voice: Local Radio and Television in Europe*, edited by Nick Jankowski, Ole Prehn, and James Stappers, 7–15. London: John Libbey, 1992.

Horwitz, Robert B. "Negotiated Liberalisation: Stakeholder Politics and Communication Sector Reform in South Africa." Paper presented at the Rethinking Public Media in a Transnational Era Conference, New York University, January 2001.

Horwood, James N., and Allison L. Driver. "Public Policy Update: Court Decisions and FCC Rulings." Spiegel & McDiarmid, 2002, at www.spiegelmcd.com/pubs/jnh_public_policya.htm (accessed October 14, 2002).

House of Representatives Standing Committee on Communications, Transport and the Arts. "Local Voices: Inquiry into Regional Radio." Canberra: The Parliament of the Commonwealth of Australia, 2001.

Huesca, Robert. "Conceptual Contributions of New Social Movements to Development Communication Research." *Communication Theory* 11, no. 4 (2001): 415–33.

Jacka, Liz. "'Democracy as Defeat' the Impotence of Arguments for Public Service Broadcasting." *Television and New Media* 4, no. 2 (2003): 177–91.

Jakubowicz, Andrew. "Speaking in Tongues: Multicultural Media and the Constitution of the Socially Homogeneous Australian." In *Australian Communications and the Public Sphere*, edited by Helen Wilson, 105–27. Melbourne: Macmillan, 1989.

James, Estelle. *The Private Provision of Public Services: A Comparison of Sweden and Holland*. New Haven: Institute for Social and Policy Studies, Yale University, 1982.

Jankowski, Nicholas W., ed. *Community Media in the Information Age*. Cresskill, N.J.: Hampton Press, 2002.

Jankowski, Nick, Ole Prehn, and James Stappers, eds. *The People's Voice: Local Radio and Television in Europe*. London: John Libbey, 1992.

Jauert, Per, and Ole Prehn. "State Subsidies—Added Value?" Paper presented at the annual meeting of the International Association of Media and Communication Research, Barcelona, July 2002.

Katz, Elihu, and Paul F. Lazarsfeld. *Personal Influence: The Part Played by People in the Flow of Mass Communications*. Glencoe, Ill.: The Free Press, 1955.

Keane, John. *Civil Society: Old Images, New Visions*. Cambridge: Polity Press, 1998.

———. *The Media and Democracy*. Cambridge: Polity Press, 1991.

Kleinsteuber, Hans J., and Urte Sonnenberg. "Beyond Public Service and Private Profit: International Experience with Non-Commercial Local Radio." *European Journal of Communication* 5 (1990): 87–106.

Klug, Heinz. "Extending Democracy in South Africa." In *Associations and Democracy*, edited by Erik Olin Wright, 214–35. London: Verso, 1995.

Knight, Alan. "Won't Get Fooled Again: A Paper Detailing 25 Years of Brisbane's 4ZZZ." *Australian Community Broadcasting Series*, no. 1 (2001), at www.cbonline .com.au.

Kukathas, Chandran. "Are There Any Cultural Rights?" *Political Theory* 20, no. 1 (1992): 105–39.

Kymlicka, Will. *Contemporary Political Philosophy: An Introduction*. 2nd ed. Oxford: Oxford University Press, 2002.

Kymlicka, Will, and Wayne Norman. "Return of the Citizen: A Survey of Recent Work on Citizenship Theory." *Ethics*, no. 104 (1994): 352–81.

Leach, Robert. *Political Ideology in Britain*. Basingstoke: Palgrave, 2002.

Leiner, Barry M., Vinton G. Cerf, David D. Clark, Robert E. Kahn, Leonard Kleinrock, Daniel C. Lynch, Jon Postel, Larry G. Roberts, and Stephen Wolf. "A Brief History of the Internet ISOC." 2000, at www. isoc.org/internet/history/brief.shtml (accessed October 2, 2001).

Lerner, David. *The Passing of Traditional Society*. Glencoe, Ill.: The Free Press, 1958.

Lessig, Lawrence. *Code and Other Laws of Cyberspace*. New York: Basic, 1999.

———. *The Future of Ideas: The Fate of the Commons in a Connected World*. New York: Random House, 2001.

Lewis, Peter M. *Community Television and Cable in Britain*. London: British Film Institute, 1978.

———. "Whose Experience Counts? Evaluating Participatory Media." Paper presented at the annual meeting of the International Association of Media and Communication Research, Barcelona, July 2002.

Lewis, Peter M., and Jerry Booth. *The Invisible Medium: Public, Commercial and Community Radio*. Basingstoke: Macmillan, 1989.

Liddell, Craig. "Diversity on the Airwaves: Histories of Australian Community Radio." 2SER and the Community Broadcasting Foundation, 2005, at www.cbonline .org.au (accessed February 1, 2005).

Linder, Laura R. *Public Access Television: America's Electronic Soapbox*. Westport: Praeger, 1999.

Lyons, Mark. *Third Sector: The Contribution of Nonprofit and Cooperative Enterprises in Australia*. Sydney: Allen & Unwin, 2001.

MacIntyre, Alisdair. *After Virtue*. 2nd ed. Notre Dame, Ind.: Notre Dame University Press, 1984.

Mansbridge, Jane. "A Deliberative Perspective on Neocorporatism." In *Associations and Democracy*, edited by Erik Olin Wright, 133–44. London: Verso, 1995.

Marcato, Peter. "Different Values for Changing Times? The Melbourne 2001 Community Broadcasting License Grants." *3CMedia*, no. 1 (2005): 50–57.

McConnell, Bill. "TV's Terrestrial Imperative." *Broadcasting & Cable* 130, no. 7 (2000): 14.

McKay, George. *DiY Culture: Party & Protest in Nineties Britain*. London: Verso, 1998.

McQuail, Denis. "Mass Media and the Public Interest." In *Mass Media and Society*, edited by James Curran and Michael Gurevitch, 66–80. London: Arnold, 1996.

———. "The Netherlands: Freedom and Diversity under Multichannel Conditions." In *Television and the Public Interest: Vulnerable Values in West European Broadcasting*, edited by Jay G. Blumler, 96–111. London: Sage, 1992.

Meikle, Graham. *Future Active: Media Activism and the Internet*. Sydney: Pluto Press, 2002.

Melkote, Srinivas R. "Reinventing Development Support Communication to Account for Power and Control in Development." In *Redeveloping Communication for Social Change*, edited by Karin Gwinn Wilkins, 39–54. Lanham, Md.: Rowman & Littlefield, 2000.

Melkote, Srinivas R., and H. Leslie Steeves. *Communication for Development in the Third World: Theory and Practice for Empowerment*. 2nd ed. London: Sage, 2001.

Michaels, Eric. *The Aboriginal Invention of Television in Central Australia 1982–1986*. Canberra: Australian Institute of Aboriginal Studies, 1986.

———. *For a Cultural Future: Francis Jupurrurla Makes TV at Yuendumu*. Vol. 3, Art & Criticism Monograph Series. Melbourne: Artspace, 1987.

Mody, Bella. "The Contexts of Power and the Power of the Media." In *Redeveloping Communication for Social Change*, edited by Karin Gwinn Wilkins, 185–96. Lanham, Md.: Rowman & Littlefield, 2000.

Molnar, Helen, and Michael Meadows. *Songlines to Satellites: Indigenous Communication in Australia, the South Pacific and Canada*. Sydney: Pluto Press, 2001.

Monshipouri, Mahmood. "State Prerogatives, Civil Society, and Liberalisation: The Paradoxes of the Late Twentieth Century in the Third World." *Ethics and International Affairs* 11 (1997): 232–51.

Moran, Albert. "Multiplying Minorities: The Case for Community Radio." In *Public Voices, Private Interests*, edited by Jennifer Craik, Julie James Bailey, and Albert Moran, 147–64. Sydney: Allen & Unwin, 1995.

Mouffe, Chantal. "Democratic Citizenship and the Political Community." In *Dimensions of Radical Democracy*, edited by Chantal Mouffe, 225–39. New York: Verso, 1992.

———. "Democratic Politics Today." In *Dimensions of Radical Democracy*, edited by Chantal Mouffe, 1–16. London: Verso, 1992.

Nancy, Jean-Luc. *The Inoperative Community*. Minneapolis: University of Minnesota Press, 1991.

Neeson, J. M. *Commoners: Common Right, Enclosure and Social Change in England, 1700–1820*. Cambridge: Cambridge University Press, 1993.

Negroponte, Nicholas. *Being Digital*. Rydalmere: Hodder & Staughton, 1995.

Newman, Otto, and Richard de Zoysa. *The Promise of the Third Way: Globalisation and Social Justice*. Basingstoke: Palgrave, 2001.

Noam, Eli. *Television in Europe*. New York: Oxford University Press, 1991.

Norris, Pippa. *Digital Divide: Civic Engagement, Information Poverty and the Internet Worldwide*. Cambridge: Cambridge University Press, 2001.

O'Connor, Alan, ed. *Community Radio in Bolivia: The Miners' Radio Stations*. Lewiston, N.Y.: Edwin Mellen Press, 2004.

———. "Mouth of the Wolf: Anthropology and Radio." Paper presented at the OURMedia I Conference, Washington, D.C., May 2001.

O'Donnell, Vincent. "Community Broadcasting: In Its Twenties Now." *Overland*, no. 158 (2000): 94–98.

O'Regan, Tom. "Some Reflections on the Policy Moment." *Meanjin* 51, no. 3 (1992): 517–32.

O'Regan, Tom, and Ben Goldsmith. "Meeting Cultural Objectives in a Digital Environment." Paper presented at the Rethinking Public Media in a Transnational Era Conference, New York University, January 11–14, 2001.

O'Siochru, Sean, and Bruce Girard, eds. *Communicating in the Information Society*. Geneva: United Nations Research Institute for Social Development, 2003.

Pearson, Noel. "From Campbelltown to Cape York—Rebuilding Community." The Brisbane Institute, 2000, at www. brisinst.org.au/papers/noel_pearson_rebuilding/print-index.html (accessed October 9, 2000).

Petersen, Vibeke G., Ole Prehn, and Erik N. Svendsen. "Denmark: Breaking 60 Years of Broadcasting Monopoly." In *The People's Voice: Local Radio and Television in Europe*, edited by Nick Jankowski, Ole Prehn, and James Stappers, 45–61. London: John Libbey, 1992.

Poster, Mark. "Cyberdemocracy: Internet and the Public Sphere." In *Internet Culture*, edited by David Porter. New York: Routledge, 1997.

Prehn, Ole. "From Small Scale Utopianism to Large Scale Pragmatism: Trends and Prospects for Community Oriented Local Radio and Television." In *The People's Voice: Local Radio and Television in Europe*, edited by Nick Jankowski, Ole Prehn, and James Stappers, 247–68. London: John Libbey, 1992.

Productivity Commission. "Inquiry into Broadcasting." Canberra: Ausinfo, 2000.

Prometheus Radio Project. "Low Power Signal: Special Interest Noise." 2000, at www.prometheusradio.org/artnoise.shtml (accessed March 12, 2003).

———. "The Next FCC Giveaway: Digital Radio." 2000, at www.prometheusradio.org/artdigital.shtml (accessed March 12, 2003).

Putnam, Robert. *Bowling Alone: The Collapse and Revival of American Community*. New York: Simon & Schuster, 2000.

Rennie, Ellie. "Creative World." In *Creative Industries*, edited by John Hartley, 42–54. Malden, Mass.: Blackwell, 2005.

———. "The Story So Far: Digital Storytelling, Narrative and the New Literacy." Paper presented at the Image Text and Sound Conference, RMIT University, Melbourne, September 2004.

Rennie, Ellie, and Saba El-Ghul. "Supporting the Democratic Voice." Paper presented at the annual meeting of the International Association of Media and Communication Research, Porto Alegre, July 2004.

Rennie, Ellie, and Sherman Young. "Park Life: The Commons and Communications Policy." In *Virtual Nation: The Internet in Australia*, edited by Gerard Goggin, 242–57. Sydney: UNSW Press, 2004.

Rheingold, Howard. *The Virtual Community: Homesteading on the Electronic Frontier*. New York: Harper Perennial, 1994.

Rifkin, Jeremy. *The Age of Access*. London: Penguin, 2000.

Rodriguez, Clemencia. "Citizens' Media and the Voice of the Angel Poet." *Media International Australia*, no. 103 (2002): 78–87.

———. *Fissures in the Mediascape*. Cresskill, N.J.: Hampton Press, 2001.

Rogers, Everett. *Diffusion of Innovations*. New York: The Free Press, 1962.

Rose, Nikolas. *Powers of Freedom: Reframing Political Thought*. Cambridge: Cambridge University Press, 1999.

Ross, Karen, and Virginia Nightingale. *Media and Audiences: New Perspectives*. Maidenhead, U.K.: Open University Press, 2003.

Sandel, Michael J. *Democracy's Discontent: America in Search of a Public Philosophy*. Cambridge, Mass.: Harvard University Press, 1996.

Servaes, Jan. *Communication for Development: One World, Multiple Cultures*. Cresskill, N.J.: Hampton Press, 1999.

———. "Introduction: Participatory Communication and Research in Development Settings." In *Participatory Communication for Social Change*, edited by Jan Servaes, Thomas L. Jacobson, and Shirley A. White, 13–28. Thousand Oaks: Sage, 1996.

Slack, Roger S., and Robin A. Williams. "The Dialectics of Place." *New Media & Society* 2, no. 3 (2000): 313–34.

Slater, Don, and Jo Tacchi. *ICT Innovations for Poverty Reduction*. New Dehli: UNESCO, 2004.

Smith, Anthony. "The Public Interest." *Intermedia* 17, no. 2 (1989): 10–24.

Spinello, Richard A. "The Future of Intellectual Property." *Ethics and Information Technology* 5 (2003): 1–16.

Spragens, Thomas A. "Communitarian Liberalism." In *New Communitarian Thinking*, edited by Amitai Etzioni, 37–51. Charlottesville: University Press of Virginia, 1995.

Stallman, Richard. "The GNU Project." In *Free Software Free Society: Selected Essays of Richard M. Stallman*, edited by Joshua Gay, 15–30. Boston: Free Software Foundation, 2002.

Stein, Laura. "Access Television and the Grass Roots." In *Radical Media: Rebellious Communication and Social Movements*, edited by John Downing, 299–324. Thousand Oaks: Sage, 2001.

———. "Can the First Amendment Protect Public Space on U.S. Media Systems? The Case of Public Access Television." Paper presented at the annual meeting of the International Communications Association, Washington, D.C., May 25–27, 2001.

———. "Democratic 'Talk,' Access Television and Participatory Political Communication." Paper presented at the twelfth EURICOM Colloquium on Communication and Culture, "Communication, Citizenship and Social Policy," University of Colorado at Boulder, 1997.

Stoney, George. "The Essential George Stoney." *Community Media Review* 24, no. 2 (2001): 29–31.

Streeter, Thomas. *Selling the Air: A Critique of the Policy of Commercial Broadcasting in the United States*. Chicago: University of Chicago Press, 1996.

———. "Technocracy and Television: Discourse, Policy, Politics and the Making of Cable Television." Doctoral thesis, University of Illinois, Urbana-Champaign, 1986.

Sullivan, William M. "Making Civil Society Work: Democracy as a Problem of Civic Cooperation." In *Civil Society, Democracy and Civic Renewal*, edited by Robert K. Fullinwider, 31–54. Lanham, Md.: Rowman & Littlefield, 1999.

Tacchi, Jo. "Transforming the Mediascape in South Africa: The Continuing Struggle to Develop Community Radio." *Media International Australia*, no. 103 (2002): 68–77.

Tebbutt, John. "Constructing Broadcasting for the Public." In *Australian Communications and the Public Sphere*, edited by Helen Wilson, 128–46. Melbourne: Macmillan, 1989.

Thompson, Michael. "Some Issues for Community Radio at the Turn of the Century." *Media International Australia*, no. 91 (1999): 23–31.

Thornley, Phoebe. "Early Voices: Divergent Philosophies/Aspirations of the Original Participants." Paper presented at the annual conference of the Community Broadcasting Association of Australia, Hobart, November 2001.

Turner, Graeme. *British Cultural Studies: An Introduction*. 2nd ed. London: Routledge, 1996.

Verba, Sidney, Kay Lehman Schlozman, and Henry E. Brady. *Voice and Equality: Civic Voluntarism in American Politics*. Cambridge, Mass.: Harvard University Press, 1995.

Vine, Jeni. "Community Media Training: A Tool in Combating Social Exclusion." MA diss., Hallam University, U.K., 2001.

Vittet-Philippe, Patrick, and Philip Crookes, eds. *Local Radio and Regional Development in Europe*. Manchester: European Institute for the Media, 1986.

Walker, Jesse. *Rebels on the Air: An Alternative History of Radio in America*. New York: New York University Press, 2001.

Walzer, Michael. "Citizenship." In *Political Innovation and Conceptual Change*, edited by Terence Ball, James Farr, and Russell L. Hanson, 211–19. Cambridge: Cambridge University Press, 1989.

———. "The Civil Society Argument." In *Dimensions of Radical Democracy*, edited by Chantal Mouffe, 89–107. London: Verso, 1992.

———. "The Communitarian Critique of Liberalism." In *New Communitarian Thinking*, edited by Amitai Etzioni, 53–70. Charlottesville: University Press of Virginia, 1995.

———. "The Idea of Civil Society: A Path Towards Social Reconstruction." In *Community Works: The Revival of Civil Society in America*, edited by E. J. Dionne Jr., 129–43. Washington, D.C.: Brookings, 1998.

———. "Pluralism: A Political Perspective." In *The Rights of Minority Cultures*, edited by Will Kymlicka, 139–54. New York: Oxford University Press, 1995.

Weber, Steven. *The Success of Open Source*. Cambridge: Cambridge University Press, 2004.

Wilkins, Karin Gwinn. "Accounting for Power in Development Communication." In *Redeveloping Communication for Social Change*, edited by Karin Gwinn Wilkins, 197–210. Lanham, Md.: Rowman & Littlefield, 2000.

———, ed. *Redeveloping Communications for Social Change*. Lanham, Md.: Rowman & Littlefield, 2000.

Wolfe, Alan. "Is Civil Society Obsolete? Revisiting Predictions of the Decline of Civil Society in *Whose Keeper?*" In *Community Works: The Revival of Civil Society in America*, edited by E. J. Dionne Jr., 17–23. Washington, D.C.: Brookings, 1998.

Wurzer, Wilhelm S. "The Political Imaginary." In *On Jean-Luc Nancy: The Sense of Philosophy*, edited by Darren Sheppard, Simon Sparks, and Colin Thomas, 91–102. London: Routledge, 1997.

Young, Iris Marion. "The Ideal of Community and the Politics of Difference." In *Feminism/Postmodernism*, edited by Linda J. Nicholson, 300–323. New York: Routledge, 1990.

Yúdice, George. *The Expediency of Culture*. Durham: Duke University Press, 2003.

Index

About the Author

Ellie Rennie is a Research Fellow at the Institute for Social Research, Swinburne Univeristy of Technology. Her academic and industry work focuses on community communication, as well as the broader public philosophies and policy trends associated with broadcasting and new media.